The Private Eye Story

The cover of the 500th issue of Private Eye, *13 February 1981 illustrated by Willie Rushton.*

The Private Eye Story

Patrick Marnham

The first 21 years

'Men are seldom so serious as when they are making jokes, and seldom so funny as when they are talking seriously.'

Claudel (I think)

ANDRE DEUTSCH

Also by Patrick Marnham

Road to Katmandu
Fantastic Invasion: Dispatches from Africa
Lourdes: a modern pilgrimage

First published in Great Britain in 1982 by
André Deutsch Limited
105 Great Russell Street London WC1
and Private Eye Productions Limited
34 Greek Street London W1

Copyright © Patrick Marnham

Printed by Ebenezer Baylis and Son Ltd, Worcester

ISBN 233 97509 8

To my big brother
lots of love
Joanna /x

Contents

Introduction

A magazine that has been published for twenty-one years has not been published for very long, but *Private Eye* is such an unusual institution that it is possible to justify an account of this short life. It prints what other papers will not print. At a time when the British press is constantly tempted to risk less by publishing less, and is so heavily influenced by lobbies, public relations men and advertisers, *Private Eye* joins no lobby, rubbishes the PR industry and is completely independent of its advertising revenue. More important, the distorted world inhabited by its familiar cast of fictional characters makes people laugh.

When I started to write this book I asked one young reader what she wanted to know about the magazine and she replied, 'All the dirt.' It must be a taste she has acquired from reading it. I am afraid she may be disappointed because rather than seeking 'all the dirt' – which in most cases would be too trivial to be worth digging up – I have instead merely tried to write about *Private Eye* in that papers own spirit of disrespectful inquiry.

I first started to work for *Private Eye* in 1966. One gloomy afternoon in March I was sitting in the library of Gray's Inn pretending to prepare for the Bar finals when my friend David Dodd, later a lecturer in criminology at Georgetown University, Guyana, wandered in with a copy of the latest issue. In those days he was as bored with study as I was, and together we had constructed a social life that revolved around the weekly programme at Ronnie Scott's – with daily intermissions in the billiard room thoughtfully provided by the kindly benchers of Gray's Inn. The future lecturer pointed out an advertisement for 'editorial assistant, preferably graduate with knowledge of politics and journalism' which he suggested I should answer. There was a telephone outside the library door. By the time the exam results came through, it was too late. I had escaped from the laws of England disguised as a journalist, an occupation which in those informal days required no more than a mild display of aptitude and interest.

Soho that summer made a pleasant contrast with the library. No. 22 Greek Street was divided into offices above a betting shop and the Naked City strip club filled the basement. Opposite was the tall, blank wall of the Prince Edward Theatre. *Private Eye* occupied the top two floors, high enough to observe the crowded social calendar of the local pigeons, rattling through their heroically frequent courtships with clenched beaks, the frenzied moments of intercourse causing their few eggs to descend from time to time onto the human heads beneath.

In less frantic moments we could lean out of the window and watch the Maltese ponces, Jamaican gamblers and English strippers who formed the local working population. Appalling arguments sometimes broke out. Once during my lunch hour I found myself, the centre of an interested crowd, trying to re-glue about one-third of a club owner's scalp to his skull, my efforts being hampered partly by the blood, partly by the brilliantine. Eventually an arm emerged from a window and handed me a grubby towel. I remember that the ambulance could not get through because a delivery driver, no friend of the club owner, insisted on unloading his van before clearing the way. The club owner, unable to see through the mess, but hearing every word of the conversation, remained calm. His premises had formerly been occupied by 'The Establishment' – London's first satirical night-club.

The strippers always carried little vanity cases and were easily distinguished in the crowds as they hurried from one club to the next. That the routine of undressing from their street clothes, dressing in their costumes, removing them on stage, scooping them up as they stumbled into the darkness and then replacing their clothes, only to go through the whole thing again twenty minutes later in another tacky basement, that this bored them witless, was only too evident from the expression of disgusted indifference on their faces as they performed. But at least they were alive, unlike the mechanical aids and inflatable shapes which have replaced them, and they were well paid. When the average annual wage was £1500, they could earn £5000 or £15,000 just by tottering around Soho for about sixty hours a week, and taking off their clothes.

The sound I remember best from No. 22 in the sixties was the mournful cry of the barkers. 'Live show. Live show. Twelve lovely girls. They're naked AND they dance. Come along in boys. Live show.' This drifted up to our window every ten minutes or so with the regularity of ice-cream chimes, providing a gentle background accompaniment to the editorial day. As editorial assistant my task was to sort through unsolicited contributions, to write paragraphs for the 'Colour Section', and to interview the mixed bag of criminals, bankrupts and other victims of life who walked in off the street asking to see 'a reporter'.

The office at No. 22 was divided into two floors, the lower one presided over by Tony Rushton, shortly to become managing director, the upper one supporting the editorial personnel. The business affairs of the paper were conducted eccentrically. Board meetings, for instance, were announced merely by the appearance of Tony Rushton with a carnation in his buttonhole. But I had a clearer view of the editorial arrangements. To Richard's room there came a changing cast of collaborators, most frequently William Rushton, John Wells and Peter Cook. Barry Fantoni occasionally appeared. Christopher Booker at that time was more usually a voice on the telephone. Paul Foot occupied the room across the corridor. There were also innumerable casual visitors from Fleet Street or even less salubrious haunts. One wall was covered with a garish oil painting by Gerald Scarfe, Ralph Stedman, Fantoni and Rushton, showing various people connected with *Private Eye*. The landlords eventually removed this work of art, muttering about 'vandalism'. The presence of Rushton or any of the card-carrying satirists was usually enough to ensure a stream of inspired jokes that were funnier than any public performance then available, and which I was being paid (admittedly only £7 a week) to watch.

The humorous sections of *Private Eye* have always been produced in a peculiar way. With rare exceptions they are based on collaboration, a technique developed by the editors from the earliest issues. The technique was not planned, it just grew. The process resembles more than anything the composition of short, dramatic scripts, since the phrases are spoken aloud and in character. One person at the typewriter, or with pen in hand, will edit the result and will appear to an onlooker to be the dominant member of the partnership. The others will chip in whenever inspiration takes them. But the appearance of domination can be misleading. John Wells says that *Private Eye*'s methods of collaboration have always been 'genuine', unlike writing television scripts with Ned Sherrin, when jokes were accepted on a 'win one, lose one' basis. Christopher Booker says that, 'although at any given time one person's ideas may be dominant, the thing really is a collaboration. One person could not do it on his own. It requires the presence of the others to draw out something which could only exist as a joint enterprise.' The collaboration has been extended even to cartoons; many of the early Rushtons were worked out between him and Booker, 'before Rushton put his master stamp on them'. And the 'Great Bores' series today is a collaboration between Michael Heath, Ingrams and Fantoni. The management of the collaboration is a delicate matter. Too many participants and the atmosphere becomes too competitive, resulting in one person's jokes being elbowed off the ledge, and consequent ruffled feathers.

The characters that have emerged from these collaborations over the years provide a summary of the collective editorial opinion, if such a thing is possible. Mrs Wilson, Denis, Lord Gnome, Lunchtime O'Booze, Glenda Slagg, Dave Spart, Ron Knee, E. J. Thribb, the Rev J. C. Flannel, Bamber Gasket and Sylvie Krin are all an original response to the conventional roar of events and to the circumscribed attitudes towards reality which other papers impose – as the illustrations that follow in this book will demonstrate. Most of the lampoons take the form of a newspaper article. And *Private Eye* imitates Peter Simple, Michael Frayn and Beachcomber in using 'joke' journalists such as O'Booze, Slagg and Spart.

Today the most usual arrangement is Ingrams and Fantoni, with Booker being present for one or two afternoons a fortnight, and John Wells coming in for the 'Dear Bill' series which he does with Ingrams alone. Ingrams, Booker and Fantoni have worked in this way for the last twelve years, with the occasional dazzling intervention by Peter Cook. Together they have produced almost all the humorous pieces in the paper during that period. The true voice of their collective subconscious is said to be that of Sir Herbert Gussett, the chronic letter writer to newspapers, whose most characteristic phrase is 'My dear wife, whose name for the moment escapes me'. When the script is finished it is read aloud to enthusiastic applause from those who have written it, which adds to its dramatic character. Next it is typed out in a room below and applied to the page with cow-gum by Tony Rushton. It is then ready to be printed.

The simplicity of these arrangements has always been an important feature of *Private Eye*. By making everything as informal and cheap as can be, it has been possible to avoid most of the great constraints on freedom which adult life usually imposes. It is a feature of this relaxed manner that the paper is produced on a fortnightly basis – one week 'on', one week 'off' – and by a part-time editorial staff. This means that many people can contribute at their own convenience, but it may encourage a rather too casual approach to some of the factual contributions.

The design of the paper is close to that of a children's comic, apparently off-putting, once cracked very approachable. It has grown up organically. What is now the centre of the paper was originally the whole of it, a sequence of jokes, cartoons, spoofs, scripts, lampoons and parodies. This is now preceded by the 'Colour Section', a selection of short paragraphs, newspaper cuttings, gossip and cartoon strips; and it is followed by the longer, less easily digestible news items, lightened by Auberon Waugh's 'Diary'. This blend of gossip, satire and hard information has evolved under the direction of Richard Ingrams over the years. He seldom adds to or subtracts from it; his instinct in the matter is deeply conservative. Generally speaking, innovation will only follow if someone is available. He prefers this to dreaming up new schemes and then finding someone to execute them. All unsolicited contributions to the paper have to fit somewhere into the existing format, with very rare exceptions. This may sometimes become repetitious but it works.

The 'Colour Section', Christopher Logue's 'True Stories', Auberon Waugh's 'Diary' and 'Business News' are produced in the conventional way by single contributors. Logue's 'True Stories' started from an obsession with newspaper cuttings which he inherited, together with a bulky file, from his father. He receives from fifty to seventy-five letters a fortnight and estimates that he has read twenty thousand stories submitted by about fifteen thousand people. For Logue, the message of 'True Stories' is 'what you read on page one of the newspapers is not life. It is what goes onto the inside pages that you have to deal with.' The supply of 'True Stories' shows no sign of drying up. Similarly Auberon Waugh's 'Diary' started as a parody of Alan Brien's 'Diary' in *The Sunday Times*. The original inspiration has long since been abandoned as utterly irrelevant, but the 'Diary' continues, a simple idea that has taken on a life of its own, and become a parody of itself.

To make my own position clear, I have since 1966 contributed to the 'Colour Section' and 'Footnotes'. I left the paper in 1968 to take a job in Fleet Street, but returned as a regular contributor in 1970. I wrote the original 'Grovel' column, when it was criticised for being more amusing than factual. I also wrote an occasional series for the back pages called 'Fifth Column'. I have in short contributed anonymously to the paper for sixteen contented years. This position as both observer and participant should have given me an advantage in trying to write an 'authorised history' from a detached point of view. I find, having finished the book, which I was invited to write by Richard Ingrams, and which is published by André Deutsch and *Private Eye* jointly, that my account is sufficiently detached to have evoked strong and critical disagreement from some of those who founded the paper. It remains my account and I bear the usual responsibility for any inaccuracies it may contain. Nonetheless, my thanks are due to the following who have assisted me in my inquiries.

Mark Amory, Jeffrey Bernard, Anthony Blond, Christopher Booker, Cyril Bottomley, Mark Boxer, Sarah Burns, Catherine Carpenter, David Cash, Diana Clark, Peter Cook, Kate D'Arcy, Nigel Dempster, André Deutsch, Barry and Tessa Fantoni, Paul Foot, George Gale, Nicholas Garland, Michael Gillard, Germaine Greer, Maurice Hatton, Michael Heath, Peter Hillmore, Richard and Mary Ingrams, Christopher Logue, Nicholas and Elizabeth Luard, Candida Lycett-Green, Peter McKay, Sukie Marlowe, Andrew and Stuart Osmond, Venetia Parkes, Jim Perry, Tony Rushton, Willie Rushton, Martin Tomkinson, Peter Usborne, Alan Watkins, Auberon Waugh, John Wells, Richard West, Michael Wharton and Sam White.

I must acknowledge the courtesy of Montgomery Hyde, who allowed me to consult his unpublished typescript about 'Sir James Goldsmith and his battle with *Private Eye*'. I have found both *Children of the Sun* by Martin Green and *Gossip* by Andrew Barrow to be of great assistance in describing the social background of the sixties.

Finally I would like to thank the various people who agreed to speak to me only on condition that they remained anonymous; desperate men and women eking out a ruined life in exile and poverty, waiting night after sleepless night for a knock on the door, and the snuffling of a Dobermann pinscher.

Long, long ago 1

The early sixties have become an historical period, like the nineteenth century. It was a time when the young could still believe that the British Labour party would renew their world. It was a time when an Old Bailey jury was asked, confidently, to ban *Lady Chatterley's Lover* because the word 'fuck' appeared 'no less than thirty times'. The newspapers declined to print the essential word. The jury declined to convict. Rudolf Nureyev had just skipped through the customs hall at Le Bourget airport shouting 'I want to be free.' Mr Harold Macmillan had appointed his nephew, the Duke of Devonshire, as a junior minister for the Commonwealth. John Osborne had written to *Tribune* to say 'Damn you England'. Bertrand Russell had spent a week in Brixton after persistently obstructing the highway by sitting in it. Christine Keeler was discovered swimming naked in Lord Astor's pool at Cliveden. She was nineteen. Viscount Hailsham had been photographed swimming in the sea at Brighton wearing goggles and flippers. He looked ninety-eight. And I went to Soho to see *L'Avventura* directed by Antonioni. One of the advertisements projected onto the screen was for a nearby coffee bar called Le Macabre. 'Coffee on a tombstone?', the sepulchral voice inquired. So I left and had a cup of espresso on a black wooden table and read a copy of a magazine that I had not seen before. The cover showed a picture of the Albert Memorial and the headline read, 'Britain's First Man Into Space – Albert Gristle awaits blast-off'; it was Issue 4 of *Private Eye*. Things began to look up.

The young are dumped into an inhabited country. They have not been supplied with maps. The natives speak in cipher, a chilly welcome is the most they can expect. In this predicament most are tempted to bide their time. But a few, over-endowed with confidence, conduct a frontal assault entirely on their own terms. It is a bluff but surprisingly often it works. Looking back on the early issues of *Private Eye*, it seems to be an example of the successful frontal assault. It was the creation of outsiders who did not want to stay that way for long.

PRIVATE EYE

incorporating THE FLESH'S WEEKLY

VOL I No 4   Wednesday 7th February 1962   Price 6d.

BRITAIN'S FIRST MAN INTO SPACE

ALBERT GRISTLE AWAITS BLAST-OFF

ho ho very satirical

The world that faced them was still dominated by the events of twenty and thirty years before. Most of its politicians had been soldiers in the war against fascism or, if they were dissenters, they had spent their youth opposing fascism in the thirties. Perhaps because their youthful experience had been so vivid it seemed to a later generation entirely out of date. The political world had been frozen since 1945. It was time for a change. In 1965, *The Times Literary Supplement* drew up a list of key words. It included the Common Market, Lady Chatterley, Buchanan, Rachman, Profumo, Congo, Snow, Smethwick, the Beatles, Eichmann, Education, Violence, Colour Magazines and Computer. The practice of making such lists and finding them significant was itself characteristic of the sixties. The only notable political innovation had been peaceful direct action, copied from Gandhi and fashioned by the Campaign for Nuclear Disarmament into a statement of mainly youthful conscience that was truthful, innocent and futile.

When *Lady Chatterley* was cleared by an English jury the book became an immediate best-seller. The number of paperback titles in print increased between 1960 and 1965 from 5866 to over 14,000. Among them was the *New English Bible*, a translation which drained Scripture of its symbolic power. In Rome a council was meeting to do the same for the Catholic liturgy. Reactionary old men were becoming harder to find, something which progressive younger ones were slow to realise. It was the perfect time to launch a magazine that used a cheap new process, based on the steam typewriter, in place of traditional printing methods. No previous generation had been so exposed to mass communications or was so fascinated by the press and television. A new term was popularised to cover this area of activity, 'the media of communications'.

The generation of the sixties was not the first to discover the 'media', but they provided it with more original copy. When the fashionable young of the fifties were frivolous there was something eerily old-fashioned about it. As perceived through the social columns, they seemed almost formal in their abandon. In May 1953, Mark Boxer, the Cambridge undergraduate and editor of *Granta*, was rusticated for publishing a blasphemous poem. He was twenty-two. In January 1954, Isabel Patino eloped with James Goldsmith, who was aged twenty. Her father, a Bolivian tin millionaire, pursued them to Kelso – where they were married. In 1955, Kim Philby, a 'senior Foreign Office diplomat', was cleared of the suggestion that he was a Russian spy by Harold

Macmillan, the rather frivolous Foreign Secretary. Philby held a press conference in his mother's flat in Drayton Gardens, where he must have thoroughly enjoyed himself pulling the wool over the eyes of the hapless reporters. Unknown to press and public he was still being protected by the code of personal relations which bound the members of his class even if they had betrayed their country and murdered its agents. He was the most extreme example of that rebelliousness which had divided an earlier generation of clever young men. But the world of the fifties continued as though the thirties had never occurred.

In 1956, Emma Tennant gave a Persian fancy dress party in Cheyne Walk. The Duke of Kent attended, in oriental costume, and the guests danced to 'Rock Around the Clock'. In 1958, John Aspinall and his mother, Lady Osborne, were charged with running an illegal gaming house at her home in Eaton Place. Their defence, that they were only holding private parties, succeeded. Meanwhile, Dominic Elwes ran away with *his* heiress, Tessa Kennedy. They were married in Havana, and ran out of cash in Florida, six weeks later. In Cyprus Cornet Auberon Waugh of the Royal Horse Guards, in a memorably frivolous moment, wandered within range of his own armoured car and was near-fatally wounded. His former headmaster commented that he had never been notably athletic. In 1959, a party at the Whisky A Go Go was attacked by would-be gatecrashers who hurled bottles at the host, Anthony Haden Guest. In 1960, Viscountess Lewisham, formerly Mrs Gerald Legge, née Raine McCorquodale, the daughter of Barbara Cartland, later to be the Countess of Dartmouth and then Countess Spencer, signed the pledge in order to obtain cheaper car insurance, for one.

All of these figures were eventually to play some part in the lives of the schoolboys who would found *Private Eye*, and who were already voraciously reading newspapers.

The editors of *Private Eye* first met at Shrewsbury School in 1951. P. M. Foot and C. J. P. Booker proceeded from their respective prep schools (Ludgrove and the Dragon School) to take the Shrewsbury scholarship. On their arrival they found to their irritation a boy called R. R. Ingrams also taking the scholarship, although he was already within the school. However, the story has a happy ending for all three boys received awards. Booker remembers a later occasion when the school debating society considered a motion 'that this House deplores the decline of the landed gentry'. It was proposed by

Booker and opposed by Foot. The school magazine was called *The Salopian* and was under the editorship of Ingrams and another boy, W. G. Rushton, a precocious cartoonist. It soon took on a humorous character. When their period of editorship was over Ingrams and Rushton were succeeded by Booker and Foot. Already something of a pattern was forming. Some years after they all left, their headmaster, John Peterson, issued the following report:

> These people were quite unnoticed when they were at Shrewsbury. . . . Ingrams was a very able boy, a classical scholar . . . no trouble at all . . . a model boy. Christopher Booker was an extraordinarily staid young man, reserved and studious, who used to spend his Sundays collecting fossils. Paul Foot had all the makings of an angry young man, but he was not in fact a difficult boy at school. William Rushton was undistinguished (until he took the part of Lord Loam in *The Admirable Crichton*). He was an enormous success and after that experience of the limelight never recovered. He *was* Lord Loam. But he had one talent: he was a good cartoonist. . . . They were the mid-fifties generation, and pillars of happy citizenship compared to the generation that followed them at Shrewsbury.

Early drawings by W. G. Rushton on the cover of the school magazine, May 1955.

Reporting in turn on his headmaster, Richard Ingrams later said, 'John Peterson was a tragic figure. He was very shy. He should never have been a headmaster. He should have been a clergyman.'

In 1955, boys who left school went almost without exception into the armed forces for national service. Foot became a second lieutenant and spent some of the time in Jamaica where his father Sir Hugh Foot had previously been governor. Ingrams attempted to gain a commission but never rose higher than the rank of sergeant in the Royal Army Educational Corps. In that capacity he was sent to both Korea and Malaya. Rushton refused to apply for a commission and spent much of his time with the Army on the Rhine in Bad Oyenhausen, 'holding back the Russian hordes from the NAAFI'. Booker was excused military service on medical grounds. Instead he was recruited as a 'personal assistant' in a solicitor's office and was instructed to sit in on the professional conferences of a Mr Arnold Goodman.

After two years of national service Ingrams went to Oxford and found to his surprise that Foot was also at University College. They were the last of the national service undergraduates, which meant that the freshmen of succeeding years

The undergraduate Osmond, by Rushton.

The 'watercress issue', with hessian cover.

were at least three years younger than them. This gave them an additional authority and confidence, even contempt, in their dealings with official university life. Foot became notorious in his first term for receiving a telegram from his father: 'Get a first stop Be President of the Union.'*

Foot's ambition at the time was to be an actor rather than a politician, another purpose he shared with Ingrams, but instead they found themselves becoming involved with a paper called *Parson's Pleasure*† which was owned by Adrian Berry, whose father was the proprietor of the *Daily Telegraph*. There are traditionally two Oxford undergraduate papers, *Cherwell* and *Isis*, but at this time there was a fashion for starting new ones, and *Parson's Pleasure* was read by the editor of another rival paper, *Mesopotamia*, a Balliol undergraduate called Peter Usborne. Since childhood Usborne had been fascinated by funny writing. His father constantly recited Belloc and Lear to him, and he was allowed to browse through his Uncle Richard's study, which contained every book P. G. Wodehouse had written. When *Parson's Pleasure* closed down, due to financial difficulties, Usborne invited Ingrams and Foot to join his paper. '*Mespot.* was supposed to be funny but frankly it wasn't,' said Usborne. 'So I asked Foot, Ingrams and Andrew Osmond to come over and join *Mespot.* and also their friend Willy Rushton who was not at Oxford but who spent the week in London and came up to draw the cartoons at weekends.'

Andrew Osmond had been to Harrow, but he had met Ingrams before Oxford.

For me the whole story began in a library of the Royal Army Educational Corps in Malaya. I was an officer in the Gurkhas, dressed in all my finery, and I remember there was this utterly hopeless-looking sergeant sorting out books with a Chinese girl. I looked at him and thought, 'You poor sod'. He looked at me in my little hat and obviously thought, 'You bastard'. Later we met in the Blue Angel in Berkeley Square (what the hell was *he* doing there?). Then at Oxford I became the resident idiot on *Parson's Pleasure*. The proctors objected to one of our

* *The Guinness Book of Records* states that the Foot family holds the record for presidencies of the Oxford and Cambridge Unions, since Foot, his father and his three uncles were all elected to one of these posts.

† Named after a bank on the River Cherwell where male dons and undergraduates were able to bathe in the nude.

cartoons which was of a giraffe standing at a bar saying, 'The high balls are on me'. I was a writer. Once I spent an entire vacation working on a serial story and I took it to Ingrams who rejected it at once.

Uz was The First Tycoon. He had one of his usual brilliant ideas which was to make *Mespot.* a magazine for Oxford and Cambridge and so transform its financial basis. Uz was the editor. He did all the organising and we just wrote the jokes. I remember lying on the floor of Uz's rooms in Balliol, helpless, weak, with laughter. One issue was bound in sackcloth in which mustard and cress seeds were embedded. 'Apply water and grow your own mustard and cress.' The point was it grew.

Usborne also recruited 'the funniest chap in Oxford', who was a year ahead of the others and was called John Wells. 'He knew none of us then. He was an academic and a very different person.' He had a reputation as a brilliant mimic. Wells also remembers seeing Ingrams before Oxford during national service. (As a soldier Ingrams was obviously a memorable sight.) 'I first saw him in Korea. I was up the sharp end as a second lieutenant in the Royal Sussex. I used to see a Captain Ambrose in the Education Corps once a week. He said there was a sergeant back at base who I should meet. This was a gorilla-like figure, playing the harmonium at church service with fingers too big for the harmonium keys. I noticed and remembered, but did not meet him for another three years.'

Mespot. also engraved a gramophone record into the cover of the first proper issue. 'It sold like the clappers.' Usborne organised 'hundreds of girls to go round college rooms selling it, early on Sundays. I remember just after it came out walking across the quad in Balliol and hearing John Wells' voice coming out of every other window.'

One of these girls was Candida Betjeman who was then doing a sculpture course at Oxford Tech. She was officially a friend of Wells but found herself nursing an unrequited passion for Ingrams.

I first saw him in the Town and Gown in Oxford. It was an awful little egg and chip place. With neon lights. It became my home from home. I went there every single day for six months because I knew Ingrams would be there. Foot, Peter Jay* and Rushton would be there as well. Then in the

Wells by Rushton; the prototype of 'Little Gnittie'.

---

* Later to become Jim Callaghan's son-in-law, and Callaghan's British ambassador in Washington.

evenings we used to hang around at his flat. Ingrams was very serious about an actress in Nottingham in those days. There was a large photograph of her in his room. He never showed any sign of knowing about my love for him. Once I saw him when I was on my bike and I fell off, but he did not notice.

People didn't sleep with people in those days much. Footy was totally grown up and terrifying when he was with Monica (who he later married). And I thought Margaret Callaghan and Peter Jay were doing it. But I was certainly a virgin and I'm sure Wells was as well. I used to miss most of my sculpture lessons to go to the Town and Gown. One exciting thing that happened was when Noel Picarda came round to our flat and heard me singing 'Love for Sale' in the bath. When I came out he said, 'You've got it, Kid', and leered. Actually I used to lurch from one octave to the next.

Not all the undergraduate journalists were members of this group however. Before *Parson's Pleasure* folded Ingrams and Foot were approached by a man at Christ Church called Auberon Waugh who wanted to buy the title and turn it into 'the organ of the bloodies'. Waugh's advances were rejected, but during his visit he took sufficiently strongly against Paul Foot to make him the central figure in a short story which he submitted to *Isis*. It was about scruffy men in roll-neck sweaters who lay about on the floor of their lodgings late at night talking left-wing politics, drinking cocoa and trying to seduce girls who were also wearing roll-neck sweaters.* Shortly after this Waugh abandoned Oxford and published his first novel, *The Foxglove Saga*.

After three years at Oxford a terrible thing happened to the editors of *Mesopotamia*. They found they were expected to leave. Contrary to every expectation raised by the university since their arrival, they were not immortal and Oxford was not for eternity. The last meeting of the mutual admiration society was held in a hayfield near Aynhoe. It was hot, exams were looming, and around them were singing all the birds of Oxfordshire and Gloucestershire. The mutual admirers drank their claret and finished their picnic and went to sleep. Only one, Rushton, who was already out in the real world, realised

The editors of Parson's Pleasure: *Ingrams, (Brahms), Foot.*

* According to Ingrams, Foot was already 'widely suspected of taking things too seriously'. He had found a Marxist guru who was evangelising him during weekly sessions in his digs in the Woodstock Road.

that it did not have to end here after all. '*Mespot.* could continue. You should do it,' he said seriously; then he fell asleep too.

Before leaving there was one last adventure. After finals they got together and took a review to the Edinburgh Festival. At Oxford there had been a famous production of Marlowe's *Tamburlaine*. The producer was another under-graduate, John Duncan, and Osmond and Usborne had played minor roles blacked up down to the waist. Ingrams had played the mad King of Persia. Now, confident from this success and led by Noel ('You've got it, Kid') Picarda, they retired to a stable block near Thame and started to write and rehearse. Usborne had gone, but Ingrams, Osmond and Rushton, together with 'amazingly pretty girls' (Candida, Wendy Varnals and Danae Brook), set to work. All the bookings were made but there was no script. Rushton and Osmond nearly died from sleeping on the stable floor when the tap of the gas cooker was left on. The money ran out, and so did the food. But all was saved when with a toot of the horn Candida's mother drove up, threw open the boot and said, 'I thought you might be hungry.' They looked in to see it bulging with food.

Ingrams and Rushton at the Edinburgh Festival.

Ingrams as 'the Mad King of Persia' in Tamburlaine.

They only heard about the necessity for the Lord Chamberlain's permission when they had reached Edinburgh and so had to return to the regional office in Newcastle for their script to be approved. Most of it was. The first night lasted two and a half hours and was a smash. It was in Edinburgh that the undergraduates realised the power of publicity in the world outside Oxford, and the ease with which it could be generated.

Candida remembers that before their revue started they had to take parts in Aristophanes' *The Birds*. She and Osmond used to ham it up. 'The producer was in tears in the wings. Osmond used to make me corpse all the time. He made me laugh more than any of the others. If he walked into the room today I think I'd immediately start laughing just as much again.' Ingrams, Rushton and Picarda were the stars. John Osborne's *Luther* had recently opened as part of the regular festival. The play included various references to the saintly heretic's trouble with constipation.

We had a skit where Ingrams squatted in the middle of the stage dressed as a monk, heaving and groaning, and

Osmond came on also dressed as a monk. Osmond slowly approached the groaning Ingrams and finally said 'Luther?' Whereupon Ingrams groaned even more and then replied, 'NO . . . . Tighter!' One night Albert Finney came over from *Luther* and actually played it himself. I remember very well how I felt when the show closed. Everyone went off in different directions. It was awful.

It was the end of Oxford.

Candida Betjeman and Danae Brook at the Edinburgh Festival.

2 A rage for satire 1961–1963

What is England? .... From Swift to Huxley our writers have been giving us private tuition courses in self-hatred.
Gerald Brenan, *The Face of Spain* (1950)

There is a place in society for nasty-minded, rude people.
Peter Cook

eyond the Fringe first fell upon London like a sweet, refreshing rain on the tenth of May, 1961. It must have been St Jonathan's Day, because it has rained satire ever since, day and night, harder and harder, spreading outwards from London to cover the whole of the British Isles in one steady downpour of soaking jokes, until, as Peter Cook said recently, the entire realm seems about to sink sniggering beneath the watery main.'

The opening words of Michael Frayn's introduction to the text of *Beyond the Fringe* describe the 'real' world which greeted those who left Oxford and Cambridge in 1961. The sixties opened with 'the satire boom', a short-lived phase which accustomed people to a greatly increased freedom of abusive expression. *Beyond the Fringe* had started life at the previous year's Edinburgh Festival. It made an immediate reputation for its four devisers, Alan Bennett, Peter Cook, Jonathan Miller and Dudley Moore. For the first time, as it seemed, war, patriotism, professional ethics, capital punishment, religion and the royal family – all the adornments of a self-confident ruling class – were treated as suitable subjects for ribald humour. Its point of view was anarchic rather than 'satirical' in the classic sense, but satire is what the press called it, and that is what it became. The main achievement of *Beyond the Fringe* was that it made its metropolitan audience laugh at their new helplessness and at the pretensions that history had bequeathed them. This was a subversive act. *Beyond the Fringe* changed social conventions. Its most popular imitator was eventually to be the television show *That Was the Week That Was (TW3)* which sufficiently diluted the original inspiration to make it acceptable to a national audience.

While at Cambridge, Cook and a friend, Nicholas Luard, had thought of the idea of opening a satirical nightclub in London which would mount political review and provide jazz. At first they were unable to find a site, but in the summer of 1961, during the first success of *Beyond the Fringe*, Cook heard of a strip club in Greek Street, Soho, which had closed after a police raid. He contacted Luard who was by that time in New Orleans, researching a thesis on Hemingway. Luard returned and The Establishment opened in October. Meanwhile the former editors of *Mesopotamia* had not been idle.

Eschewing the Edinburgh Festival, Usborne, with characteristic determination, had plunged straight into real life when the Oxford term ended in June. This meant tramping the streets of New York looking for some sort of job. On one of those days, in another part of New York, Henry Luce, the mogul of *Time-Life*, rose from his bed, read the newspapers and issued a directive that if any right-wing Cuban exiles were to apply to his papers for a job they were to be accommodated. As an afterthought he added that if any Englishmen did the same, the same went for them. Unaware of this, Usborne chose that day to enter the *Time-Life* building and almost immediately found himself on the twenty-sixth floor in a room full of Cuban exiles, cutting up newspapers. But he was unable to rid himself of the idea of *Mesopotamia* and, having heard of Christopher Booker through his friends at Oxford, he sent him a long and very businesslike letter. Booker considers that the letter was so practical that it made Usborne 'the one man, if any, who started *Private Eye*'.

After a month or two, Usborne tired of cutting up American newspapers and returned to England to work in a vast advertising agency, Mather & Crowther. While there he met Booker for the first time and was much impressed with his sophistication. Booker seemed to know all kinds of smart people, the sort of people who were about seven years older and whose names were constantly figuring in the *Evening Standard*'s gossip column. Booker was at that time working on *Liberal News* where he had joined up with Rushton and with a young Australian journalist called Bruce Page. They too had been discussing the possibility of starting a new magazine, which would specialise in political gossip and disclosures. The model they chose was *Le Canard Enchaîné*, the title Page favoured was *Bent*.

But starting papers requires administrative ability and so

the initiative passed to Usborne. He had started a paper before and he began to look around for the simplest and most practicable means to do it again. He needed no more incentive than daily life at Mather & Crowther. He recalls,

> Nobody seemed to like working there. I was a trainee account executive, and we were always being humiliated by our clients. I remember in particular the Shell International account. We had to have regular meetings with them and these seemed to turn into a weekly exercise in the petty humiliation of my boss. But while there I became familiar with a new printing process that was just in the news. It was called 'offset-litho', and it meant that an office typewriter and a jar of cow-gum could take over much of the traditional business of producing a newspaper. By the autumn I had assembled Booker, Rushton and a bit of John Wells, and Danae Brook. We had got as far as meeting in The Bunch of Grapes and arguing about a possible title. I wanted to call it *The Yellow Press*. I'm a gimmick merchant, and I had thought of this yellow paper. But this was all rather premature as none of us had any money. So I sent a telegram to Osmond who was in Paris.

'That was the day my life changed,' Osmond says.

> I had gone to Paris to learn French before taking the Foreign Office exam. This telegram arrived. It read, '*Mespot.* rides again. Come home. Uz.' By the time I got back and had found which pub in Chelsea they had moved to, they had completely forgotten about the telegram. They were still arguing about the cover. Anyway I had £450 and I agreed to back them with it. I became the original Lord Gnome. Ingrams was there too, although he was then far more interested in a touring theatre he had started with John Duncan, the producer of *Tamburlaine*. Anyway, we rejected *The Yellow Press*, *The British Letter* and the *Flesh's Weekly*. Ingrams wanted to call it *The Bladder*. I wanted to call it *Finger*. I had been looking at the Lord Kitchener recruiting poster. We would be putting the finger on people. Then I looked at Kitchener's eye. So I thought of *Private Eye*. Rushton was against *Bladder* because his grandmother was dying of a bladder disease. So Ingrams was overruled. I think he still broods about it sometimes.

PRIVATE EYE

Vol I Nº I   Friday 25ᵗʰ October   Price 6ᵈ

CHURCHILL CULT NEXT FOR PARTY AXE?

Butler for Gambia?

by Pravdaman Edouvard Khrankschov

Sensation follows sensation in the campaign to isolate the "anti-Party group" inaugurated at the recent 22nd Party Congress at Brighton. The latest, and most startling move is Selwyn Lloyd's 'public confession' that he must "share the blame" for the current economic crisis.

Perhaps more ominous, however, is the series of articles by new Party Boss and Praesidium Leader Ivan MacLeod in the Party organ The Sunday Times, in which he is rehabilitating the reputation of ex-Premier Chamberlain.

Chamberlain was in the doghouse throughout the Churchill era, for his pre-war "appeasement" policy at the time of the notorious Anglo-German Pact. The Munich Pact is now viewed in top Party circles as a heroic attempt to buy time from Hitler before a war which Chamberlain saw was inevitable.

Purge

Obviously this campaign can only mean further humiliation for the man who ousted Chamberlain, ex-Premier Winston Churchill, and all those associated with him. Premier Macmillan has already relegated many of those who rose to power in the Churchill era to minor diplomatic and industrial posts, but hitherto the Churchill Cult itself has remained virtually inviolate.

(continued on page 2.)

YOU'VE BEEN SOLD A DUMMY

- of what we hope, after further experiment, will be a weekly newspaper to appear regularly in the New Year.

IF YOU HAVE ANYTHING TO OFFER

money, advice, goodwill or even contributions

CONTACT THE EDITOR, PRIVATE EYE, 28, Scarsdale Villas, London W8.

---

contents

BORE of the WEEK
(back page)

Usborne recalls that Osmond's enthusiasm was decisive. Once he had decided to return from Paris and back them, they had to go ahead. The meetings continued in Usborne's Islington flat, in a room in Rushton's mother's house in Scarsdale Villas, and in the studio at the foot of the garden of Ingrams's mother's house in Cheyne Row. Using the advertising agency's telephone to a scandalous extent, Usborne located an offset litho press in Neasden owned by Rank Xerox. Eventually, on October 25th, in the same month that The Establishment opened, the first issue of *Private Eye*, printed on yellow paper (now rather pointlessly), was carried from the press to Scarsdale Villas, where it was collated and stapled together. None of its perpetrators' names appeared in it (an illegal omission), but there was a reference to an editorial address.

Most of the first issue had been written late at night in the Cheyne Row studio by Booker. It was the week of Kruschev's denunciation of Stalin and probably the most hopeful week for world communism since the end of the Nazi–Soviet pact. The new paper was not about to get bogged down in reflections of that sort. The lead headline was 'Churchill Cult Next for Party Axe' and there was a front-page announcement appealing for funds. One item has remained unchanged. In the top left-hand corner the figure of a pathetic mediaeval crusader with a bent sword, parodying the Beaverbrook

Booker, Rushton and volunteers working on an early issue.

crusader, peered out. (This character, 'Little Gnittie', had previously appeared in *Mesopotamia*. He bore a satirical resemblance to John Wells and had been depicted as an innocent in Oxford, learning about sex from Ingrams.) Every single piece of type was stuck down by Rushton, who even drew the lettering for some of the headlines. Page 2 had a serious news item, 'The Ship That Never Was'. The story promised further revelations in the next issue, a promise that was never intended to be kept, since no one had any idea of how or where to find such revelations. Page 3 had an embryo gossip column that was always intended to be a regular feature, but that too disappeared. Most of the work was done by Booker and Rushton, but Wells contributed a spoof interview with Sir John Gielgud ('Feelgood') and Ingrams a musical column about Hermann Mousjak. The back page carried an attack on Mr Punch, 'Bore of the Week'. The decrepitude of *Punch* was a constant inspiration to the editors of the new paper, who intended to provide their readers with everything that *Punch* had ceased to attempt decades before. They were greatly assisted in this by the editor of *Punch*, Mr Bernard Hollowood, who used to censor many of the best cartoons that were submitted to him. It was not long before cartoonists discovered that *Private Eye* would invariably print these.

Having assembled the first issue, the next problem was to distribute it. This task fell to Osmond who owned a mini-car, and who set out for the part of London he knew best – the South Kensington coffee bar strip. That was the favourite stamping ground of Osmond, Booker and Rushton and that was where they tried to sell their paper. It was the land of striped shirts and hair lacquer where, after games of rugby and squash, public schoolboys faced up to grim reality and each other's sisters. Osmond took his copies to cafés in the Gloucester Road and Earl's Court, such as The Troubadour, a CND stronghold. 'The first issue had a cover price of 6d (2½p). They were virtually given away. I would put a stack out in some likely spot with an honesty box. Later on I came back. The copies were always gone and the box was always empty. We did not mind. We decided that if we could live the way we had lived at Oxford we would have found supreme bliss. We wanted advice really. And we wanted to be told we were brilliant.'

With the second object in mind they also distributed the copies to people thought to be influential. Kenneth Tynan is the example most frequently recalled. Of the first print order of three hundred about one hundred were given away. This ploy attracted some publicity, and the editors seem to have been brilliant enough at least to inform the *World's Press News* that the first print order had been for five thousand copies and had sold out, a misinformation which the *WPN* dutifully repeated. Something closely resembling a publicity stunt was mounted as the first yellow issue was succeeded by two more in November. A few newspapers were induced to run stories along the lines of 'British Satire Industry Expands'. It was 'moving off the stage and into print under the leadership of Mr Christopher Booker' who was 'more or less the editor'. Further attention was attracted by Candida Betjeman, Sukie de la Mare and Danae Brook who agreed to distribute a hand-painted poster in the London underground. Usborne's ostensible idea was to avoid the costs of printing. London Transport duly obliged by banning such posters on the grounds that they were 'not waterproof', and a story in the *Daily Herald* was the successful result. The mixture of innocence and guile which succeeded in launching this amateurish-looking effort is quite disturbing. The gossip column in Issue 2, 'The Stained Glass Monocle', included the names of Jocelyn Stevens, David Hughes, Mai Zetterling, Clive Labovitch, Michael Heseltine and Mark Boxer, and this time the authors were listed in the style of a school magazine as W. G. Rushton, R. R. Ingrams and C. J. P. Booker. By now the appeal to readers had been expanded to include money and writs.

Candida Betjeman remembers how at this time she spent the day subbing copy about fur coats on *Queen* magazine and then in the evenings went round to Mary Morgan's house in Pavilion Road and stapled together the copies which Mary, a friend of Richard's, had collated.* Then she got out her address book and started to post the copies to her friends. John Piper was the first person from her book who took out a subscription. 'I just did a heck of a lot of manual labour. And laughing. That never stopped. Then Jocelyn Stevens found out I was moonlighting on *Private Eye* and sacked me.' The first feud had been born.

By the second issue a design breakthrough had been achieved with the discovery of 'R' type which Rushton remembers as 'terrible stuff like sellotape', but which he could alternate with hand-drawn letters and words cut out of newspapers. Issue 3 had the first 'bubble' which was suggested by an old Cambridge friend of Booker, Peter Cook. It

---

* Richard Ingrams and Mary Morgan were married in November 1962.

PRIVATE EYE

Vol I N° 3   Thursday 30th November 1961   Price 6ᵈ

A MERRY CHRISTMAS TO—

Ad Majorem Dei Gloriam

Chris Chataway
Ken Tynan
Dominic Elwes
Penelope Gilliatt
Stansgate
Snowdon
Timothy Beaumont
Kenneth Allsopp
Jeremy Thorpe
Jocelyn Stevens
Aristides. P. Gnome and
all Ad-men, Brubeck fans,
P.R.O's, Bow Groupers,
striped shirts and pseuds
everywhere

GOD REST YOU MERRY...

was dated November 30th and sold as a Christmas issue. The cover also bore a list of names, 'Tynan, Chris Chataway, Dominic Elwes, Penelope Gilliatt, Stansgate, Snowdon, Timothy Beaumont, Kenneth Allsopp, Jeremy Thorpe, Jocelyn Stevens'. They were the fashionable younger generation immediately above the editors and therefore, in Booker's phrase, 'the early hate figures', although in retrospect they appear more as objects of envy. Having started by circulating such people for their support, the magazine had now decided that the time had come to attack them. Sooner or later there must be, blessed moment, the first writ. The infant was learning fast.

At an early moment Usborne went to Paris to interview the editor of *Le Canard Enchaîné*. It had been noted and discussed in hushed tones that *Le Canard* sold 350,000 copies, which sounded like money for everyone and a bit to spare. When Usborne told the editor that Britain, unlike most European countires, had no satirical organ of disclosure, he said that he thought the paper would eventually succeed. But, he warned, 'you will have to wait until you are all aged forty-five. That is because your friends in government will not come into power until then. We on *Le Canard*,' he explained, 'survive by getting the hot potatoes from our friends in power.'

There had been some moments of doubt, when Booker and Osmond had considered giving up, and only Usborne and Rushton wanted to continue. But they were all sufficiently encouraged by the editor of *Le Canard* to go ahead in the new year with fortnightly issues. They needed a new design and new printers since Lord Rank had found out about their use of Huprint Ltd, his Neasden plant, and banned them. Ingrams had pretty well dropped out, having become still more involved with Tomorrow's Audience, the touring theatre which visited schools. He had sunk several thousand pounds of his own money into the project and was seeking an Arts Council grant. But Rushton was particularly keen to continue with the paper. He had been fired from his other job as cartoonist on *Liberal News*, and in retaliation had drawn his last strip of the character Brimstone Belcher in such a way as to spell 'Fuck Off'. And Booker had been turned down by 'almost every paper in Fleet Street'.

Issue 4 came in February. It was on white paper in a slightly larger format. The cover was the picture of the Albert Memorial, entitled 'Britain's First Man in Space'. Osmond remembers that the picture was taken by Lucy Lambton who had probably seen the photo of Osmond wearing only a

Rushton's farewell to Liberal News.

nightie in the previous issue, and had decided that if they were going to print that kind of filth she might as well have a hand in it. Osmond drove Lucy to the Albert Memorial to take the shot and after a while, growing somewhat bored with the assignment, she said: 'I'm going to take one upside down, Andrew. You hold my skirts while I stand on my head.' So she did and he did, though he wondered vaguely at the time why she did not just reverse the print.

Issue 4 also carried the first genuine advertisements which had to be distinguished from the jokes by a black border. They were warmly welcomed by Lord Gnome in his first column. There was also the first proper masthead, which firmly identified Booker as the editor. This was the last issue to be printed by Huprint, but new printers had been found, the Wembley music-printing specialists John Thorpe & Son. There was to be a regular print order of five thousand. From now on the magazine was in business and the first salaries were paid by Osmond. Booker and Rushton started on £5 a week, subsequently increased to £15 a fortnight. Usborne left Mather & Crowther.

Five thousand copies were not going to be sold with a mini-car and honesty boxes in a few cafés, but Usborne had solved this problem by discovering another crucial figure, a van driver for *City Press* called John Harness, who was re-christened Sir Charles. Sir Charles agreed to put a few bundles on the back of his van and to drop them in at some of his newsagents. At the same time there was a rave review on the back page of *The Observer*. This said that the new paper was 'almost impossible to obtain except at a few eccentric

Editor, typist: Christopher Booker. Art Editor, catering manager: William Rushton. Photographer: Lucy Lambton. Business Manager: Peter Usborne. Proprietor, driver: Andrew Osmond. Half secretary: Candida Betjeman.

shops' and also identified 'Andrew Osmond's chain store father' as the proprietor; a treble inaccuracy since his father did not own the paper, his father had never owned a chain store and his father was, in any case, dead. There was also recognition in *The Times*, the *Daily Mail*, the *Glasgow Herald*, the *Daily Sketch* and the *Evening Standard*. This, together with Sir Charles's bootleg van, made a fine start.

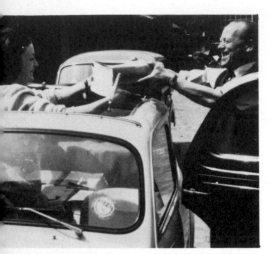

John Thorpe handing over copies of the early Private Eye *to Mary Ingrams.*

John Thorpe & Son had printed Issue 5 under their own name, but after a long, cool look at the contents, particularly at the cover, John Thorpe decided that for many reasons it was time 'Son' made his own way in the world and accordingly set up a shell company, Leo Thorpe Ltd, to bear all responsibility for future issues. The Thorpes made a remarkable firm. John had been a bandmaster in the Indian Army and had then become a conductor of the Regent Orchestra. In 1950 he decided to start a profitable sideline photocopying music. This went so well that he took over a disused stables behind a spring-making factory in Wembley, and then expanded into a converted kipper factory nearby. He then invented a secret method for setting music copy and turned to full-time music printing. He was clearly just the sort of man to handle a paper which was edited by people who knew nothing about printing and who could not be bothered with the niceties of photographic enlargement, or even with presenting their unjustified and typewritten pages in a shape generally resembling a square.* He was sufficiently ingenious to deal with all this and to make a profit from a print run that was to move from five thousand to one hundred thousand copies. This part-time job was eventually to change the whole shape of Thorpe's business. And for Sir Charles too a change was coming. *City Press* found out about his moonlighting and fired him, but with the necessary support from *Private Eye* he was able to start his own distribution firm.

The success of the paper now became a problem in itself. It was one thing to be told you were brilliant and to enjoy publicity provided by the trend-spotters. It was much harder to turn the new paper into a sound business which was able to meet the expanding demand for satirical journalism. What was needed most was money. A false dawn was provided by

---

* It was once suggested to Willie Rushton that *Private Eye*'s design was an exercise in 'neo-Brechtian realism.' He replied that it had always reminded him of a betting-shop floor.

Gareth Powell, who Osmond remembers as a crazy Welsh publisher who had moved from delivery boy to millionaire via soft pornography. Powell offered to take over the distribution of *Private Eye* and sell it nationally. While this was being worked out he offered the staff an office in Neal Street, Covent Garden. 'I remember at our first meeting, when it seemed that all our problems just might be solved by this wonderful man, how Usborne turned round as we were leaving and said, "Oh by the way. Could you let us have a photocopier for the next three weeks?" Uz was always pushing his luck abominably.' The deal never came off but the office did.

The office at 41, Neal St., Covent Garden.

We never paid a penny's rent. All we had to promise was to lock it up at night because of the insurance. It was the nicest office we ever had. I remember the pavements covered in banana skins and Vera's café. Then one night someone forgot to lock it up and Gareth Powell kicked us out.

By that time I had passed my Foreign Office exam and had to face the final board. Nine men sat around a crescent-shaped table. As I walked in they all turned up a copy of *Private Eye* and said, 'Are you responsible for this?', and tittered. I knew then I was in. At that time they were under fire for being too stuffy. I decided that I was going to join the FO. I was very worried about money, and we had just hired two secretaries, Mary Morgan and Elizabeth Longmore. I was utterly exhausted. I seemed to spend half the night doing the accounts and used to fall asleep at meals. The only thing I needed was a buyer.

Issue 6 had started a series which was to run for many issues. It was called 'Aesop Revisited', it was lovingly worked out and drawn over a whole page, and the first subject chosen was 'The Satirist'. He was called Jonathan Crake, but he most closely resembled Peter Cook. Crake progressed from school plays to Cambridge magazines to a satirical revue, television fame and his own satirical nightclub. This was followed by sycophantic audiences, the bottle and finally copying out jokes from *Punch* 1890. The moral was 'Humour is a Serious Business' but the sharpest jibe was against the satirical club's upper-middle-class audience baying in uncomprehending laughter when Crake called them 'ugly, boneheaded bastards' and murmuring proudly to each other that 'of course' they 'knew all the Fringe boys'.

ÆSOP revisited 1. The Satirist

Young Jonathan Crake shows early talent for raising laughs in School Play ...

... at Cambridge his gay, witty, little pieces in all the mags have the chaps in fits ...

... sparkling revue "Short Back and Sides" mentions Prime Minister. Crake acclaimed as biting satirist of our time ...

... instantly beseiged by press, TV men seeking views on Monarchy, Mr. Gaitskell, Common Market, Schedule A, the Bomb ...

... stage, TV, film offers pour in. Featured in five glossies simultaneously. Opens satirical nightclub in Fulham .. strain becomes terrific ...

... cannot open his mouth without everyone collapsing at brilliant satirical comment...

MORAL:

HUMOUR IS A SERIOUS BUSINESS

Despite this apparent lack of sympathy, the owners of The Establishment were the obvious people to buy *Private Eye* when Osmond decided to sell it. Peter Cook and Nicholas Luard had formed a company called Cook–Luard Productions Ltd, which owned, apart from The Establishment, the magazine *Scene*. Luard was at this time referred to by the press as 'the Emperor of Satire'. For £1500 Cook and Luard acquired seventy-five of Osmond's shares in Pressdram Ltd. Pressdram was simply the name of a ready-made company which Osmond had purchased for £26 'from a bloke in Fleet Street'. Originally Osmond had ninety-nine shares in Pressdram and had given the other one to Usborne. Now he sold seventy-five shares to Cook–Luard, kept most of his other shares, but gave some more to Usborne and to Gareth Powell. In addition, of the £1050 profit he had made on the deal, he gave Rushton, Booker and Usborne £250 each, keeping the remaining £300 for himself. When Osmond left the circulation was, he thinks, about eighteen thousand, which had been built up in the first ten issues. He remembers that Rushton told him he was crazy and that he was only leaving to please his mother. He remembers also 'how everyone was suffering greatly from Booker who was terribly highly strung. Keeping up with our own success was driving us all into the ground. Being brilliant every fortnight was a strain. I left them feeling that they wouldn't survive and feeling slightly treacherous.' He was the first member of the hayfield mutual admiration society to leave. He had never written a word of the paper or contributed one joke except: 'Losing the hairs in your ears? Try ear wigs.'

The first decision Luard made was to change the cover of Issue 11. Matthew Carter designed the new masthead, which is still in use today. Luard then had to address himself to the problems of personnel. By this time Ingrams had become a full-time contributor. Tomorrow's Audience had proved a failure. Despite the enthusiasm and talent available, it proved impossible to make a go of it. The Arts Council had refused a grant and the success which they had with a new Spike Milligan play, *The Bed Sitting Room*, came too late to save the company. Osmond remembers a conversation he had with Ingrams at about this time on the top deck of a bus in the King's Road. 'Ingrams said, "I've learnt one thing. Never put your own money into anything."' He had lost much of his capital, about £3000, and must have wished that he had put it into *Private Eye* instead. But the stage remained his first love,

37

and if Tomorrow's Audience had succeeded he would have stayed with it in preference to *Private Eye*.

With Ingrams and Cook available the editorial arrangements were changed. Booker, who had been sole editor, now became one of a four-man editorial board. Luard remembers that one of the problems was the constant quarrelling between Booker and Ingrams. 'They weren't a happy little band of satirists. Booker was once locked out of the office by Ingrams and he came to me to complain.' The press announcement of May 7 had said that Luard had acquired 'a partnership interest' in *Private Eye*, and that he would 'be assisting them financially'. He also said, 'it needs more writers.'

Luard's idea was to form a link between the *Eye* and the resident team at The Establishment which included John Bird, John Fortune, Eleanor Bron, and Jeremy Geidt (the man who coined the word 'poove'). Unfortunately this plan was doomed to failure because of the mutual jealousies involved. The *Eye* editors thought that The Establishment was a rather dubious and highly trendy enterprise, an object for attack rather than partnership. They were anxious for their independence. The Establishment team thought that the *Eye* was written by public school chancers. Luard tried to get the two sides together over lunch. Wells remembers the hostility and a division between the Oxford journalists and the more committed Cambridge actors. During the year that *Private Eye* was housed by The Establishment the staff shared the waiters' changing room. The only way out was across the stage, and if a performance was in progress it was impossible to enter or leave the office. Among the waitresses employed by the club at that time was an *ingenue* newly arrived from the antipodes, Miss Carmen Callil, later to become a co-founder of the publishers, Virago.

Private Eye now settled down for a period of more than a year to attack the old England that still in the early sixties appeared to be the dominant one. The new atmosphere of cynicism and frivolity had quite failed to penetrate the governing classes. Food rationing had only ended in 1954. More and more new restaurants were opening, the Stock Exchange was embarked on its greatest boom backed by small investors, hire-purchase restrictions were removed. It was, in short, an excellent time to attack the old standard-bearers who had brought all this about. One of the earliest and most effective outrages was published in Issue 13, a sequence of pictures of R. A. Butler, devised by Peter Cook, describing him as 'a flabby-faced old coward' for, among other things,

I admit the Immigration Bill ran
counter to all my principles . . .

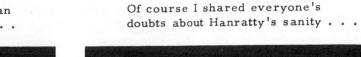

Of course I shared everyone's
doubts about Hanratty's sanity . . .

And I know that flogging lunatics
in gaol doesn't do anybody any
good . . .

The fact remains - I'M JUST
A FLABBY FACED OLD COWARD

P.S. And what's more, he's such
a flabby faced old coward he won't
even sue us.

P.P.S. And even if he does sue us
he's STILL a flabby faced old coward.

doing nothing about the Hanratty murder verdict (though they got it wrong by suggesting that it was Hanratty's sanity that was in question before he was hanged).

Another coup was in Issue 8. It was a photograph of Harold Macmillan sitting in his shirt sleeves on a chintz sofa with anti-macassar, gazing mournfully up at the camera. This astounding scoop had been obtained by the film director Maurice Hatton, who happened to be passing a hotel bedroom in Blackpool and had glanced in to see the Prime Minister in this position. Unfortunately, when it appeared everyone assumed that the photograph was a brilliant composite and Maurice's scoop did not receive a standing ovation.

The paper's early attitude to Fleet Street was displayed in one 'Aesop' which was devoted to Arthur Christiansen, 'The Expressman'. It turned into an attack on investigative reporters of the foot-in-the-door type – 'I have a sacred trust to expose you to my readers' – and ended with the dispiriting moral: 'Once you've gone on the Street you've got to stay there.' Issue 16 contained an even fiercer comment on Fleet Street in the form of a premature spoof Apology to Lord Beaverbrook. 'Thousands of journalists, many of them talented, intelligent were . . . sucked into the maw of creeping servility, sycophancy and grovelling amorality with which he has been surrounding himself ever since he came to this country. . . . Not a shred in their secret hearts of self-respect. While they are up in the sun they laugh at the Baron's little idiosyncrasies, they sneer at those who mock. They think they are living life to the full – until suddenly they find that there is nothing left but Bell's Scotch whisky and thirty long years to kill.'

The editorial board was divided on some matters. Ingrams recalls two arguments with Booker at this period. 'One was on abortion; Booker was for. The other was on Mozart; Booker was against.' There is no doubt that the first editor of *Private Eye* was beautifully attuned to his times.

Rushton and Ingrams were Christians, Booker and Cook were atheists. Cook remembers that some jokes could not be printed. He feels that he now has far more freedom to make blasphemous jokes and cites *The Dead Sea Tapes*, which was acceptable in 1974 but which would probably have sent him to prison if it had been published in 1963 when it was written. In Issue 19 Christopher Logue, a lapsed Catholic then as now, devoted his 'True Stories' to a spirited satire on the Roman Catholic Church and in particular to its Stations of the Cross. Whatever the religious views of the editors, the peripheral liturgy of the Roman church was entirely acceptable as a target. As far as that sort of eccentricity was concerned, it would have been universally agreed that a Brave New World was on the way. Political affairs were different; they involved serious issues which had to be fought for.

Rushton remembers Booker's excitement at the time of the Liberal victory in the Orpington by-election. 'He hadn't been Muggeridged then. He hadn't got religion.' Ingrams remembers Booker's work on the Eric Buttock column, based on Eric Lubbock, MP, the victor of Orpington. This was a St Trinian's-style report on the House of Commons, inspired by the work of Ronald Searle. He also remembers the number of pieces Booker would tear up in mid-flow, the smashed telephones, and how they all worked hardest on 'Aesop' which got most of the best jokes. Booker remembers how much they wanted to distance themselves from the trendy sixties which they were considered to be part of. 'The paper was still written by outsiders,' he says. 'Sometimes we were paid £10 a fortnight and then as much as £30 a fortnight, but we still received most of our income from elsewhere. Willie and I were getting £80 a week at one time from *TW3*.'

In fact it is not always easy to see how this distance between the *Eye* and the upper-middle-class generation that had seized cultural power was maintained. The early line suggested by a cartoon in Issue 6 ('Nigel, I think we're going to have an abortion'), which was placed beside a spoof ad

"Nigel, I think we're going to have an abortion"

I'm sorry but the ethical position is quite clear. Thalidomide was a legal prescription, but what you suggest is an illegal operation.

recommending happy families to contain no children, was soon replaced by the more conventional progressive view of Issue 17. This was a Trog cartoon of a doctor and a girl patient. He is saying, 'I'm sorry but the ethical position is quite clear. Thalidomide was a legal prescription, but what you suggest is an illegal operation.' And elsewhere in that issue there is a letter satirising the attitude of those who opposed abortion and thereby allowed more thalidomide children to be born.

Another early contributor did not last very long. Issue 19 contained a piece entitled 'The Hounding of the Pooves'. Unfortunately it was signed by 'Dr J. Miller' and his picture appeared. The resulting howl of outrage, all the way from Washington, D.C., was enough to sour relations between Jonathan Miller and *Private Eye* from that day to this. 'You stupid bloody irresponsible cunts,' began the letter from the eminent neurologist and thespian, and he went on to protest about the possibility that he might be struck off the medical register for advertising; a suggestion so satirical when one examined the original article as to ensure that his note would immediately be pinned to the office notice board where – yellowing and torn – it can still be seen.

At some point during this period Booker remembers that he had a conversation with Ingrams in which he asked him what he wanted to do with his life. 'I want to edit a magazine,' Ingrams replied. 'Little did I realise,' says Booker, 'which magazine he had in mind.' Also at some time in this period Paul Foot, by now an earnest trainee reporter on the *Glasgow Daily Record*, with memories of Oxford fading fast, received a letter from Ingrams offering him the editorship of *Private Eye*. The letter stressed the importance of editing it 'from left of centre'. Foot replied, rather pompously as he now says, pointing out that he could not accept the offer since his own future lay with the workers' struggle. 'I'm part of a Movement now,' he explained.

Other notable events in the first year were a piece, of which Booker is particularly proud, in Issue 9, a ferocious attack on tower blocks. And a typical response to International Reverence in Issue 8 – a Rushton cartoon of an unknown man rushing into the courtroom in the middle of the Eichmann trial shouting, 'Hang on, I did it.' In its first year *Private Eye* also printed two stories of an investigative and sensational nature. In America, Cook, who was appearing in *Beyond the Fringe*, was informed that President Kennedy was a divorced man, and accordingly set in train a series of inquiries which culminated in the discovery of a book entitled *The History of*

THE HOUNDING OF THE POOVES

AN INVESTIGATION

BY DR J Miller

"Pooves, pooves! Que pouvez-vous dire? Sont-ils ils ou elles?" Not even Montaigne himself, the balding sage of old Dordogne, could fathom the ways of the crafty poove.

Doctors have realised, in recent years, that there are many more pooves in society than meet the eye at a glance, many of them running the country, as intellectuals, politicians, artists and even masquerading as women. More than four out of every twenty men you meet on the top of a bus are pooves. While we all know of the married poove, with several children, who has married simply as a vile disguise - to conceal his poovish practises from his wife.

After intensive research, both in this country and in America, we know that your average poove is a sick man. He should be treated as such by society - with aspirin or whatever comes to hand. It is simply ridiculous to say that he is abnormal. Your normal poove is in no way unnatural. Indeed, as pooves come, he is probably considerably more normal than your average so-called heterosexual.

There has been considerable agitation in recent years by irresponsible left-wing elements, pooves etc., for a reform of the so-called Labouchere Amendment which makes the filthy and depraved practices of the poove a criminal offence. It must be remembered, however, that this trivial Amendment was merely the after-dinner caprice of a well-known Commons eccentric, passed well over seventy years ago. To drag this dusty issue up again would be to deprive the celebrated Poove Squad, the most successful Division of the Yard, of its last vestiges of official power. The ever-watchful Poove Hounds would no longer roam the streets and conveniences of London on their ghastly mission. While our women and children could no longer sleep soundly in their beds.

Female practice which could drive a young man to poovery.

Pooves, or 'queers', at their filthy practices.

Men of the Poove Squad in plain clothes prepare for a raid.

Drag Queen avoiding publicity.

Columnist John Gordon reproving young poove.

Pooves receiving occupational therapy at Poove rehabilitation centre.

ERIC BUTTOCK WRITES
.HOME . . .

JO →

Dear Mummy

 larst wek transport house (thats Gaters house) had
there house Fate in the park. it was called the
festival of Laber ha ha and evryone had to mak
flotes of there one, to sho there House Spirit Spirit.
It was orl joly xpensive about £700 per flote
so george Brown he'sthe Skool Buly think how
can we pay for it orl. he also think how can i be
more poplar at the sam time, sinc he hav ben
somewot in the doghouse recerntly.

then he com up with this brite weeze why dose
he not get old bert rusell to pay for it. so he
sa 'bert' i see you hav not paid up yore 6d.
sub. to the deb.soc. and anihow you are just
a peenut and a komunist. so were going to
xpel you or else.

then he find that old Gaters hav not paid up
either so quikly he get gaters to pay up, then
he find that old Bertie hav frends, Chorley
and Colins (he's the Skool Chaplin) and Matron
wooton but Ruthless Gorge disregard them orl
and stil go on trying to tak the Mikey out of
Bert. then he find that 150 thousand other men
hav not paid up for Deb.Soc either but StILL
he go on with his litl game. Finerly Bert sa
"but i hav paid up", so anyone with sens would
think Gorge mite pull out and xxxxx save his
face wots left of it. but he kik out old bert
anihow and dosnt even get his 6d.

now George is evn more in the doghouse xh than
ever almost as bad as Ian macloud in tories
house, xxxxx so old mac, hes Hed of Skool,
sa joking to Gaters why do we not xchange
George brown and macloud. but noone is having
ani so it look as if noone is going to win the nex
elekshun at orl xept posserbly the xxxx scotish
xxxxxxxxx Nashnerlists ha ha

me   luv
     eric

← Old Black Gaters he say:
'I kno all about defence
I've been sitting on it foryears

EICHMANN
NEW
EVIDENCI

HANG ON,
I DID IT!

DON'T THROW STONES

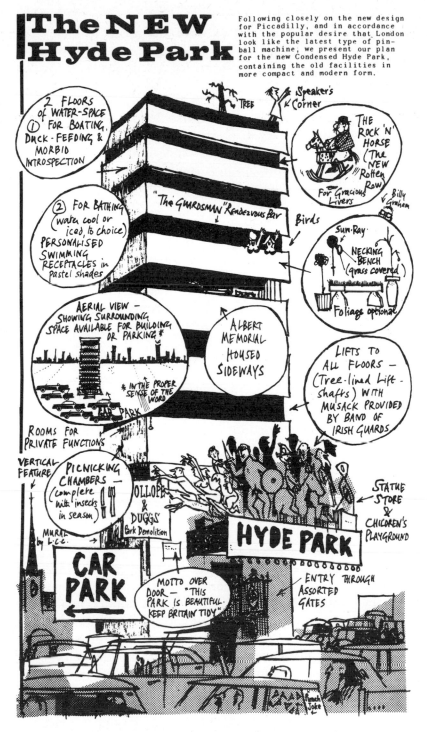

The NEW Hyde Park

Following closely on the new design for Piccadilly, and in accordance with the popular desire that London look like the latest type of pinball machine, we present our plan for the new Condensed Hyde Park, containing the old facilities in more compact and modern form.

the Blauveld Family. This stated that JFK had made a secret first marriage to a lady who was named. Feeling disinclined to deal with such persons as the outraged Roman Catholic President might send in his direction, Cook posted this sensational information to *Private Eye* where it appeared in

45

Issue 20 above a note, 'We have attempted to check the validity of this grotesque story.... Unfortunately [we have failed] so, as usual, we have printed it without verifying our facts.'

The following issue contained a story written by Booker, who remembers with some surprise that he actually went to the newspaper library at Colindale to expand it. It revealed that Lord Beaverbrook's famous appeal for cooking pots and pans to be turned into Spitfires and Hurricanes in July 1940 – part of the mythology of wartime spirit – was completely useless. There was a surplus of aluminium in the country at that time and it is doubtful whether, despite Beaverbrook's promise to the Women of Britain, a single aeroplane was fashioned from the massive donation.

Issue 23 in November 1962 is remembered by Booker as 'the best ever', with the board in hysterics of laughter for most of the time. It contained the curiously prophetic piece on the Cuban missile crisis in which *Private Eye* revealed exclusively that the whole affair boiled down to a plot by the Cubans to flood the USA with pooves. The figure of 'Grocer' Heath was launched (with reference to the Common Market negotiations) and this portly vessel was then manoeuvred to a disused dock ready for use at a later date. At some time during this week the editors agreed to publicise a new board game called 'Diplomacy'. Pictures appeared in the national press of Booker and Ingrams wearing funny hats and playing it in Sukie de la Mare's flat in Maida Avenue.

The 24th of November 1962 saw the climax of the fashion for satire. *TW3* was launched by the BBC. With its successor, *Not so much a programme...*, it made national figures out of such unlikely characters as Rushton, the poet P. J. Kavanagh and Bernard Levin, as well as Lance Percival, Millicent Martin and of course the unutterable Frostie, soon to be dubbed 'the bubonic plagiarist' by Cook. Booker became one of its main script writers. 'For me and Willy this was the most heady phase. I wrote *TW3*, Rushton appeared on it. We had money, fame and a booming circulation. *TW3* helped *Private Eye* a lot. We had a lot of the "fortnightly version of *TW3*" type of publicity. The upper classes took us up. I married Emma Tennant.'*

Nicholas Tomalin once wrote that at Cambridge Booker

---

* In fact television was to some extent in competition with *Private Eye* for the services of its contributors. Rushton, then primarily a cartoonist, was turned into 'a personality' following the enormous success of his *TW3* impersonation of Harold Macmillan.

THIS PICTURE COULD MEAN
WAR
MEAN

3" NAILS PROB.
CHINESE

2⅜" x 4¼" ULTRASONIC
VALVE-DETECTING DEVICE
OF TYPE BELIEVED TO BE IN USE

PROB. N. KHRUSCHEV IN TENT

PROB. CARDBOARD BOX

PEACELOVING COW
PROB. OF RUSSIAN MAKE
(1) and (2) AN UDDER

PROB. CRATES

PROB. TREE

WARMONGERING SHEEP

LORD HOME AGREES

YES, THIS IS THE PICTURE THAT COULD MEAN
WORLD WAR III.
To the ordinary peaceloving reader it may look just
like an ordinary clump of trees in any old field.
Which is, of course, what it is.
But the trained observer looks beyond the simple
peaceloving blades of grass, the few freedom-
hungry sheep. For when this picture is blown up
24,000 times it shows nothing less than an enormous
underground missile site. On neat racks lie hundreds
of nuclear missiles, each one carefully labelled with
the name of an individual American city and the words
"Made in Russia".
THESE ARE THE SECRETS REVEALED BY THE
EVER-VIGILANT EYE OF THE PEACELOVING U2
PILOT AND THE CAREFUL USE OF WHITE INK
IN THE PENTAGON PHOTOGRAPHIC SECTION.

● These are also the pictures, it was revealed last
night by the Danish newspaper Dagbladet, that were
taken last year of a Montana chicken-ranch for its
millionaire owner Homer Q. Tilt.

*　　*　　*

Miami, Florida

There is an air of indescribable tension in this
waterfront town here tonight.
During the past few days, half the United States
Army has moved into Florida to play its vital
part in the forthcoming Naval blockade.
"Operation Peaceloving", as it is known, is
proceeding smoothly, despite last night's revelation that President Kennedy's pictures were
all fakes.
Said Kennedy himself: "What the hell - the show
must go on".
Commented cigar-chewing, grenade-throwing
7-star General Otis P. Kneethug, in charge of
naval operations: "These Chinese must be taught
a lesson".
Lord Home expressed concurrence with these
sentiments. "It is quite right to point out that
these pictures are fakes; but I am right behind
the President in any move he cares to make".

FISHBEDS   9 FAGOTS   12 FISHBEDS   8 FAGOT

*

Among the installations spotted
by the U2 in Cuba are several
'Nests of Fagots' (or Pooves, as
they are known in this country.)
In Washington yesterday, I was
shown pictures of the Pooves
taken from 97,000 feet and mag-
nified 4,500 times. (see picture above.)
"They are bearded little men"
said the Washington spokesman,
"wearing swimming trunks".
It was probable, he went on, that
they were being trained by Soviet
Fagots (flown into Cuba last
month) to undermine the moral
strength of the peaceloving Western hemisphere.
As the Vassall case demonstrated
only this week, the Russians have
employed the same devices to
great effect in our own armed ser-
ces.
esident Kennedy stated in his
eech last night:
here can be no doubt at all

that these Fagots are of a hostel
and offensive character, and as
such constitute a definite threat
to the peace of the Western world.
It is our opinion that they are
being trained in Cuber with the
intention of eventual infiltration
into the United States to subvert
and sabotage the Constitution -
as we have already seen from the
film Advise and Consent, Communist influences in Hollywood have
long since blueprinted the course
such subversion may take".
OUR MEDICAL CORRESPONDENT
Writes:
"The Washington pictures show
very clearly the characteristics
of the Fagotus Cubanus Castratus,
or lesser bearded poove, one of
the most deadly and carniverous
species of poove. Any contact
with this species causes moral
decay, and eventually imprisonment and death".
The Earl of Home expressed full
agreement with this view.

Fig. 1
Harmful, warmongering
Russian ship to be stopped
at all costs.

Fig. 2
Harmless, peaceloving
American ship that will
do the stopping.

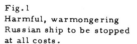

(The difference is apparent from the smoke)

had declared three ambitions: to edit his own paper, to marry a duke's daughter, and to appear on television. In the summer of 1962 it all seemed to be coming true. Sukie de la Mare (now Marlowe) remembers the wedding for the party afterwards, which was held in Mark and Arabella Boxer's house in Holland Villas Road. 'The highlight was a drag act by two window dressers from C&A (since better known as Rogers and Star). They wore chandelier ear-rings, they were dressed as cinema usherettes and they sang a song with the refrain

> Would you like a lick of my lollipop?
> Would you like a suck on my sweet?'

Boxer recalls that Booker loved the show.

Just as Booker was then no Christian, his wife was not yet a Marxist, and was still to earn Maurice Hatton's description as 'the girl who put the Ché in Cheyne Walk'. But Noel Picarda at least must have seen trouble ahead. He was then reading for the Bar, and his wedding present to the Bookers was a 'free divorce voucher'.

Ingrams also started to write for *TW3*, but he found Frost rather difficult to admire. 'For a short time I went to Frostie's flat and wrote scripts but then I had a traumatic experience with Frostie and ceased to contribute.' (The traumatic experience was when Frost retired from the conference to go to the lavatory but continued to make suggestions from the throne, having left the door open.) In Ingrams's view, Booker and Rushton lifted a lot of *Eye* material for *TW3* without attribution.

Rushton also enjoyed his first years of fame. He appeared on *TW3* because of a revue at the Room at the Top nightclub. This was a relic of *The Bed Sitting Room* in which he had starred in the pre-London run. An agent called Willy Donaldson (later better known as 'Henry Root'), who had promoted *Beyond the Fringe* and was looking for another hit, took the undergraduate revue to this nightclub in Ilford, which was situated at the top of a tower block. The cast were Rushton, Ingrams, Wells and Barbara Windsor, and the audience were mostly East-Enders. 'I can't believe it,' said Barbara Windsor when Rushton and Ingrams turned up for the first night in their tweed jackets. Ingrams actually said 'Fuck' during his John Gielgud imitation. The only night the house was full was Saturday night and the whole cast were given the bird except for Barbara Windsor. The only consolation was that Donaldson was paying everyone £30 a week. One night the Kray twins turned up. 'We thought they were frightfully nice,' says Rushton. 'We couldn't understand what Barbara was panicking about. She wouldn't come out for a drink that night because they had summoned her.' Despite Barbara, the show closed after its three-week run, and never transferred to the West End.

Undeterred by this further theatrical failure, *Private Eye* continued to go from strength to strength. There had been a very important early piece of publicity in the 'Atticus' column, which was handed over to the editors to do what they liked with in April. The results were heavily censored by the editor of *The Sunday Times* but that did not matter. Rushton remembers that Booker's idea at that time was that doing it 'would make us all terribly famous and then we could move on to something else. What happened instead was that Ingrams and I got jobs of a sort on a paper called *Time & Tide*, a weekly newsmagazine.' Ingrams became the theatre critic. The editor and proprietor was W. J. Brittain. One of his minions was Ian Sproat, now an MP, who had just come down from Oxford. After a while Sproat sent Ingrams a memo saying: 'Mr Brittain asks me to remind you that you are writing for a great magazine and not for yourself.' Shortly afterwards Ingrams was sacked. There was also a rave review in *The Observer*'s 'Daylight' column which was written by Thomas Pakenham. This noted that after only a year *Private Eye* was printing fifty thousand copies a fortnight and had thereby overtaken such papers as the *Spectator*, and that this had been achieved despite a ban from W.H. Smith and with the aid of only two old delivery vans.

The width of attack in the *Eye*'s material was one of the paper's earliest hallmarks. Tynan wrote a scathing note asking, 'When are you going to get a point of view?' but this was really to miss the point. It was partly because the joke went in, whatever the point of view, that so many people had a chance to find themselves in agreement as well as under attack. There was a great deal of confusion about which parts of the magazine were intended to be jokes and which were meant to be either straight advertisements or factual news items, but again the editors did very little to dispel this confusion. The only way to speak with authority on the matter was to become a regular reader. Cook considers that the paper has always had a point of view on particular issues. 'It has always had the same point of view about the world of finance. Its attitude in that area has always been left-liberal. There are a large number of crooks about. Let's tell you about them.' And in 1962 the editors told *The Observer* that they were prepared to agree on the need for a more democratic educational system.

In the autumn of 1962, *Private Eye on London*, published by Weidenfeld & Nicolson at 16/– (0.80p), appeared. It was a rare example of a *Private Eye* book that was not simply reprinted material. It had been reworked into a narrative. 'We really tried on that book,' remembers Rushton. The acknowledgements read:

> Our thanks are due to the following gay young things, who assisted in the preparation of this book: To Miss Caroline Rodgers, Miss Pamela Deane, Miss Mary O'Morgan, Mr. Andrew Osmond, Mr. Richard de la Mare and Mrs. Richard de la Mare (who appears by kind permission of her husband) and Mr. Harold Macmillan who modelled for pictures.

The book had been written at great speed after an approach by George Weidenfeld over 'drinks at the Ritz'. It had been an outstanding example of successful collaboration. Booker recalls how he and Rushton had taken immense trouble and considerable time to meet the deadline, writing one draft only and working together at both the cartoons and the text. 'It brought out Willie's capacity to do detailed and brilliantly observed caricatures and also some of his finest puns.' Booker thinks that Rushton may have resented the work, but that it was worth it, even if it meant overcoming his more easy-going and lovable side. The book was 'by *Private Eye*, Christopher Booker, William Rushton and Richard Ingrams with photographs by Maurice Hatton'.

The first writ finally arrived in response to a spoof on *The Guardian* in Issue 25. A man called Colin Watson objected to being described as 'Colin What's-'is-name the little known author who . . . was writing a novel very like Wodehouse but without the jokes'. He was eventually paid £750. Two issues later Noel Picarda, writing as 'Retinus', referred to the Liberal candidate in the Rotherham by-election as 'the most uproarious Mayor in living memory and keener on the Good Things of Life than the bad things in Rotherham'. This figure emerged from the North to identify himself as Alderman Tarbit. He issued a writ but then passed away,* possibly overcome by good living, before he could collect his pennies. And so the first full year in the history of *Private Eye* drew to a close. In the first birthday issue (22) Lord Gnome announced that sales had reached thirty-five thousand, which

*A mishap which later gave rise to the legend of 'The Curse of Gnome'.

was not bad for a magazine that had been started on £450. Gnome also noted that the *New Statesman* and Lord Buggeridge of Snide had said that with such sales it must be obvious that the satirical mission was failing since 'if it was proper satire, people would be far too offended to buy it at all'. To which Lord Gnome ventured the obvious retort that if no one bought the paper 'he could not be the bloated tycoon he was today'.

Lord Buggeridge of Snide was of course Malcolm Muggeridge and the reference was to a piece he had written entitled 'The Hollow Tooth'. The magazine satirists, wrote Muggeridge, were 'delightfully and offensively rude to one and all', but they used 'a bazooka rather than poisoned arrows', and he added that no one had accused Swift's satire of being sick, and suggested that with their 'largely Top People clientele' they would soon become accepted as part of the establishment. Booker replied to this attack in a letter to the *New Statesman* comparing Muggeridge's aged attempts to understand satire with an old lady who slips on a banana skin. (It is interesting that he should have chosen to attack Muggeridge on grounds of age since he was later to devote many pages of his first book, *The Neophiliacs*, to an attack on the cult of youth.) *Private Eye* itself, with typical speed, responded by including the phrase 'Top People clientele' in a leaflet that was circulated to advertisers.

Muggeridge by Rushton.

Even those infants who set out to misbehave need mentors. Muggeridge was one of a group who the young satirists could hold in high regard. Randolph Churchill was another. Together with such contemporaries as Evelyn Waugh, Tom Driberg, Graham Greene, Claud Cockburn and Maurice Richardson, they had built up an enviable reputation for persistently blotting their copybooks. Waugh had satirised the orthodox aspirations of an earlier 'young generation' with greater skill than any other English writer of the century. Greene's fictions had illuminated the lives of sinners, Cockburn had adopted Communism and spent his life undermining established views in any way he could, Maurice Richardson was noted for his destructive social presence and for a conversational style similar in effect to Cockburn's journalism. Muggeridge was almost universally detested for his opinions – than which there could be few higher recommendations. Driberg was a sexual anarchist and gossip of the first water with a warm interest in the activities of young men. Randolph Churchill had missed no opportunity to ensure that, wherever high ability and superb connections could be expected to work their magic, his behaviour would be sufficiently offensive to guarantee failure.

All these venerable figures had started on their careers between 1925 and 1930. When they had come down from university they had rejected the usual careers of the governing classes, in the Army, the Foreign Office, banking or the Treasury, even though each of these institutions tolerated actvities such as gambling, homosexualism, Communist espionage or extreme right-wing authoritarianism. But if the earlier rebels had set a disruptive example, they had also shown that the essence of interesting opinions is their unpredictability. In an extraordinary article in the *Spectator* of 13 April 1929, Evelyn Waugh, writing as the spokesman of the under-thirties, mounted an attack on the concept of 'a younger generation' and therefore on the youth cult which then, as in the sixties, seemed a basic ingredient to the success of cultural rebelliousness. Observing that the Great War had imposed second-rate standards on the children of that time, Waugh wrote:

> The only thing which could have saved these unfortunate children was the imposition by rigid discipline, as soon as it became possible, of the standards of civilisation. Unfortunately [the young schoolmasters returning from the War] returned with a jolly tolerance of everything that seemed 'modern'. Every effort was made to encourage the children at the Public Schools to 'think for themselves'. When they should have been whipped and taught Greek paradigms, they were set arguing about birth control and nationalisation. Their crude little opinions were treated with respect. Preachers in the school chapel week after week entrusted the future to their hands. It is hardly surprising that they were Bolshevik at eighteen and bored at twenty.
>
> The muscles which encounter the most resistance in daily routine are those which become most highly developed and adapted. It is thus that the restraint of a traditional culture tempers and directs creative impulses. Freedom produces sterility. There was nothing left for the younger generation to rebel against, except the widest conceptions of mere decency. Accordingly it was against these that it turned. The result in many cases is the perverse and aimless dissipation chronicled daily by the gossip-writers of the Press.
>
> What young man today, for example, in choosing a career, ever considers for one moment whether, by its

nature, any job is better worth doing than any other? There was once a prevailing opinion that 'the professions', which performed beneficial services to the community, were more becoming to the man of culture than 'trades' in which he simply sold things for more than he gave. Today that prejudice is suppressed and shopkeeping has become a polite hobby.

The remarkable thing about this article is its applicability to the sixties. Lack of discipline in schools, *trahison des clercs*, even the issues of birth control and nationalisation, are raised. With the complaint about the social acceptability of trade, the boutiques and bistros and antique markets of the sixties are also anticipated. Waugh's invective, written only one year after the publication of *Decline and Fall*, sets his satire in a moralistic context. He had evidently chosen his targets with the intention of reforming them in the classic satirical manner. And beneath an apparently modish revolutionary surface his rebelliousness was already the expression of thoroughly reactionary opinions.

Muggeridge's article was the first direct comment made by the black sheep of that older generation on their successors. They were all still busy men at the height of their influence. In the month that *Private Eye* was launched, for instance, the *Spectator* had carried numerous contributions from them. Graham Greene had written a letter advising Lord Home, the newly appointed Foreign Secretary, 'not to lick his lips on the television' since it hardly gave 'the impression of a Foreign Secretary negotiating from strength, the role which he was so hopelessly attempting'. Evelyn Waugh wrote a long letter defending Angus Wilson's *The Old Men at the Zoo* from hostile criticism, and he also reviewed Greene's travel book *In Search of a Character*. His own new novel, *Unconditional Surrender*, had been reviewed by Kingsley Amis, adversely. Other reviewers included William Golding and Stevie Smith. Elizabeth David wrote a cookery column, and the cartoonists included Trog, Timothy, Heath, and ffolkes, all of whom were shortly to become contributors to *Private Eye*. One of Trog's *Spectator* cartoons, drawn at the time of the Tory party conference, showed the doorman at The Establishment assuring customers of a seat as most of the regulars were away at Brighton.

But the idea that 'there were giants in those days' did not occur to the editors of *Private Eye*. They chose to satirise the *Spectator* in Issue 12. The featured target was 'Children's Books from Ireland' with contributions from Sean Lemass,

Now that even the Pope is a bloody liberal, I think the time has come for me to die

Sean O'Kenny, Lunchtime O'Booze, Nancy O'Spain and Father Eainid O'Bloightain. This issue of *Private Eye* was circulated to members of The Establishment and the subsequent print order was doubled.

After a suitable interval the *Spectator* responded by inviting the editors of *Private Eye* to write an eight-page supplement for the 1962 Christmas number. (*Private Eye* had already carried out similar assignments for *The Sunday Times* and *Queen*.) The supplement they wrote for the *Spectator* included a Rushton cartoon of Evelyn Waugh, as a member of the Senile Club, saying, 'Now that even the Pope is a bloody liberal, I think the time has come for me to die.' Apart from being an unfortunate piece of prophecy, this was an inspired reference to a piece in the same issue of the *Spectator* written by Evelyn Waugh and entitled 'The Same Again Please', a sustained and brilliant attack on the direction the Roman Catholic Church was taking following the Vatican Council. In attacking this trend Waugh was of course attacking the new orthodoxy, and in satirising him *Private Eye* was assisting that orthodoxy. (Issue 22 for instance carried a Trog cartoon of two cardinals discussing the pill, one saying, 'Well I suppose it's got to come sometime, but at least we can urge that the instructions on the packet be printed in Latin.')

At about this time Evelyn Waugh was sent a copy of *Private Eye on London* for review by *The Observer*. He declined to review it on the grounds that it exposed him as 'a hopeless old fogey' and that 'not one of the objects of its jokes' was known to him. (He suggested that it be sent to his son Auberon Waugh, of Chester Row, SW1, who was in touch with modern London; an idea which *The Observer* did not follow up.) The odd thing was that *Private Eye on London* did not contain a single reference to Evelyn Waugh. The only place where the cartoon had been published at the time when that book was sent to him for review was in the *Spectator*.

The reasons for his hurt are evident. But the fact that the *Private Eye* attack had taken place on his own ground must have been particularly hard to take. For fifteen years Waugh had used the *Spectator* as his own private squib factory, the place where he could start trouble for those whose lives he wished to make more interesting. Later the national press could be relied on to take the matter up, by which time, having lit the blue touch paper, he would have retired.

Another father figure to react frostily to juvenile attention was Peter Simple. He was teased in Issue 10 with the suggestion that he had made an extreme right-wing speech at

British Letters

We have received many letters on the courtesy of coloured bus conductors, the first cuckoo in Clackmannanshire, C.P.Snow and other traditional sources of ribaldry which we are unable for reasons of legibility to publish.

PETER SIMPLE
As one imagines him ... and as he is

The Daily Telegraph
and
Morning Post

TELEGRAMS
TELENEWS, LONDON.

FLEET STREET.
LONDON. E.C.4

TELEPHONE
FLEet STreet 4242.

3rd May, 1962.

Dear Sir,

The funnier parts of your magazine show that you have made a close, even systematic, study of the "Way of the World" column. Even more systematic study might have shown you the following facts:

I have never at any time expressed any prejudice against "niggers" or "the working classes", as such, for the good reason that I do not feel any. "Angry Young Men" have, I think, not been referred to in this column since the term became obsolete some years ago. I admit to a slight distaste for "beatniks" and a strong distaste for protest marches.

Incidentally, the joke about Lady Pamela Berry being the author of this column was first made (by, I think, Randolph Churchill) about six years ago. It was quite amusing at the time but seems hardly worth reviving now.

To be effective, humour demands some knowledge and understanding of what one is trying to be humorous about. Otherwise it tends to be merely silly.

The best of luck to you.

Yours faithfully,

Michael Wharton

PETER SIMPLE

---

spike milligan   9th May

Dear Sir,

Floriet ocule secretus. My cri de coeur has been heard. In the wake of your word "Shame" I have been granted a place on this Sceptred Isle. I have been granted Welsh Citizenship, provided I stay on a mountainside and only say 'Baaa'.

Respectfully,

Spike

A Marino Ram

68, Watney Road,
Mortlake, SW 14.

Dear Sir,

May I suggest that you introduce a "Readers' Letters" feature in your magazine and pay a guinea for each letter published? Please send my guinea to the above address.

Yours Faithfully,
Robin Jones.

This week's guinea has gone to Mr. Peter Simple of THE DAILY TELEGRAPH a racialist rally and that his speech 'was written as usual by Lady Pamela Berry'. Simple, alias Michael Wharton, responded with gratifying speed and his letter was reproduced in Issue 11. His point was that this was an old and untrue accusation first made by Randolph Churchill. He also said: 'The funnier parts of your magazine show that you have made a close, even systematic, study of the "Way of the World" column.' There was some truth in this accusation. Rushton and Booker were particularly fond of reading *Mad* magazine, and Rushton recalls that 'Michael Wharton was right. Ingrams and I were terribly fond of Simple, which *was* very funny.'

Booker was also influenced by Bernard Levin's 'Taper'* column in the *Spectator* (1957 to 1961), by Peter Sellers's sketches on the record *Songs for Swinging Sellers*, by Malcolm Muggeridge's book *The Thirties*, and by his editorship of *Punch* (1953–1957). He also admired Ronald Searle's series 'The Rake's Progress'† which had appeared in *Punch*, and which inspired the *Eye*'s series 'Aesop Revisited'. Another influence on Ingrams and Rushton was Beachcomber of the *Daily Express*.

Having dealt with Waugh and Simple, *Private Eye* next turned its attention to another old man, Randolph Churchill. But this time it was the new teases who proved incapable of matching the old one. *Private Eye* had already taken one bite at the cherry with the cartoon in Issue 16, by Rushton, of Randolph on *Panorama* holding a glass, and two BBC men saying: 'Old Randolph certainly knows how to hold his drink.' 'Trouble is he never lets go of it.' This proved a curtain raiser to the 'Aesop' of Issue 30. Entitled 'The Greatest Dying Englishman', and devoted to Randolph's biography of his father, it showed him presiding over a bowdlerised version of Winston Churchill's life, compiled by an army of hacks, who were omitting all reference to such blots on the Churchill career as Tonypandy, Gallipoli and the Dieppe Raid. Randolph's response was swift. Woken from his torpor by this unsolicited testimonial, he worked through the night. He issued writs, retained four out of six of England's leading libel counsel and mounted a watch on the magazine's offices.

In February 1963, Nicholas Luard had just started his

---

* 'Taper' was a political column which blended satirical comment, serious analysis and investigative reporting.

† This was itself an updated version of the original series by Hogarth.

honeymoon in the Ritz Hotel, Paris. He had married
Elizabeth Longmore at St Margaret's, Westminster, and after
the ceremony there was an 'unexpectedly formal' reception at
Claridge's attended by Edward Adeane, son of the Queen's
Private Secretary, and James Butler, son of the Home
Secretary, whose father had been the victim of a cruel satirical
attack in *Private Eye* the previous June. The suite at the Ritz
had been provided by the bride's grandmother, who had told
her that they could have it for as long as they wanted. Two
days after their arrival a telegram was delivered requesting Mr
Luard's return for an urgent conference with the staff of his
magazine on the subject of Randolph Churchill. In the words
of Mr Luard, 'the boys had panicked'. Attendance at the
conference was an unwelcome duty for the paper's twenty-
five-year-old proprietor who reflected that it was not often
that one was offered a suite at the Ritz for an unlimited
period. It was even more irritating for his bride, who had left
a junior position at *Private Eye* in order to get married.

When Luard got back he deployed the staff in the
appropriate directions. Usborne was instructed to collect
evidence. He heard that an Oxford historian called Martin
Gilbert might act as a friendly mediator. Usborne travelled to

*Ingrams, Rushton, Booker and Luard
on the steps of the High Court at the
time of Randolph Churchill's libel
action.*

57

ÆSOP revisited

OVER NOW to the factory in Suffolk, where the keel has just been laid of the 500-volume Official Biography of the Greatest Dying Englishman. The Great Bumpkin himself, Rudolph Rednose, is enthroned . . .

Here beginneth the First War

It's not me that's the hack - it's the people who write my books

W.S.C

. . . never was so much written by so many for so little. But, as the Bumpkin and his hirelings pay nightly homage with readings from the Great Book, as fat offers for serialisation flow in from the scoop-hungry Sunday Telegraph - a dreadful doubt arises. That like all Official Portraits this one too will bear little resemblance to the original . . . that it will, for instance, forget to mention how the Greatest D.E. devoted his life to . . .

TONY PANDY 1911 · DADDY AT TREASURY 1926 · DADDY AGAINST THE INDIANS 1936

Let them eat coke!

PHOTO BY TONY PANSY

MOTOR CARS ARE BUNK

Spend money on roads'. Nonsense! It was the railways that made Britain Great !

Your Gandhi and Soda, sir

I have not become the Tory's First Rebel to watch over the liquidation of the British Empah

. . . smashing the workers (shooting Welsh miners, General Strike etc) . . .

. . . putting back clock in all directions (back to Gold Standard, Free Trade) . . .

. . . opposing every manifestation of 20th Century in favour of long-lost glories of 19th, 18th, 17th etc. . . .

DADDY AT WAR 1942

WSC

Disaster at Dieppe, sir

Only 5000 dead! You should have seen what we did at Gallipoli !

You didn't think I meant all the United Europe rubbish, did you? Only did it to get the Freedom of Strasbourg

. . . wild and futile military gestures, regardless of cost . . .

. . . and that even when he chanced on a radical idea for the only time in his life - he was careful to betray it again as soon as he came into office . . .

. . . but it will concentrate instead on the one short period of his life from which he can be painted as the Great Patriot who did more for his countrymen than anyone else in the 20th Century.

You have now reached the end of this magazine. You are asked to rise and sing the National Anthem

Oxford, called on him and had a most encouraging chat with the hospitable young don. But when he returned home he found that his file, containing most of *Private Eye*'s papers on the case, was missing, and presumed that he had left it with his host.

Excited by the success of the quarrel – which was getting wide publicity – *Private Eye* had mounted an exhibition in the display case outside the office. Randolph's spies reported that this, too, was defamatory. Churchill then applied for an injunction and there was a hearing in chambers at the High Court for which Churchill's counsel, Gerald Gardiner, QC, was late. As they all sat waiting they heard his measured footsteps approaching down the stone-flagged corridor. Rushton kept time with the paces saying: 'TEN guineas, TWENTY guineas, THIRTY guineas, FORTY guineas ... ' This caused even the judge to laugh. But to little effect. the injunction was granted, the exhibits were removed and replaced by a graffito, 'Killjoy was here.'

Shortly afterwards the missing libel file was returned to the office with a note: 'Yours, I think. R.C.' It was clear that the time had come to sue for terms.

Luard accordingly decided to go down to Bergholt within the hour, taking with him Rushton, whose task was to amuse the great man, and a gift. This was the framed original of the Butler 'flabby-faced coward' joke, since it was known that Churchill hated Butler more than almost anything.

When they arrived they were greeted by the well-known figure with the words, 'Who the hell are you?' His second remark was, 'No one's going to have a drink until we've settled this.' Luard's spirits rose, since it was already 11.30 in the morning. It soon became apparent that the sticking point was the apology. There was no disagreement about the withdrawal, but beyond that it was a question of whether or not there should be an apology. Luard remembers,

As the hours passed, he started to sweat. He was clearly in poor shape and needed some refreshment. In order to keep himself distracted he would occasionally snap his fingers at the hacks (or 'researchers') who were gathered in the same large room and would instruct them to read aloud from the great work in progress. 'Get to your feet,' he would say to some moderately distinguished scholar. 'Read from the lectern what I have written for the *News of the World*.' He would then correct their emphasis. Alternately he would go off at bizarre tangents. Finally at 4.45 we reached a settlement. We would withdraw on a full page of the

The Editor,
Private Eye,
22, Greek Street,
London, W.1

Stour,
East Bergholt,
Suffolk.
14 February, 1963

Sir,

I write to call your attention to the lies and libels about my father and myself contained in your issue of February 8.

I   Your allegation that I am planning to write a biography of my father of a tendentious character amounting to a falsification of history is unfounded; and flies in the face of all the known facts (see transcript of my broadcast on B.B.C. Television, January 31, and article of Page 5 of the SUNDAY TELEGRAPH of February 3).

II   Your suggestions that I intend to omit or gloss over unpleasant alleged episodes in my father's life are abominable.   I shall certainly paint a truer picture than you have done. Your further statement that I am not going to write the book myself is also false and constitutes a libel not only on myself, but on those who are associated with me in this enterprise.

The lies you tell about my father are exceptionally gross and offensive.

III   Your allegation that my father was responsible for "shooting Welsh miners" is not only a lie, but the reverse of the truth.

(See account of Tonypandy riots in Annual Register for 1910 and in Peter de Mendelssohn's THE AGE OF CHURCHILL.)

IV   Your suggestion that my father had a callous disregard for loss of British and Canadian lives in two world wars, and in particular that he made light of the casualties at Dieppe, is the vilest libel I have ever seen.

I only draw your attention to the lies you tell about my father since, being his official biographer as well as his son, I have a special responsibility for maintaining his reputation against defamations such as yours.

I shall be glad to have your observations on the foregoing as soon as possible.

yours faithfully,
Randolph S. Churchill.

We the undersigned wish to withdraw the false allegations we made and implied against Sir Winston and Mr. Randolph Churchill, and the latter's assistants in the issue of Private Eye of February 8th.

Christopher Booker	*Mrs. O'Morgo Ingrams*
William Rushton	*Anne Chisholm*
Richard Ingrams	*Sir Charles Harness*
Nicholas Luard	*Brian Moore*
Peter Usborne	*Pressdram Ltd.*
Tony Rushton	*Leo Thorpe Ltd.*

Evening Standard, but not in *The Times*. There would be no apology. It was all we had hoped to get out of him. The saving of money was considerable. And by breaking the mould of the traditional newspaper apology I hoped to sustain our apparent freedom from writs for longer. He then relaxed, brought out the whisky and even introduced the hacks who were arranged around the premises very much in the way that we had suggested in 'Aesop'. Finally he asked us if we wanted to see the garden. It was pitch dark and pouring with rain but he found a torch and led us outside. There we stood in the mud looking at a rosebed in the torchlight.

Rushton remembers the extraordinary similarity between the visit and the supposedly libellous strip. 'But we had no idea what we faced with Randolph Churchill. In those days we could never have raised the money if he had stood on his rights. Apart from anything else he seemed to have retained every available lawyer in the country. We couldn't find anyone notable who was free.' In fact more of that 'Aesop' has since been proved correct. Martin Gilbert, whose historical reputation was made by his work on the Churchill archive, has recently said that certain letters on the subject of Tonypandy were omitted from the book that Randolph supervised.

Luard remembers the Churchill libel case as the great experience of the early *Eye*. The publicity was such that it transformed the status of the paper. 'Until then we had been hanging on the coat tails of the satire boom. After that we were on our own. With the full-page retraction in the *Evening Standard* we increased the print order again.'

Surviving the Churchill libel action left the paper in the perfect position to take advantage of the events that were to follow in 1963. As the year passed the rumours that later became known as the Profumo affair began to circulate in London and, as is generally the case with a British political scandal, nothing was reported. Since the War, journalists, perhaps drilled by the exceptional conditions of the Emergency, had become accustomed to finding out what was going on and then keeping it to themselves. That was, after all, one of the great insidious attractions of being a journalist. By suppressing the information one automatically increased the value of it to those chosen few who were let in on the secret. The days of the Abdication Crisis – when the press had eventually proved impossible to control – were long since over. It seems likely that the government's news managers in 1963 were reasonably confident that, as the Profumo story developed, they would be able to manoeuvre it into some convenient *oubliette*. Certainly they can hardly have been expecting it to cause the kind of trouble for the government and the Tory party which it did.

Even now it is hard to see exactly why this should have been so. A subsequent scandal, 'the Lambton affair', with rather similar facts, caused very little harm to the Tory party, merely resulting in the resignation of three junior ministers. The only additional factors in the Profumo affair were a minister being caught lying to the House of Commons, and a slightly bogus security angle, in that the minister not only visited a prostitute but shared her with a Russian naval attaché. These additions, while fun, were hardly enough to explain the extraordinary public interest in the story and the eventual damage to Macmillan's government. These only seem explicable in terms of the age. For various reasons, 1963 was the perfect year for such a scandal. *Private Eye* played some part in drawing attention to the story, but re-reading the magazine's coverage now it is hard to see what the readers of the paper were getting to justify their confidence that this would be the one paper that would tell the truth if any would. What is indisputable is that sales rose from thirty-five thousand to eighty thousand during the course of that summer.

The first hint of what was to come for *Eye* readers was a satire. It was a letter ridiculing the incomprehensible statement of a junior government minister who had resigned apparently for lending his motor car to a young man who had subsequently been involved in a minor collision. The minister (Charles Fletcher-Cooke) subsequently described his trifling act of generosity as 'a serious error or judgement'. Issue 33 coincided with the resignation of Profumo from the War Ministry 'for personal reasons', and 'Idle Talk' had satirical references to Lucky Gordon, Christine Keeler (who appeared to be the real-life embodiment of the *Eye*'s Miss Gaye Funloving, the twenty-one-year-old 'model'), Stephen Ward, Vladimir Ivanov, or Bolokhov, Lord Astor and Mr Montesi (i.e., Profumo).* By referring to the rumours in this way *Private Eye* was not making a statement that anyone could understand unless they had already heard the rumours themselves, but it was enough that those who had heard them could find this written confirmation, however garbled, for the magazine to win its first reputation as an important source of gossip.

It was in the next issue with Profumo on the cover that the paper went some way towards explaining things, with a

* Lucky Gordon was a West Indian pimp. Christine Keeler was the hooker in question. Stephen Ward was a fashionable osteopath accused of procuring prostitutes for his rich friends. Vladimir Ivanov was the relevant Russian naval attaché. Lord Astor had entertained Keeler and Ward.

double-page spread drawn by Timothy Birdsall and written by Booker, entitled 'The Last Days of Macmillan'. Here was the Prime Minister dressed as a Roman emperor and lying by a swimming pool surrounded by naked girls and attended by 'Juvenile', a clear reference to David Frost. The Fleet Street reporters were shown as geese who followed Lord Boothby for their diet of rumours. But it was in the motto written above the pool that the real news came. It read, 'Per Wardua ad Astor', and it was enough to bring Dr Stephen Ward hurrying round to the office on the assumption that *Private Eye* had discovered all. The truth was that the editors were pretty well in the dark. Rushton remembers that Ward's line was, '"I see you know everything," so we said "just refresh our memories", which he did because he needed help.' Booker, the chief authority on the Profumo affair, was away that morning and the interview was conducted by Rushton and Ingrams, but although they were able to find out more of what was going on very little of it appeared in the subsequent paper.

It was in the same issue as 'The Last Days of Macmillan' that *Private Eye* distributed a leaflet advertising the forthcoming visit of Lenny Bruce to The Establishment. This was unusual in the annals of publicity in that it actually attacked many of the club's members.

The Establishment is still the only place to hear a legend called Lenny Bruce. Last time they came from Belgravia. They listened to the finest modern jazz and danced and drank until the early morning at the lowest prices in London. But they hadn't driven thirty miles to hear that word. There was tumult and riot. They wrote poison pen letters to us, and letters of protest and outrage to the newspapers. One of them belted the doorman, which was misguided: he had recently been cruiser-weight champion of Wales. Ultimately they returned to Eaton Square. Lenny Bruce comes back for four weeks on April 8th. '... the most original, free-speaking, wild-thinking gymnast of language this inhibited island has ever engaged to amuse its citizens. ... Hate him or not, he is unique, and must be seen.' (Kenneth Tynan: *The Observer*). The best jazz is still there. So are the drinks. This time we'd like you to join.

The annual subscription was three guineas and membership

X-IX-VIII-VII-VI-V...

BELLUM CAPUT

NON IMPERIO IN FACTUM

INTERCONTINENTAL BALLISTA
Another of the Emperor Macmilian's humiliations at this
time was the acquisition, at
enormous expense, of large
numbers of these weapons
from his Persian allies. The
missiles failed to leave their
cubicula jacenda or launching
pads.

the last day
MACMILI

AN EXTRACT FROM "THE DECLINE
AND FALL OF THE BRITISH EMPIRE"
WITH NO APOLOGIES TO MR.
EDWARD GIBBON

MIXED BATHING PER WARDUA AD ASTRA

NYMPHS MODELS DISPORTING THEMSELVES WITH FAMOUS NAMES

HAVEN'T I MET YOU SOMEWHERE BEFORE?

By the early days of the year 1963, the twilight of the British Empire provided a sorry spectacle of collapse and decay on every hand.

It is evident from history that there is no nation which, having extended its sinews and vigour in the conquest and administration of empire, can then, on relinquishing that empire, maintain its previous standards of morality and efficiency in the prosecution of its remaining activities.

* * * * * * *

A strange mood walked abroad in Britain of that year, the eighth of the reign of the Emperor Macmilian. The ability and desire of the Emperor and his advisers to undertake the proper responsibilities of government seemed to have quite evaporated.

GEORGIUS LIBIDAULT THE ELUSIVE GALLIC REBEL

Vast tracts of the Northern provinces had fallen into desuetude. Along the great rivers of Tyne, Clyde and Mersey, the hammers of the shipyards were stilled. The busy workshops that had once provided the sinews of imperial prosperity were silent. The people moved in uneasy groups through the streets, deprived of bread, craving in vain for circuses, sensitive to that stirring of the instincts of the mob that finally erupted in open rioting outside the Senate at Westminster.

Throughout the country the broad roads went unpaved. The iron roads that had once been the proud arteries of a brilliant civilisation were uprooted to give way once again to the weeds of the forest.

Even in the furthest reaches of the Empire unrest was slowly ripening into bitter contempt for the symbols of authority that had for so long held sway. When Macmilian's consul, the horse Elizabetha, made a progress through the province of Australia, few bothered even to stop in the streets to observe the passing of the tattered imperial standards. Among the placid farms and latifundia of Rhodesia, black rebellion was brewing up in the hearts of the African slaves, exacerbated by the iron rule of the Governor Winstonius Ager, and unassuaged by the smooth ambivalence of Macmilian's proconsular envoy Butlerius Africanus.

* * * * * * * *

But it was in Britain itself, and in Londinium that the air was heavy with the smell of indulgence and decay, with searchings after strange Gods, with rumour and counter-rumour and with a drifting sense of doom.

The old faiths of the Republic had lost their hold. Even the High Priests no longer proclaimed the existence of the Gods. The legions had abandoned their once fierce bull-worship almost entirely. Only Son-Worship still flourished, in outlying regions of Suffolk.

In place of religion, there came at this time a great spate of omens. An outbre of the plague among travellers, one of the first for many years. Rumours of strange cults and black magic practiced in ruined temples spread through the land. On the coast of the province of Sussex, a woman was attacked by a gre squirrel. Even the harshness of the winter, one of the coldest and most prolonged for hundreds of years, merely added ominous misery and bewildermen to the fears of the people.

But it was in Londinium, at the very heart of the Empire, that rumour, dist and corruption had finally broken out ir the open. After years of an uneasy indulgence, the people were restless and dissatisfied - a spirit which reache into all quarters of society. Even the

WRITTEN ANY GOOD RUMOURS LATELY?

YES, LORD BOOTHBY JUST TOLD ME ALL

HACK HACK

HONK HONK

SNIFF SNIFF ...

THE GEESE of the Via Fleeta who gave their name to the pamphleteers and satirists whose warnings of the evils of Macmilian were never heeded.

flower of the legions, the Praetorian Guard, were in mutinous mood at their camp at Pirbrittius.

After his final defeat in the Gallic campaign, after the prolonged and tiring battle of Brussels upon which all his ambitions had been centred, the Emperor Macmilian himself lounged increasingly powerless at the heart of this drift and decay. His Ministers fought and intrigued over the succession, no longer mindful of the great perils that lay without. While the proper administration of the country languished utterly.

Wild rumours flew nightly through the capital. Of strange and wild happenings in country villas out in the country. Of orgies and philanderings involving some of the richest and most powerful men in the land. In the private diaries of a well-known courtesan of the times, we can read the names of many leading members of imperial society - ranged in order of sexual prowess.

But while natural debauchery became the small talk of a capital long sated with public offerings of vice and harlotry of every description, among the clerks and eunuchs of the administration the old standards of the Republic had vanished altogether. Men proclaimed their love not for their wives, but for each other - and the strange loyalties thus formed, stretching up into some of the highest places in the land, allowed laxity, indulgence and even treason to flourish unchecked.

At this time too, the Chief of the Praetorian Guard, Sextus Profano, came under widespread suspicion for his admission in the Senate that he had been acquainted with Christina, a beautiful girl known well to many of the great figures of society despite her lowly origins, and whose lover, a negro slave, had been sentenced to seven years in the sulphur mines for threatening to kill her in a fit of jealous revenge. It was a sign of the times that few expressed surprise at such an admission.

MUTINOUS LEGIONARY or Praetorian Guard of the type which rose in protest against an excess of official Bull-Worship.

All these happenings brought the capital into a frenzy of speculation that was far from healthy for the continued reign of Macmilian, and the scribes and pamphleteers were only the leaders and articulators of the widespread hostility and contempt aroused by the Government in the hearts of the great mass of the people.

But it was finally the sight of one of Macmilian's more despised advisers, Henricius Domus Secretarius, making himself a private triumph through the streets, leading from his chariot the proud and chained figure of a great African chief Enobarbo, that drove a weary people into deciding that the Emperor's tyranny and disregard for any sentiments but the cheap, the opportunist and the ignoble must be put aside for ever. And that these small men who had disgraced all the noble and glorious history of the British Empire with their petty deeds should be humiliated and forgotten.

TRUE STORIES

After making love to his friend's wife, Mr Johann Heer of Vienna took a felt-tipped pen and drew a romantic landscape on her bum.

Less harm would have come of this recreation if Mr Heer had not signed his work.

"I am a regular Sunday painter", said Mr Heer, "and, after we had enjoyed ourselves, Frau Garubul wanted to watch *Gone With The Wind* on television.

"Love stories do not interest me", he continued, "so I took up my pen. I did not ask her permission as she likes being tickled. Later I went to sleep. She was gone when I woke up".

Returning home, Frau Gambul got into bed just before her husband, Franz, finished his stint as a late-night taximan.

"As my wife was asleep when I got in, I thought I would give her a goodnight kiss. It was then I saw the landscape - signed with Johann's name. It was his signature," Franz went on, "and to prove it, I woke my wife up and we compared it to another signature on a painting he gave us that hangs in the dining-room."

He was granted a divorce.

was restricted to those over eighteen. It was a deliberate attempt to water down the hearty element who had latched onto The Establishment by appealing to the supposedly more intelligent and relaxed readership of *Private Eye*. Unfortunately all came to nothing when the Home Secretary, Henry Brooke, prevented Bruce from entering the '***try', as *Private Eye* put it. Identifying with the absent genius, *Private Eye*'s masthead bore a new recommendation, 'A fortnightly symposium of sick jokes and lavatory humour', which was a quote from the Home Secretary's explanation for his ban on Bruce.

In the same issue Christopher Logue launched the *Eye*'s first attempt at fund-raising in his 'True Stories' column. He told of how a retired street sweeper had been forced to demolish his own house and had thereby incurred a debt of £100. Logue proposed that readers should help the sweeper to pay this debt. The fund remained open for one month and closed at £37.

Logue's 'True Stories', which had started in Issue 15, had originally been suggested by Peter Cook. In 1962 Logue had been sentenced to one month's imprisonment, together with Bertrand Russell and other members of the Committee of 100, for refusing to be bound over to be of good behaviour. (They had been obstructing the highway.) They had served their sentences in an open prison, Drake Hall, and had appropriately been put to work demolishing a nearby munitions factory. Robert Bolt was in the same prison and suffered the indignity of being removed in Sam Spiegel's lilac Rolls Royce. Bolt was then writing the screenplay for *Lawrence of Arabia* and Spiegel, horrified to hear where he was, told him that unless he agreed to be bound over shooting would have to stop. Before this episode Logue had written songs for The Establishment, and when he was released he found a letter waiting for him from Osmond, inviting him to work for the *Eye*, which was by that time owned by Luard.

There was an early move to establish independence from the advertisers in May 1963. The previous issue had carried an advertisement from Longmans for Wolf Mankowitz's new novel, *Cockatrice*. 'Wolf Mankowitz bites the hand that feeds him' ran the copy line. *Private Eye* took its cue promptly and devoted the next 'Aesop' to Mankowitz, suggesting that his new book was 'A lot of cock written in a trice'. This was to result some time later in another writ. Mankowitz was less amusing when his own hand was bitten.

In June 1963 there was an obituary for Timothy, who had died of leukaemia at the age of twenty-four. 'Timothy

Birdsall died shortly after our last issue went to press. We miss him very much.' He had first come to *Private Eye* when the *Spectator* censored one of his cartoons. His last work had appeared in the previous month, an enormous double-page spread entitled 'Britain Gets Wythe Itte, 1963'. June (Issue 40) also saw the last appearance of Booker's name as a member of the editorial board. It was the end of the first phase in the magazine's history.

Summing up the period when he presided over *Private Eye*, Booker emphasises that it was a creature of the sixties and of the England of Macmillan. The paper was against Macmillan and therefore radical, but it was also against the upper-middle-class world of striped shirts and the Saddle Room, *Town* magazine and The Establishment's dominant members. 'That was really the only time the upper middle classes ran the show,' says Booker. 'And our line was simply that whatever was the received wisdom, we were against it. You can't do that for ever.'

Looking back on the first years of *Private Eye* Peter Cook remembers that it was always considered to be 'the most ephemeral part of the satire movement'. It was generally agreed that the paper would close down long before people tired of *TW3*, or the many imitations of *Beyond the Fringe*.

3 Sow the seeds of discord

Satirists are like spiders. We are always devouring each other.
Peter Cook

Nobody looking for evidence that 'the establishment' is dead, as Richard Ingrams has claimed, would be much encouraged by the network of those who have worked for *Private Eye*. The paper has frequently shown how the world of property development or artistic patronage resembles a web of personal connections in which all the decisions are taken by spiders who are either related to each other or were at school together. Consider the patterns which would be revealed if the same test were to be applied to *Private Eye*.

The magazine is the direct heir to the Shrewsbury School magazine, *The Salopian*, of the early fifties. That was edited by Christopher Booker, William Rushton, Richard Ingrams and Paul Foot. Also at the school at the time was Tony Rushton, William's younger cousin. Astonishingly, none of these boys had been to the same preparatory school.

Of this group Ingrams and Foot went on to the same college at Oxford, where they wrote for various magazines and illustrated them with jokes by ... Rushton. At Oxford and on these magazines they met Peter Usborne (Eton and Balliol), Andrew Osmond (Harrow and Brasenose College), John Wells (Eastbourne College and St Edmund Hall). They also met Auberon Waugh (Downside and Christ Church). All were eventually to be involved with *Private Eye*. Booker, boldly, went to Cambridge. There he met Peter Cook (Radley and Pembroke) and Nicholas Luard (Eton and Magdalene). Over the years this rich mixture has been progressively diluted, but nonetheless, when, under Osmond, an advertisement was placed for an additional member of the advertising staff, the person chosen, Sarah

Burns, turned out to be the sister of Professor Gerald Cadogan, once Osmond's fag at Harrow.

One complete outsider who has broken in is Barry Fantoni, who claims to represent the urban working classes and Jewish-Italians. In the view of Fantoni everyone else on *Private Eye*, having been educated at public school, has identifiable oddities. 'There is the speed at which they classify people, for instance as "a roaring poof". And they all analyse things better than I do. I'm more intuitive. Originally I just went along there and suggested that they use my drawings. I was attracted to *Private Eye* because it was against extremist oppression. But I've never had any idea of where it stood on anything. Who does?'

Fantoni has since become one of the central figures at *Private Eye*, but he was originally hired as an odd-job man, his first job being to re-paint Usborne's door. His own background was not 'public school'. He was born and brought up in south London, and in 1953 went to Camberwell School of Art. While there he stopped eating and got TB. Then he was expelled, as far as he knows the only person ever to have been expelled from that institution. He says this happened because the newspapers were full of stories about rebels and he was worse than most of the other rebels at Camberwell. Also 'there were some strange experiences with women, in the clay bins.' Then he went to work in a menswear shop, Barrie's of Brixton, making suits and selling clothes. After a while he decided to re-apply to Camberwell so that he could teach; there was nothing else to do. 'There were only four illustrators and they all worked for the *Radio Times*, and if you were a cartoonist you were seventy and worked for *Punch*.' So he started to do satirical paintings. Then in one week in 1963 he had a one-man show which sold out, he wrote a piece about modern art in *Scene* and he had a drawing accepted by *Private Eye*, at the suggestion of Tony Rushton. So then he left Camberwell all over again. Later that summer Fantoni and Willy Rushton submitted a satirical portrait of three establishment types to the Royal Academy Summer Exhibition, where it attracted considerable attention. This hoax was signed by 'Stuart Harris', a name later to become an editorial pseudonym.

Over the years Fantoni has been many things. His friends recall Fantoni the pop singer, Fantoni the television personality, Fantoni the cricketer and footballer, Fantoni the jazz band leader, Fantoni the satirist, Fantoni the straight actor and Fantoni the music critic. There was Fantoni's 'Stanley Spencer period' and the time when he toyed with the charismatic renewal movement. At one point it was thought that he might found 'The First Church of Christ Sensualist'. Then he seemed to branch off into vegetarianism and Jungian philosophy. Next he published a slim volume of poems, *Tomorrow's Nicodemus*, which was privately printed and has become a rare collector's item. It reminded some readers of T. S. Eliot's very early years. He is currently establishing a reputation as a writer of detective stories, but only a rash man would suggest that he has at last found his true vocation.

Fantoni sees most of his colleagues as teachers. 'Wells and Martin Tomkinson literally were teachers. Foot is a natural teacher. So is Booker. His parents are teachers. I wanted to be one. I really should have been a rabbi, dealing with people's problems. Writing is the nearest I've ever come to it. Making parables. I now understand why the Jews prohibited painting. It's a terrible waste of time. Only about fifty people have ever altered someone's life by painting a picture.' As a Londoner, Fantoni provides the nearest *Private Eye* has ever come to the common touch. It is hard to imagine Ingrams being able to write pieces about footballers or pop groups without Fantoni's cooperation. He is also, with Ingrams and the cartoonist Michael Heath, one of the regular team who devise the covers. Each press day, a Monday, the three shuffle through a selection of news photographs and suggest possible 'bubbles'.

Christopher Booker remembers that Fantoni just walked in off the street. 'He interpolated himself. The rest of us all knew each other. He was a complete outsider and he is now one of the collaborators, and at the heart of the magazine. The only person ever to have done it. Remarkable. I feel fondly towards him for that reason among others.'

Although as the founding editor of *Private Eye* Booker still bitterly regrets the manner in which he was separated from his paper,* he points out that if he had remained he would never have had the opportunity to write in the way he wished. He also considers that Ingrams was 'undoubtedly put on earth to be editor of *Private Eye*', and was the right man to keep the paper going in 1963. Deprived of the paper, and then of *TW3*, Booker spent the next six years preparing a densely argued account of his times that turned into a history of the

* He told Philip Oakes in 1967: 'I left because they hated me.'

sixties and was called *The Neophiliacs*. It still has a cult following, though Rushton described it as, 'all his *Private Eye* stuff with the jokes taken out'.

Writing that book was a difficult period for Booker but one compensation was his friendship with Muggeridge. They had first met in Michael Astor's house in 1963 and had 'hit it off at once'. When Booker had a religious experience in 1965 he found that it coincided with an experience of Muggeridge's, who had written an article on the subject. From then on Muggeridge's influence over him increased. The old man's iconoclasm was an inspiration, and when Booker suffered a financial crisis in 1968 Muggeridge invited him to stay in Sussex for three months, and then put him up in the village for another three months at his own expense. At this time Booker was also mending the quarrels he had had with the old Salopians, which had been carried on in a curiously oblique manner. *The Neophiliacs*, which mentions many rather obscure figures of the sixties, does not mention Ingrams anywhere in the text, although he is thanked in the acknowledgements, immediately after the manager of the National Westminster Bank. Ingrams in turn, when he was writing the history of the first ten years of *Private Eye*, sent Booker a draft of the text which only mentioned Booker's role in a cursory way.

Oddly, these quarrels have not necessarily interrupted their collaboration. Even Paul Foot thought the manner in which Ingrams and Booker conducted their quarrel at the time of the Goldsmith case rather eccentric, with each slanging the other in the *Spectator* but continuing to collaborate as usual in Greek Street. Ingrams did not object when Booker described *Private Eye* then as 'on its day a strong candidate for the most unpleasant thing in British journalism'. While that opinion was entirely tenable, it was rather unfortunate that Booker should have chosen that moment, June 1976, when *Private Eye* was under very heavy attack from Goldsmith, to voice it. But Ingrams regards this as merely an example of 'Booker's admirable tendency to bite the hand that feeds him'.

Earlier Booker had said that he once left *Private Eye* for six months 'in protest at the repulsive side, the salacious gossip'. Booker also criticised the paper for 'the practice, from time to time, of publishing stories, purporting to be entirely factual and without any saving grace of humour, which are based on dubious evidence, which no serious attempt is made to check, and which turn out in the end to be not true'. One remembers with a start that the same Booker, when he was the *Sunday Telegraph*'s jazz critic, had enthusiastically reviewed an

Erroll Garner concert which had – in truth – been cancelled at the last moment.

William Rushton at work at Neal St.

Of the original Salopians, William Rushton has had the least to do with *Private Eye* for many years. His cartoons, puns and collaborations were an essential feature of the paper's early success. He invented the *Eye*'s gastronomic correspondent Walter Blezard, himself the inventor of an astounding pudding known as 'La Bombe Blezard'. He also invented Lunchtime O'Booze, who started life, though this is not generally known, as a Catholic priest, Father Lunchtime O'Booze. He was subsequently unfrocked and turned to journalism. The idea of O'Booze came to Rushton when he was on a bus one day and saw a cinema advertising Tuesday Weld, which he considered 'a damn silly name'.

Rushton, a man heavily disguised by his bluff exterior, has an interest in serious ideas but a dread of pretentiousness. This prevents him from ever discussing anything in other than humorous terms. A rare principle he will own to is, 'I will not draw for *Punch*. It is the only thing I wouldn't do.' He admits to being 'more civil to W.H. Smith than I ought to be. But my excuse is I'm into books.' His other principle concerns the education of his son. There was no question of sending him to a boarding school. To explain why, he points to a cartoon he drew in Issue 8. It shows a father taking his little son to meet the headmaster on his first day at boarding school. The father is saying: 'I want him to have all the disadvantages I never had, Headmaster . . . '*

One of Rushton's most vivid memories is of an extramural activity, which was the attempt to get him into Parliament instead of the man known by *Private Eye* as 'Baillie Vass'. The 14th Earl of Home had disclaimed his title in order to become Prime Minister and the MP for Kinross. *Private Eye* decided that this had to be stopped and Rushton was accordingly despatched to the Scottish borders to fix it. Bernard Levin wrote his election address and Gerald Scarfe drew a grotesque caricature of the Baillie which was printed on car bumper stickers. The campaign was to be *Private Eye*'s first experience of the national press at work. Rushton arrived at the home of a sympathiser, the publisher John Calder, to find two gentlemen from Fleet Street already inside the empty house and making themselves comfortable. George Gale was

---

* Oddly enough this joke was thought up by Ingrams, who did send his children to boarding schools.

sitting at the piano wearing a top hat and an *Express* photographer was in attendance. A certain amount of whisky had already been consumed.

For the first week Ingrams came up to assist him and Foot came over from Glasgow. 'But then they left. And the Tories who were beginning to get a bit worried by our attempt to ridicule the Baillie sent up a hard man, an MP from the south, to heckle me. The only joke I am proud of making during the entire campaign was when this man shouted out, "What about winter keep?" – the whole electorate were sheep farmers as far as I could see – and I replied, "I don't read John Buchan." I invited the heckler up onto the stage but he was unable to manage the steps. He was too pissed.' The next notion Rushton put around was that Vass would only represent Kinross until the General Election and would then move closer to London. 'Finally I urged all my supporters to vote Liberal. This nearly worked because the Liberal candidate came second. I still got about forty-five votes. It was the last time we took *Private Eye* into the field. Not a good idea. I still dream of it and wake with a chill hand clutching my bowels.'

John Wells, who went to an humbler public school, notices the Salopian conspiracy. 'Shrewsbury is a tremendously snobbish school. The impression one gets from its school magazine is of competing with Eton rather than with other public schools. If there are two of the Shrewsbury mafia in Greek Street no one else gets listened to. They kept a lot of my jokes out of the paper when I was on the editorial board.' Wells also notices another exclusive aspect which he cannot share. 'Most of the others had private means when they were young. Without that *Private Eye* could never have been started because no one could have afforded to work for so little, and of course Osmond's money was also essential. Ingrams was also able to buy a cottage as soon as he was married. He had a good bunk up from the generation before.'

Since he left the editorial board in 1966 Wells's contributions have been almost exclusively to single projects like 'Mrs Wilson's Diary' or 'Dear Bill'. He sits at the typewriter and begins to speak the piece aloud; Ingrams and he then continue together or alternately until the required length has been typed. Either can object to the other's words, and normally one objection is decisive.

After Oxford Wells taught languages at Eton. Because of the Eton job, Wells signed his early contributions to *Private*

Eye 'Campbell Murdoch'. When he arrived at Eton he was told 'We didn't get on with your predecessor, David Cornwell (John le Carré) because *he had friends in London*.' In fact after acting in the Ilford revue at the Room at the Top, Wells was asked to leave Eton, but the headmaster, Sir Robert Birley, rescued him and he eventually stayed a second year. Wells says, 'Ingrams's caricature of me is justified. I've been swept upwards in society. His nickname for me, "Jawn", is justified. But I don't think I take the upper classes as seriously as he does, all the same.'

Wells gets on better with Ingrams than he does with either Booker or Waugh. He sees the latter two as 'demented'. He says 'Booker is a bad influence on Ingrams; all that unbalanced sentimental Mary Whitehousery. And he shares with Waugh a peculiar kind of viciousness, more sadistic than satirical.'

Wells also pays tribute to Peter Cook. 'Cook dominated the jokes side when he was there. Alan Bennett said that he could not write for two weeks after collaborating with Peter Cook. There was such an unstoppable flood of ideas.' Nicholas Luard also places Cook at the head of the list. 'He was in talent head and shoulders above everyone else involved in the satire boom. I remember I was once with Peter Ustinov and someone introduced Ustinov as "the funniest man in the world". "No longer," said Ustinov. "*He* is now called Peter Cook."'

Cook certainly had his share of youthful fame. A silly voice he made up for a university cabaret swept through the country, so that for several years towards the end of the sixties thousands and thousands of people between the ages of seventeen and thirty must have used it every day. It got so bad at one point that instead of making jokes to each other they just carried out normal conversations and switched to the silly voice if they thought it was time for a laugh. His father was a district officer in Nigeria, and Cook was once described (by John Heilpern) as inheriting 'the lordly mien of the forest *bwana*, stiff upper-lipped at the news that the natives were getting restless'. Unlike many 'rebels' Cook does not look back on his schooldays as unhappy times. He went to Radley College, and when he won a scholarship from there to Cambridge it marked the close of an idyllic period in his life. During his last year at Radley, 'I had a life of complete luxury. . . . I don't think I've ever laughed as much. I was already in at Cambridge. I had two fags. I had breakfast in bed. I used to go to the pictures and fish for trout in the lake. And I organised bootleg games of soccer because football wasn't allowed.' While at school Cook had written a musical in rhyming couplets called *Black and White Blues*. 'It was about a Salvation Army band with a jazz beat that went to Africa to convert the natives.' After school his two best friends went to Africa. One became a missionary, the other prospected for minerals. He has seen neither of them since. At Cambridge the friend he remembers best built his own coffin and slept in it. Cook was excused national service because of an allergy for feathers.

He considers that his great strength as proprietor of *Private Eye* is his inactivity. 'Where else would they find someone like me, who does nothing?' When asked what he would do with the magazine if Ingrams went mad he said, 'Oh, he did that years ago. But Booker would be the number 1 choice as replacement.' That is a selfless choice because the bits of *Private Eye* Cook misses most today are the cartoons by Scarfe and Trog, Barry McKenzie and 'Footnotes'; Booker would be unlikely to recall any of them, except Trog. Cook is also a great admirer of Christopher Logue's 'True Stories'. He considers Logue has an extraordinary talent for being non-commercial. 'Look at that book of *Heroic Failures* by Stephen Pile. It was in the charts for months. Just the same idea as Logue had twenty years ago.'

Cook's style of humour is entirely original. When he used to contribute to *Private Eye* collaborations, completely unexpected jokes were introduced. He has been responsible for many of the most successful jokes, including bubbles on photographs, Sir Herbert Gussett and the popular singing group 'The Turds'. He also suggested 'Mrs Wilson's Diary'. He has frequently said that owning *Private Eye* is his proudest achievement.

Paul Foot sees himself and Ingrams as 'failed actors'. While not delighted when the Shrewsbury connection is pointed out, he analyses *Private Eye*'s politics in terms of whether he or Booker has more influence over Ingrams at the time. 'When I left in 1972 the tone of the paper was much more radical than it is now. That change is due to Booker. He has become more right-wing. He now puts up the ideas and marks out the targets.'

There has always been a question as to why Foot left in October 1972, to join *Socialist Worker*. It was really because his position had become impossible. The *New Statesman* wrote at the time:

He claims he felt he was going stale at *Private Eye*, but it is odd that this standard malaise of journalists should have struck so soon after his Maudling–Real Estate Fund of America–Poulson triumph. A more likely explanation could be the very real discomfort he felt over celebrated *Eye* send-ups of Foot political associates like Bernadette Devlin.

Foot now denies this explanation. 'All the stories about Bernadette Devlin are crap. I hated leaving but I was offered the job on *Socialist Worker* and 1972 had been a tremendous year for the Left. There had been the miners' strike and I felt there was a bigger role for *Socialist Worker*. And so there was. When the election came in February 1974, our election issue sales went up to thirty-five thousand copies from fifteen thousand. Leaving *Private Eye* was sad because it was a tremendous place. And there was the feeling of kicking Richard in the teeth a bit. He always produces that.'

There is no reason to doubt the idealism of Foot's decision to join *Socialist Worker*, where his salary of £28 a week was half his *Private Eye* earnings, but there is usually more than one reason for such decisions and it seems likely that the teasing process at *Private Eye* had upset Foot more than he cared to admit. It had started mildly enough in August 1971 with the appearance of Len Trott, a distant relative of Dave Spart, the intense, jargon-spouting humourless left-wing student bore. Spart bore no resemblance to Foot himself but was an accurate picture of many of his comrades. (He was actually based on Richard Neville, the editor of *Oz*.)

The teasing became more pointed with the references to Angela Davis and Bernadette Devlin. Miss Devlin was the politician Foot admired and respected above all others. And that Foot did object to jokes about Angela Davis is shown by a subsequent remark, 'My God, she was on trial for her life.' One day matters came to a head. There was a photograph of B. Devlin holding her illegitimate baby and talking to Harold and Mary Wilson. Ingrams proposed to print this with the bubble, 'I'm going to call him Harold because he's a little bastard.' When Foot saw this he said that it should be taken out because it would upset Bernadette. Ingrams refused and said that anyway it would not upset her. So Foot telephoned her and returned to say that although she had tried to laugh it off she had clearly been very hurt by it. He also said that if the bubble went in there would be no 'Footnotes' that week because he would withdraw them. This challenge, made on press day, and in public, was impossible to smooth over.

Ingrams immediately agreed to remove the joke. Many editors would find such a reverse intolerable, and from then on the days of the partnership were numbered.

In August 1972, Foot went on holiday and the satirical references to his political views increased. While he was away the *Eye* mocked the 'Pentonville Martyrs' by depicting them on a medallion as thugs. One cover showed a picture of dockers' pickets with a disrespectful joke about the high rate of theft in the docks, and there was more along the same lines within.

It was on Foot's return from this holiday that the date of his departure was agreed. Ingrams had already leaked the news to Nigel Dempster, in order to upstage any attempt by *Socialist Worker* to crow over its good fortune.

One *Private Eye* contributor who did not go to Shrewsbury but who has been part of the central direction of the paper is Auberon Waugh. Waugh is unusual among *Eye* insiders in that he first made has reputation (like Peter Cook) elsewhere. His arrival marked something of an experiment. He was primarily a humourist, but in a very different style to the *Eye*'s, and the *Eye* was traditionally intolerant of other styles. The experiment (the last that Ingrams has conducted) was a success. Waugh's fantasy 'Diary' brought a completely new dimension to *Private Eye* in 1970, and he was worth as much

Waugh's privately printed postcard used by him from his address in the South of France. The card's caption reads :

ECRIVAINS DE NOS JOURS
16-9 WAUGH AUBERON né le
17 Nov. 1939
Grand écrivain polémique anglais

to it in publicity value as Foot had been. Waugh is one of the few journalists in the country who knows what to do when offered freedom of expression. He sets out what he thinks in a terrible stream of consciousness, which thousands of readers recognise as their unexpressed, indeed carefully repressed, instinctive reactions.

A collection of his insults makes fearsome reading. So Sir Michael Edwardes, chairman of Leyland, 'Looks like a victim of forceps delivery'. Referring to Mr Denis Howell, the Labour minister in charge of emergencies, he writes: 'It is an alarming thought that if ever we are invaded by Monsters from Outer Space, the man who will be appointed to save us as Minister for Monsters will be this joke yobbo who could easily be mistaken for the traditional plumber with a cleft palate who has lost his dentures down the lavatory.' An old opponent, David Pryce-Jones, is treated to a bitter-sweet mixture:

> Another half-Jewish Welsh dwarf who seems to be in need of congratulation is 42-year-old David Pryce-Jones, the Simon Wiesenthal of English letters. After six shots at it, he has at last written a very good novel.... 'Prycey' has always been torn between identities. There is the sad and sensitive 'David' who takes high moral attitudes and is very bitter about being half-Jewish – it was this character who embarked on a strange trail of revenge against poor Unity Mitford, dead and buried these 30 years, and insulted Nick Bentley, the gentle old left-winger who illustrated this column in the last months of his life. Then there is 'Taffy' Jones, as merry and gossipy a little Welshman as ever stole telephone wire from the colliery tip at Aberfan and squabbled about the compensation afterwards.

He also has an original way with obituaries:

> Sad and terrible news about my cousin, the Duke of Norfolk. ... When a great nobleman dies we are all diminished. Far too many of the rich and powerful in this country now appear to be consumed by a mixture of avarice and squalid funk. Bernard (as I feel that I can call him now that he's dead) put them all to shame. He was a wise and godly man. RIP.

> Sir Charles Petrie, the historian, has died at the age of 82. I met him several times but never liked him much. Although it is always a sad thing for anyone to die (unless he is a

religious maniac) I can't claim to be surprised by the news. . . . As soon as I saw him shuffle into the witness box (in the Lord Russell libel case, 11 years ago) I knew that he was doomed.

Poor old Olga [Deterding]. More rubbish has been written about her than about any woman of our times, but at least she gave the gossip columnists something to write about. The last time I saw her she reminded me of Rider Haggard's Ayesha after one trip too many through the Fire of Eternal Life – hairless, shrivelled and black as a tinker's nutting bag. Linda Lee Potter opines that she may have died of a broken heart, but it seems more likely that she choked on a piece of meat while toasting the New Year – a reckless thing to attempt at her age. They don't make them like her any more.

Lord Bradwell, as Uncle Tom Driberg was known in his last few months, has collapsed and died at 71. He will be sadly missed at Gnome House, where his visits often left a fragrance behind which lasted the rest of the day. He was a man who never managed to do much harm despite being an MP for 32 years.

A great sadness descends with the news of Nicolas Bentley's death. In six years collaboration we never had a cross word or sticky moment. Nick was a gentle, modest,

Cyril Connolly's admirers gather round his deathbed, each hopefully offering 'a fond breast', an illustration for Auberon Waugh's column by Nicolas Bentley.

humorous man, with none of the usual characteristics of the highly individual genius which inspired his quiet professionalism and supreme technical ability. His first ambition was to be a circus clown, but he gave it up after six weeks.

Bentley had previously illustrated Beachcomber and Belloc. The unusual clarity of his caricatures with their air of innocent merriment was particularly effective for illustrating the grotesque incidents chronicled in Waugh's 'Diary'.

The difference between Waugh's public image as the heartless poison-pen writer, with political views which would have been considered unacceptable to intelligent men before the Enlightenment, is in sharp contrast to the impression he makes in person. He has a habit when sitting at his desk in Greek Street of flicking unstubbed fag-ends out of the window, and once managed to set alight a passer-by's hat. The woman came up to reception with her hat still smouldering, and herself in a blazing temper. She was immediately directed to Waugh's room. What happened next took place behind closed doors, but she left shortly afterwards, smiling sweetly. He is a generous and thoughtful drinking companion who can be relied on to light up the dullest day with his sunny good humour. He is also brave in the face of pain and remarkably friendly to strangers, even being prepared to talk to people with whom he has nothing in common on the hopeful assumption that they must have *something* of interest to say. All these qualities are widely ascribed to Waugh's partly Jewish ancestry.

Two more recent contributors who frequently receive a bad press are Nigel Dempster and Peter McKay. Waugh has said of Dempster that he has become 'a general punch bag for journalists wishing to prove themselves respectable'. And of McKay that 'he would cut your throat and destroy all chance of friendship for two lines in the *Daily Express*. But he is interesting and unusual.' Both consider themselves outsiders but McKay really is an outsider in his chosen world, the world of London gossip. He is a hard-bitten Aberdonian, who has fought his way up from the telephone box on the Peterhead fish quays whence, as a lad, he used to phone the Aberdeen and Glasgow papers with the latest market prices. This was a vital task. The returning fishing fleets would be directed to the port with the highest prices and if, when they docked, the fishermen found that the prices were lower than reported (a trick the fish buyers were always trying on) the fishermen's rage with the young McKay was something to behold.

McKay is a better writer than Dempster, a formidable Fleet Street office politician, and a shrewd judge of how far he can bully the boss. He is a very typical Fleet Street character. There are lots of McKays in Fleet Street, amusing, shrewd, thick-skinned, whose principles it would take some time to discover. The difference with McKay is that unlike most successful Fleet Street journalists he will print anything he finds out. He is still carrying out a journalist's basic job; sometime, somewhere he will print it. If people think he should be inquiring into different aspects of life he could reply with some justification that his job is merely to go and find out, it is the editor's job to tell him where to go.* He is the only one of Ingrams's associates who has made a serious attempt to print stories about Ingrams, and he regularly attempts to intrude into the domestic bliss of Waugh.

Asked to justify his attitude towards breaches of privacy, McKay says:

Grovel based on Dempster.

I have never breached anyone's privacy, certainly not in *Private Eye*. And when I did it was entirely on your instructions. Anyway privacy is not that important. People talk of breaching it in hushed tones, as though it were on a par with physical assault. But breaches of privacy are frequently in the public interest. When they are not, one can at least say that they are fairly entertaining. Anyway why do people engaged in this debate always suppose that newspaper readers believe all the gossip they read?

I would say that if details of your private life do appear in the newspapers then it is a random penalty you must pay for leading an enjoyable secret life. We all lead such lives to some extent. Even Ingrams. And for many people the fear of discovery is part of the illicit pleasure.

Dempster is a less contented man. He sometimes gives the impression of conducting a one-man war against the upper classes. On the point of privacy Dempster says: 'No public person has the automatic right to privacy. But if they behave well they will never be written about. Gossip columnists are social policemen. You can own twenty thousand acres and never appear in any column. But if you open your door to the public and ask for their money, we get interested.'

*As McKay rises higher this excuse rings less true.

Fluck and Law. Photography by John Lawrence Jones.

83

The Private Eye Story

In the fifties Dempster was a well-established figure on the debutante circuit – charming, energetic, very popular with the girls' mothers and rather feared by fellow guests because of his aggressive wit. Then his career in the City went dramatically wrong, and he turned for a living to writing about the only other world he knew, Society. Once embarked on that he had to keep upping the stakes. Anyone who writes gossip finds that as time passes he has to spread his net wider and wider and include in it more and more of his friends; either that or he has to be a less effective gossip. Dempster has been a top gossip for twelve years and the cost to him in friendship must have been rather high. His only consolation has been in acquiring new friends; in the case of a successful gossip columnist this means friends who are further and further up the social scale. He may have reached his apogee with his sympathetic book on Princess Margaret. Having acquired a friendly acquaintance in the royal family, he has hesitated to blow it at last.

Dempster has a cold eye, an eye like a fish on a slab, but he has a warm heart. He has been known to take a story out in order to save someone's feelings. McKay has a merry twinkling eye, he is the life and soul of any party, he singles you out on a winter's night and beckons you across the bar to his cigars and double scotch. It is only months later you may find that for most people he has no heart at all.

An editor emerges 1963–1966

4

Two years after it started Private Eye *nearly closed. There was the change in fashion which marked the end of 'the satire boom' and which terminated many similar novelties. There was the financial failure of Nicholas Luard's business, the fall of the Empire of Satire. And there was the exit of Christopher Booker, the paper's first editor and presiding genius, whose departure meant a considerable loss in confidence and sophistication. Within the space of six months* Private Eye *lost its publisher, its editor and much of its readership.*

The two personal crises came first. At the beginning of 1963 the paper was controlled by Nicholas Luard and Christopher Booker. By the summer it was in the hands of Peter Cook, Richard Ingrams and William Rushton. Luard's departure was caused by the failure of Cook–Luard Productions. This was brought about by two things: the impossibility of replacing the *Beyond the Fringe* team with an equally popular group at The Establishment club; and the enormous amount of money Luard had invested in *Scene* magazine which proved to be a white elephant. Cook was also missed as an impresario. It was he who had brought Frankie Howerd, Barry Humphries and Lenny Bruce to the club. When The Establishment's bookings began to fall and the over-ambitious *Scene* faltered it looked as if *Private Eye* too would be dragged down to disaster. Fortunately, as the creditors of Cook–Luard gathered, it was discovered that – contrary to all reports – Peter Cook had never been jointly responsible for *Private Eye*; a memorandum was unearthed which showed that *Private Eye* had been the sole responsibility of Luard. Luard was therefore able to sell his shares to Cook who became the proprietor.

In April 1963, *TW3* ended its penultimate run and Booker went on his honeymoon in May, but returned in June. He then proposed to take the rest of the summer off to write a book. Accordingly he re-packed his bags and sailed for Scotland with the *Annual Register*, to start work on what was to become six years later *The Neophiliacs*. He remembers it as the first break he had taken in twenty-one months. He planned to return in the autumn to resume work on a new series of *TW3* and the *Eye*.

His colleagues regarded the matter differently. For a start, they considered that he already spent too much time on *TW3*; but Booker was also a difficult person to work with. He started writing late and continued until the small hours. He was a perfectionist and frequently rejected work at the last minute which others found perfectly acceptable. Andrew Osmond remembers him as 'an inspirational writer who was quite prepared to keep people waiting till four in the morning in order to drive his copy down to the printers'. Mary Ingrams usually carried out this task, bearing away the few pasted-up pages in an absurdly large delivery van. Booker could be ruthless in demanding assistance when others considered that they should have long since gone home. They accordingly regarded his absence in Scotland as too good an opportunity to miss. Peter Cook's agreement was secured from New York and Booker received a letter signed by William Rushton saying that he had been fired and that henceforth Rushton and Ingrams were to be joint editors. So much is agreed. Beyond that it seems that Booker still regards the letter as an act of betrayal. He also says that the letter was actually written by Ingrams who then persuaded Rushton to sign it. Rushton confirms this point, adding that it was the first time he had seen the word 'obdurate'. There was a postscript added by Ingrams beneath Rushton's signature, in which Ingrams said, 'Sorry about this but Rushton is an obdurate old bastard.' Ingrams has little to say about the matter in the voice of a sane man, but tends to cackle gleefully and let out cries of 'Stabbed in the back! Stabbed in the back!' whenever he is asked about it.

Looking back on this event Booker says:

In a sense probably not true of anyone else involved, I thought of *Private Eye* as 'my baby'. I did not attempt to take all the credit for it but I had invested a huge amount of effort in shaping it in a certain way, and I was horrified to have it snatched from me. I took the view that it would lose a good deal of its character and backbone, and that it would decline in quality and circulation, and I was not wholly wrong. My kind of humour was based on observation and parody and exact working out of the point that was being made. I had to struggle against the more anarchist tendencies inherited from *Mesopotamia* and lazy Oxford days.

Without my capacity for taking pains, I am convinced that *Private Eye* would never have become established.

At first the seriousness of the paper's financial and editorial loss was not apparent. Booker set off for Scotland just when the Profumo affair was coming to a head and he was almost immediately replaced by Claud Cockburn, who was invited by Ingrams to take over as guest editor. There could have been no better choice; Cockburn was the ideal man for the Profumo story. Cockburn had been one of Ingrams's heroes ever since Ingrams had read *In Time of Trouble*, and he and Mary had called on Cockburn at his home near Youghal when they were on their honeymoon in November 1962.

The cover of Cockburn's issue (43) listed Lady Dorothy Macmillan, Bob Boothby and Harold Macmillan in that order, for no obvious reason. This was a covert reference to the old but unpublished story about the long-standing love affair between the first two, a passion which certainly placed the rather craggy wife of the Prime Minister in a more interesting light. This technique of apparently meaningless juxtaposition was very reminiscent of Cockburn's pre-war paper *The Week* in which he had exposed the appeasement policies of the Cliveden Set. That Cliveden was once more, with the Profumo scandal, at the centre of public attention proved highly stimulating to Cockburn's pen.

On page 3 the veteran political hooligan named, for the first time ever, the head of MI6, a practice that was to become a *Private Eye* trademark. He then floated a rumour that Dr Stephen Ward had been murdered. (A rumour is all that it has remained.) The commonly spoken but never published names of those who might have committed adultery with the Duchess of Argyll were then listed, and various connected trains of thought were pursued over a three-page editorial that was notable for *not* being written in a funny voice. Winding up at this juncture (page 7) to something approaching full speed, Cockburn printed a four-page attack on Lord Beaverbrook, written by Alan Brien – something which both he and his contributor had clearly been composing in their dreams for many years.

But it was on page 13 that Cockburn provided the *pièce de resistance*, a classic exposé of official corruption and indifference, the story of the mysterious and violent death of Mr Hal Woolf shortly after leaving police custody. The Woolf story aroused great interest. It was taken up by the national press and led to questions in the House of Commons and

'*One of the real hard men from the thirties*' : *Cockburn, by Rushton.*

eventually to an official inquiry. It had the sort of impact which *Private Eye* had never before shown signs of achieving. Looking back now, Ingrams says: 'Everyone was quite carried away by the Woolf business. I think Usborne thought that if Claud came onto the staff of the magazine we would have a Woolf story in every issue. But he never did it again.'

Cockburn's issue of *Private Eye* became justly famous and achieved a standard far higher than anything attainable by the younger members of the editorial board. It was to be some years before one of their generation was to equal the news impact of the Woolf story. The only immediate signs of a follow-up to the Woolf investigation occurred in January 1964 when Claud Cockburn rejoined the editorial board and a new column, to which Alan Brien contributed, signed 'Fascist', was started. This was the forerunner of *Private Eye*'s regular investigative journalism.

By February the name of the column had become 'The Illustrated London News' and one of its first stories told of how the 'D' Notice committee* had asked *Private Eye* to accept this form of self-censorship after the Cockburn reference to Sir Dick White as the head of MI6. The magazine had agreed to accept the notices after some persuasion, but none had been sent.

Following the departure of Booker the paper – Cockburn issue apart – went through a bad patch. Ingrams's first gift to *Private Eye* was a reliable and convenient editorial timetable, but meanwhile there was the question of the contents. The style of humour became more Rabelaisian under Ingrams and Rushton, and the working methods involved more time researching in the pub. William Rushton remembers that standards went sharply downhill. 'Booker was politically oriented. He saw events in political terms and gave his attacks an intelligent topical reference. Eventually we were saved by the return of Peter Cook who kept us going while Ingrams slowly discovered about the business of editing and getting the right people in.' In those days, Ingrams's editorial approach was admirably open. He encouraged many new people to contribute in one way or another. The overall line matched that of Cook and was left of centre. Ingrams always described himself as 'a lefty'. Foot remembers that Ingrams

Opposite. Back row: *Christopher Logue, Peter Cook, Christopher Booker;* Seated: *John Wells, Claud Cockburn, Richard Ingrams;* Front: *Gerald Scarfe, Tony Rushton; photographed for the* Sunday Times *in 1966.*

* 'D' Notices refer to various aspects of national security. Newspapers which accept them agree not to write about subjects listed without first consulting the Ministry of Defence.

voted Tory in 1959 but Labour in every election since. In Foot's view Ingrams has always held 'a sort of Roy Jenkins position; and in those days one of his tests of an MP's decency was to ask, "How did he vote on the pooves?" If the MP had voted for the liberalisation of homosexual laws he was "fundamentally" decent. If not he was "unacceptably right-wing".'

One of the weaknesses of this political piety is clearly seen at the time of President Kennedy's assassination. *Private Eye* was as nonplussed by this event as was everyone else, and after Ingrams had conferred with Malcolm Muggeridge all they could come up with was a frankly adulatory drawing by Fantoni and Rushton. With hindsight Ingrams thinks that a slightly more cynical approach might have been preferable.

For the rest of the staff the whole of 1964 was overshadowed by the financial crisis. The first signs of this had been a sharp fall in the sales figures. At the height of the Profumo affair in 1963 the sales had swollen to eighty-five thousand, and even in January 1964 the first audited figures showed sales over the previous six months of seventy-five thousand. By May this had dropped to fifty-four thousand, a rather horrifying fall, and another ten thousand had been lost by the middle of the year. In other words, the sales had halved in less than a year.

At the same time Fleet Street was adopting a new attitude to *Private Eye* and to the satire movement in general. This was largely due to television. The attempt to satisfy the insatiable, weekly appetite of *TW3* for fresh material had given the whole business a bad name. Satire was now 'old hat'. 'The boom' which the press had created in the first place was now declared to be over. In *The Sunday Times*, 'Atticus' referred to *Private Eye* as 'the last and dying echo' of the boom. George Melly, restaking his claim as the high priest of intellectual fashion, singled out the artist Gerald Scarfe as 'the only true satirist to have emerged from the whole overpublicised movement'.

'*Private Eye* at that time became the last thing to be seen carrying,' Usborne recalls. 'I had been overprinting, not having realised the speed of the sales slump, the returns started to rocket and we all had to take a pay cut. We agreed to get other jobs so as not to burden the *Private Eye* wage bill with all our living costs. I went off to *Which?*.' David Cash, who had become the bookkeeper and subscription manager at the height of the boom in April 1963, remembers that when he applied for the job Usborne said, 'You realise this magazine may not last three months.' A year later Cash recalls that the wage cuts were from £30 to £20 in some cases and that other people were having their wages halved. 'I had to go round to the bank manager, cap in hand, every Friday in order to arrange to meet the following Wednesday's wage cheques. It was a real lesson.' Ingrams became quite proficient at operating the subscribers' addressograph. But, although safer jobs were then easy to find, no one left.

In June 1964, at the height of the crisis, Cook walked into the office, as Usborne remembers, 'bubbling with jokes. We'd almost forgotten about jokes we were so depressed. He immediately put the Raft of the Medusa on the cover (with one of the cannibalistic survivors saying "This is the last time I go on a John Bloom holiday") and there was a terrific response from readers. Everything started to go right again. He was terribly kind and generous. A gentle critic and very serious about the circulation as well as just being funny.'

Eventually Usborne's efforts were successful. Severe temporary economies were adopted, the print orders was controlled, and a small capital sum was raised from some generous private backers. Somehow the paper just struggled through the year.* By November the number of telephone lines could be increased from one to three and the arrival of Lord Home as Prime Minister was hailed joyfully with a cartoon by Scarfe.

It was at this time that *Private Eye* acquired one of its most devoted readers in the form of the publisher Edward Martell who owned, edited and printed a small circulation paper called *The New Daily*. This professed fervently patriotic and free-enterprising opinions. Mr Martell never quite got the hang of *Private Eye*. He represented a British form of *poujadism*, that segment of self-employed or small business opinion which distrusts the government, believes that it is corrupt and yearns for a smaller and less complicated world. So when *attacked national leaders Mr Martell was both outraged and secretly impressed. In The New Daily* he reprinted a selection of the *Eye*'s more interesting stories and usually added some comment such as 'this is disgraceful. Either this story should lead to the fall of the government, or those responsible for these outrageous libels should be hounded through every competent court in the land.' This sort of reaction was a source of great delight at *Private Eye*, apart from being a publicist's gift, and the utterly humourless Mr Martell was immortalised. In due course Mr Martell also sued for libel.

*See Chapter 10.

What Did They Expect?

ON FRIDAY, November 15. under the heading "Mr. Powell Should See His Lawyers" I wrote as follows:
"The current edition of *Private Eye* includes, as is usual in that magazine, a list of the editorial board. It runs as follows:
    Richard Ingrams.
    William Rushton.
    Enoch Q. Powell.
"The third name on this list is, of course, new. The initial 'Q' is put into the middle of the name to shield the little men behind *Private Eye* from the suggestion that they are bandying the ex-Health Minister's name about in an obnoxious connection without his permission.
"Their shield is too small. No one who is politically conscious could fail to connect the two—as indeed they were meant so to do.
"Mr. Enoch Powell is a just, straightforward and fearless man. We could all be grateful to him if he were to issue a writ for libel immediately on the grounds that, if only one person believes him to be connected with this scurrilous, disreputable and thoroughly cowardly rag, his reputation would be harmed.
"*Private Eye* have taken a chance with Mr. Powell's name. They get away with too many of the chances they take.

THE new issue of *Private Eye* gives as its editorial board:
    Richard Ingrams
    William Rushton
    Edward Q. Martell
The announcement on our front page this morning shows that the gauntlet so ostentatiously flung down has not gone unnoticed.

BARRY McKENZIE

Australian at large

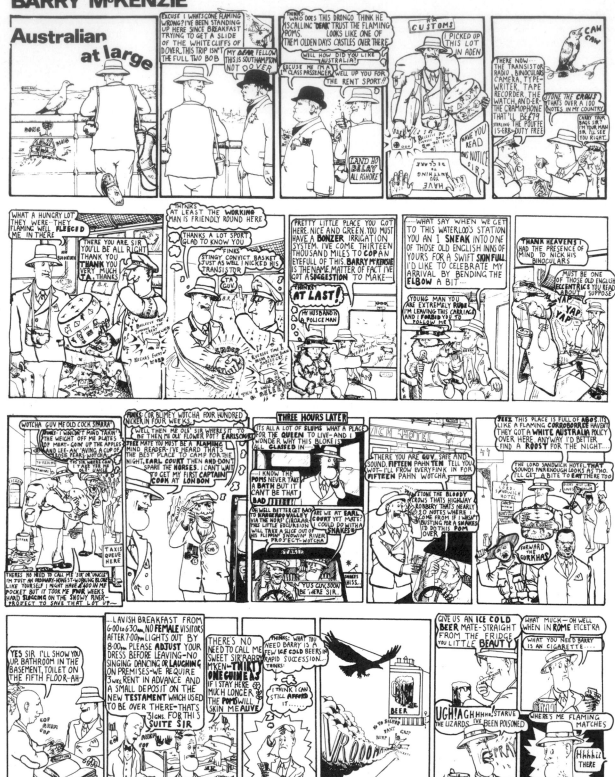

TO BE CONTINUED

No 65
Friday
12 June 64

1/-

This is the last
time I go on
a John Bloom
Holiday

The editorial revival which was marked by the return of Peter Cook became increasingly apparent throughout 1964. One of Cook's most important contributions was the discovery of Barry Humphries who started to write the Barry McKenzie strip in July. Nicholas Garland who drew it remembers discussing the idea for this large antipodean and wondering what he should look like, and then actually catching a glimpse of Barry McKenzie laying a wreath at the Cenotaph on Anzac Day. From then, he says, 'Everything fell into place.' This was also the time when one of the paper's longest running features, the 'Colour Section', got under way. The format was suggested by Malcolm Muggeridge who liked a magazine to start with a series of short paragraphs composed of news items and gossip. Muggeridge had used the same idea when he had been editor of *Punch*. The early 'Colour Section' was notable for its infrequent references to personalities, one reason being that *Private Eye* was still a magazine largely written by outsiders, and if you do not know insiders you are not tempted to write about them.

In an attempt to penetrate the 'inside' world the editors at this time pursued a number of grown-up journalists. There was then a group of writers on the *New Statesman* who were thoroughly disillusioned with Harold Wilson and contemptuous of Paul Johnson's editorship. They considered Johnson far too much of a Wilson creature and they began to call round at No. 22 Greek Street, which they found a more agreeable gossip shop in which to discuss ideas and concoct paragraphs. Regular visitors included Alan Watkins, John Morgan, Alan Brien, Richard West and Andrew Roth. In those days large quantities of alcohol were consumed at Greek Street after lunch. Ingrams used to send round to Kettners for two bottles of Scotch. On one occasion a disagreement arose between J. Morgan and A. Brien as to which of them was 'more working class'. The exchange of views turned into an exchange of working-class-style blows and a certain amount of damage was done to the electrical fittings.

By July there was sufficient money in the coffers to allow the regular editors to take a break and to be succeeded for a few issues by Peter Cook, Claud Cockburn and Malcolm Muggeridge. Cook and Cockburn named the Kray twins, somewhat cautiously. At that time the national press was full of references to an unidentified East End gang which was terrorising much of London and against which the police were powerless. Cook wrote:

Either the charges are true, in which case the newspapers should have the guts to publish them, whatever the risk of libel action. Or they are untrue or grossly exaggerated, in which case they should stop scaring the people with this horror mob movie of London under terror. The two people being written and talked about are the twin brothers, Ronald and Reginald Kray. For ten years they have been well-known figures of London life. They are rich. They have criminal records. They are credited in the underworld with immense power.

The story then went on to list the major allegations against the twins and ended by saying: '*Private Eye* is not anxious to be sued for libel, have its knee caps blown off, or get sprayed and burned as a sort of reluctant Buddhist. However, it must be recognised that if the *Mirror* reporting is accurate, this may quite probably be the last issue of *Private Eye* under the present management.'* As some form of relief from this grim warning the same issue also introduced a new character, 'Sir Basil Nardley Stoads, chief rammer of the seductive brethren', subsequently described by his inventor, Peter Cook, as 'a creation of utterly original genius'.

The next issue (69) was edited by Malcolm Muggeridge, who viewed this task with keen enthusiasm. He said that he 'felt like a respectably retired whore who had been given one night of freedom to walk down Piccadilly and see if she can still draw a whistle'. He intended the paper to be 'as *Punch* would be in a good, true and beautiful world'. Robert Pitman pointed out in his *Daily Express* column that *Private Eye* had formerly attacked Muggeridge as 'a cynical little man without any real views or beliefs who affects a worldly wisdom fashionable among ageing pundits'. Muggeridge had not been at all put out by this. He had attacked. He had been counterattacked. Could this be love?

Most of the issue was given over to Muggeridge's quarrel with his old paper, *Punch*. The cover was a drawing by Gerald Scarfe which revealed the discreditable truth about Mr Punch's prick, and there were further attacks on *Punch* on pages 3, 4, 5, 7, 8 and 9. *Punch* retaliated rather feebly by recalling the rumour that John Bloom was about to buy *Private Eye*, confirmation of a feud that had started with *Private Eye*'s earliest issues and still shows occasional signs of

---

* Cook says that the guiding principle behind this fearless act was 'Publish and be absent.' By the time the issue was on sale Claud was back in Ireland and he himself had retired to Tenerife.

SEDUCTIVE BRETHREN

Sir Basil Nardly-Stoads explains

As chief Rammer of the Seductive Brethren, (writes Sir Basil Nardly-Stoads) it is often my pleasure and privilege to seize hold of young women and clamber hotly all over their bodies.

I am often asked, by those who want to know (continues Sir Basil Nardly-Stoads) what exactly the Seductive Brethren do and what they believe in: to this there is no simple answer but to say that the BODILY SEIZING OF YOUNG WOMEN is at least part and parcel of our belief would be no exageration.

THE FUNCTION OF THE RAMMER

In my position, or rather in my numerous positions as Chief Rammer, (Sir Basil Nardly-Stoads writes) it is my solemn duty to uphold the traditions of the sect and deal with the thousand and one contingencies that need must occur in an organisation of this kind; in this I am assisted by the Holy Dragger (elected annually), Sir Arthur Starborgling. Sir Arthur saw service and, indeed, a number of other things in Dieppe. Between them the Rammer and the Dragger control the discipline of the Brethren.

HOW MANY ARE THERE OF US

The exact number of the Brethren at any given time (Sir Basil goes on) is always hard to calculate but it can be safely said that a figure of two would be exact; it is our proud claim that we are far more exclusive than our religious competitors The Exclusive Brethren and their sinister affiliates, The Elusive Brethren.

THE ORIGINS OF THE SECT

As long ago (in the words of Sir Basil) as 1961 Saint Basil (ne Nardly-Stoads) first discovered (or in the words of the Holy Stoadscript) came across the mystic words in the New Testament "Go forth and seize young women." This was taken by Saint Basil to be the essence of the message that God, in his infinite wisdom, was trying to get across. AND GO FORTH HE CERTAINLY HAS. In the words of Dragger, Sir Arthur Starborgling, "Sir Basil has certainly gone forth and seized them all right."

AFTER THE SEIZURE

Once the seizing has taken place it is the sacred function of The Rammer and Dragger jointly to achieve the SPODE of AARON. What this is can never be revealed to those outside the Brethren, but I feel (writes Sir Basil Nardly-Stoads) that the words "Rumba", "Spreading" and "Hub" might well indicate to the sophisticated reader the nature of the ceremony.

Next week I hope to adumbrate on this and explain to the general pubic exactly how they can send us money.

---

life. The only regular contributor whose copy was unused in the Muggeridge issue was Christopher Logue. Logue, then and now, considered this to be a censorship. There would have been little sympathy between them in any case. Logue was reported in *Harper's* (October 1964) to be advocating the merits of marijuana, not then the commonplace substance it has since become.

At just that point when *Private Eye* was weathering the financial crisis of 1964 the extent of its problems became visible to all. There was a marked deterioration in its general appearance and the quality of its paper from Issue 73 on. The cover price had gone up from 1/– to 1/6d for the Muggeridge issue and had stayed there.

For Peter Usborne, enough was enough. Having ensured the financial position, he felt in need of a change. In November the *South London Press* reported an extraordinary story about a student who was beaten up and robbed by his landlord after the latter found that he had been advertising in *Private Eye*. The student sued and lost his case, the magistrate considering the fact that he had placed an advertisement in the paper sufficient evidence of his bad character to make his testimony unreliable. The explanation for this was only made plain to Usborne by chance, when he himself placed an ad in *Private Eye* for his AJS 500 motorbike and was deluged with replies along the lines of, 'What about the leather gear that goes with it?' The 'Personal' column, Usborne's ewe lamb, had been infiltrated by perverts who, lacking other outlets, adopted a code. 'AJS 500' was, it seemed, a symbol of something highly unorthodox. So irritated was Usborne by this development that he began to ask himself what he was doing with his life if one of his few achievements was to provide the freaks of London with means of getting in touch with each other. Accordingly he enrolled at the Fontainebleau Business School. The *Eye* put him through Fontainebleau by paying him a retainer in return for which he remained managing director and made a weekly phone call to Tony Rushton who was his replacement. Usborne's departure, apparently the latest in a succession, was of special significance. He, possibly more than any other individual, had been responsible for turning a bright idea into a viable business. His predecessor, Nicholas Luard, had overcome his own financial crisis by this time and was on the point of departing for Spain where, having 'pulled out of satire altogether', in the words of the *Financial Times*, he was investing in a family property development and writing his first novel.

Once the paper had survived 1964 there was time to settle on a new editorial policy. The inclusion of more news did not alter *Private Eye*'s essentially irresponsible character. The 'comic' design was retained, and W.H. Smith continued to award every issue its seal of disapproval, which, though bad for sales, was of great assistance to any paper trying to cultivate a reputation for recklessness. With the Smith veto, it was not always necessary actually to be reckless; *Private Eye* enjoyed that reputation without having to run a constant risk. The grounds for the Smith ban changed with circumstances. So in December 1965 *The Penguin Private Eye* was banned on grounds of 'taste'. The firm's advisers considered Barry McKenzie to be pornographic. At the same time *Private Eye* noted that Smith's were selling large quantities of soft porn from *Playboy* and *Penthouse* upwards. Then in the following month the firm refused to accept the paper on libel grounds, and when they were offered an indemnity said that it would not be backed by adequate resources. Something about *Private Eye* offended the senior management of Smith's considerably, but what it was they were not prepared to say.

Politically *Private Eye* remained left-wing. The 'thirteen years of Tory rule' were to end in 1964, and for *Private Eye* it seemed the chance to finish off in reality every aspect of the old régime which it had ridiculed since it was founded three years earlier. Macmillan had departed but his England tottered on under the uninspiring direction of Sir Alec Douglas-Home (alias 'Baillie Vass'). *Private Eye* supported the witty intellectual who was going to re-forge the Ballie's rusty old England in the white heat of his technological revolution (Mr Harold Wilson). During the election campaign the paper took particular delight in one target, the former Viscount Hailsham, who seemed to the young sixties' radical to sum up all that was worst about the Tory party. He was pompous, provocatively old-fashioned, with a lawyer's arrogance, ambitious and odiously clever – a man who had the intellect to understand the case for socialism and whose Toryism must therefore be based on heartless self-interest. He had renounced his peerage in order to be considered for the leadership of the Tory party, and when this failed he was left with the delightfully satirical name of 'Quintin Hogg'. *Private Eye* warmly supported his attempts to get himself re-elected and even marketed a cushion set, admiringly named the 'Stuff Your Own Quintin Hogg cushion'. Hogg was eventually sufficiently rattled by this close regard to sue, and the libellous cushion had to be withdrawn from sale.

1 Claud Cockburn
2 Alan Brien
3 Ann Chisholm
  (editorial assistant)
4 Tony Rushton
5 Jennifer Wedderspoon
  (editorial secretary)
6 Bernard Levin
7 Amanda ⎫ (subscription
8 Doris ⎭ ladies)
9 David Cash
10 John Thorpe (printer)
11 Christopher Logue
12 Peter Cook
13 Ralph Steadman
14 Christine Keeler
15 A judge
16 Harold Macmillan
17 Barry Fantoni
18 Harold Wilson
19 Gerald Scarfe
20 Gill Brooke
  (classified advertising)
21 Peter Usborne
22 Charlie Harness
23 Richard Ingrams
24 William Rushton
25 Mary Ingrams
26 Fred Ingrams (son)
27 John Wells

LORD GNOME SAYS: THESE QUINTIN HOGG CUSHION KITS, IN THREE VIVID COLOURS, ON STRONG IRISH CLOTH, ARE ABSOLUTELY GENUINE, LIKE MY WELL-KNOWN CONSERVATIVE POSTERS AND CAR-STICKERS. THEY ARE AVAILABLE FROM:- "IT'S HERE" CARD SHOPS — PRESENTS OF DOVER STREET — PRESENTS OF SLOANE STREET — INGRAMS INTERNATIONAL DESIGNS, AND ALL OTHER GOOD GIFT SHOPS. OR DIRECT FROM ME AT PRIVATE EYE PRODUCTIONS, LTD., 22 GREEK STREET, LONDON, W.1. THEY ARE CHEAP AT 12/6 EACH, AND THEY WORK. INDEED, I HAVE STUFFED ONE MYSELF. I FIND IT VERY SATISFYING, AND I KEEP IT BY ME ALL THE TIME. TRY ONE YOURSELF.

At one point during the election campaign Hogg attracted national attention by making a speech in Plymouth in which he said that there were 'adulterers on both front benches'. *Private Eye* had for some time been hearing rumours about Wilson and one of his female staff and had been energetically denying the truth of them. The denials were issued on the *fiat* of Claud Cockburn, whose traditional 'party line' became particularly noticeable at election time.

An innovation brought about by the 1964 election campaign was the regular column by Lord Gnome. Gnome was a loathsome character first referred to in Issue 3. He was originally conceived of as a monstrous capitalist, a property developer, a currency speculator and a newspaper proprietor, the epitome of the greedy, ruthless, ignorant, vulgar millionaire. In July 1964 there was a dangerous innovation entitled 'Gnome Speaks', naturally on the subject of an impending price rise. In October this turned into 'Gnome Writes', this time on behalf of the Conservative Party. It is something he has done in virtually every issue since. The column is almost always written by Ingrams.

A glance at the election covers shows that, although *Private Eye* was entirely against the Tories while they were in power, not a moment was lost in turning the fire against Labour when it was successful. 'Mrs Wilson's Diary' was launched at the same time. The first installment of this was relatively weak, and it was not until John Wells succeeded William Rushton on the editorial board that the diary began to assume what was to become its permanent form.

There were other editorial changes at this time. Cockburn terminated a short term on the editorial board to become a regular contributor with a single column called 'Down Memory Lane'. It was an ingenious formula, which used memories of his childhood 'in Tring, Herts.' and his eccentric family to point up the absurdity of the Conservative approach to current events. While it ran, 'Down Memory Lane' was undoubtedly one of the best things in the magazine, and among the most effective journalistic devices Cockburn had used. His influence also ensured that when the attack started on the Labour government it was mainly an attack from the left. So the members of the new cabinet were immediately reviled for wanting knighthoods. In such apparently symbolic lapses was the Labour government's subsequent failure first hinted at, quite accurately as it turned out.

Cockburn's left-wing sympathies were shared by another occasional new contributor, Paul Foot, but *Private Eye* was still open to less socialist views. In December 1964, 'William Hickey' had reported that Christopher Booker's marriage had ended in separation after nineteen months. In May 1965, he once again started to contribute to *Private Eye* with a withering and elegant series of unsigned profiles entitled 'Pillars of Society', some of which have left scars on their victims which are occasionally visible even today. The first subject was Paul Johnson, then acting editor of the *New Statesman*. Booker suggested that he was a snob and not a very sincere socialist. The third, of Iain Macleod, contained an affectionate sideswipe at Malcolm Muggeridge, then Booker's kindly host and benefactor. The fourth was Mark Boxer, known as a youthful iconoclast, whose reaction was to phone Booker and complain. Booker congratulated him on his courage in phoning. Others included Hugh Carleton Greene ('shambling, Byzantine eunuch'), Kingsley Amis ('sub-intellectual, masturbatory'), Anthony Wedgwood Benn ('goose-stepping, crew-cut'), the Duke of Edinburgh ('cruel-mouthed') and Dick Lester ('a craze, a trend, a delusion'). Booker's anonymity ended in October when he was named in Issue 98, after two years of Stalinesque invisibility, as winner of the second prize in a readers' competition, and he was finally awarded a 'Welcome Home' contributors' credit in the 100th Issue.

Among the notable jokes in this period was the revelation that the distinguished journalist Peregrine Worsthorne, who was keen to restrict immigration, was himself of Belgian descent; his father, Colonel Koch de Gooreynd, had changed the family name and chosen an English one by sticking a pin into a map. It is also worth noting that the 'Grand Ugliest Man in Britain Competition' suggested the names of John Junor and 'Anyone called Waugh'.

During this period of fairly savage abuse the libel front was generally quiet. However, there were apologies to Wolf Mankowitz and Terry Thomas, and C. P. Snow received two apologies. The first was for a story that Snow had only attended a literary lunch on condition that he could take the chair. In the month following the apology for this story *Private Eye* stated that Snow had entertained the Nobel Prize committee to dinner in order to improve his chances of winning the prize. This suggestion too was withdrawn. The first of these apologies was prefigured by a story in the *Sunday Telegraph* recalling that Snow had himself libelled Claud Cockburn in his novel, *The Conscience of the Rich*, and that he had acknowledged this to Cockburn who had nonetheless declined to sue.

There was a taste of things to come when it was reported by the *Daily Telegraph* that 12,000 copies of the book of 'Mrs Wilson's Diary' had been recalled by the publishers Anthony Blond in order to make its authorship clear. This expensive and rather pointless exercise had been undertaken at the suggestion of an increasingly prominent solicitor, Mr Arnold Goodman, and had been preceded by 'a friendly conversation'. In October 1965 a time bomb set ticking in Issue 13 finally exploded. Lord Russell of Liverpool announced that he intended to sue. There was a friendly reference to Russell just after this announcement, but too late, too late. It seemed that no sooner was one crisis overcome than it was succeeded by another, even more threatening.

Apologise, and don't give a damn 5

To tell the truth, or what one passionately believes to be the truth, must always be worthwhile.
Patricia Cockburn, *The Years of The Week*

Apart from Randolph Churchill, the Lord Russell of Liverpool case was the first serious libel action *Private Eye* faced. But in contrast to the propaganda victory of the Churchill case, Russell was a near-disaster.

It originated in 1962, when Peter Cook, wandering around Soho, noticed that the dirty book shops contained an unexpected title. Sandwiched between *Miss Whiplash* and *Rubber News* was a book with a superficial similarity but on a very different subject – *The Scourge of the Swastika* – which was going quite well to the same clientele. 'Lord Liver of Cesspool' was consequently fashioned one sunny June day to add to the *Eye*'s gallery of semi-fictional grotesques. This piece suggested that so far from writing a serious account of Nazi war crimes, Lord Russell had been pandering to salacious and sadistic tastes.

Three years passed, Lord Russell eventually issued a writ, and *Private Eye* decided, in a wildly optimistic moment, to go to court for the first time. The decision to fight was taken by Ingrams, but he relied strongly on the advice of the *Eye*'s solicitors, Rubinstein, Nash. And Michael Rubinstein was adamant that this was the one to resist.

The result was a humiliating defeat. It was decided that none of the editors of *Private Eye* should give evidence. This would prevent them from being cross-examined about other articles, and would give their counsel, David Turner-Samuels, the last word. The only consequence of this decision was that they were abused in court for refusing to go into the witness box by Lord Russell's counsel, who was able to monopolise the court's time. Mr Turner-Samuels, for all his 'last words', might as well have been a graven image. Wells recalls that, 'at one point Turner-Samuels asked the judge if he could read an excerpt from *The Times Literary Review*. Nobody told him that the paper was not called that and he proceeded to read out the words "Lord Russell's works could be said to be pornographic." David Hirst, who was for the plaintiff, jumped to his feet and said, "Read the rest of the sentence," and Turner-Samuels rather lamely concluded, "very well I will," – "but they are not ...". Rubinstein afterwards said, "What do you think of Turner-Samuels? I think he's doing rather well."' After a four-day hearing Lord Russell was awarded £5000 damages, and costs of £3000. *Private Eye*'s immediate reaction was gloomy. John Wells told the *Daily Mail* that the magazine's total weekly income was only about £650. And Richard Ingrams expressed doubts about whether another issue could be printed. In the event, *Private Eye* discovered an entirely new source of emergency funds, the generosity of its readers. For the first time an appeal was launched, but the idea was suggested by the readers themselves, eighteen of whom, including John Betjeman, sent in contributions before any announcement had been made. This, together with a benefit concert, *Rustle of Spring*, given by Peter Cook, Dudley Moore, Spike Milligan, Peter Sellers, Manfred Mann, Bob Monkhouse, George Melly, Roy Hudd, David Frost and many others, saved the paper. The readers' appeal closed at £1325, and the concert, which had been organised by Tony Rushton, raised a substantial sum, although no one can now remember how much.

This close shave was a decisive influence on subsequent libel policy, which might be described as 'apologise and don't give a damn'. *Private Eye* carries more apologies than comparable magazines, but it takes many more risks. In considering the number of apologies, the following points should be remembered.

a. The apologies represent a tiny fraction of the inaccuracies in any newspaper.

b. Many apologies are completely misleading, and add to the inaccuracy of a newspaper.

c. Most of the information in a newspaper is generally reliable.

d. If you know anything about a news story from personal experience, it invariably contains at least one mistake.

e. None of the above statements is contradictory or even paradoxical.

News is not 'historical truth' (whatever that may be), and newspapers can still give a useful and reasonably accurate view of the general rush of events though they are riddled with minor, and some major, inaccuracies. There is nothing surprising about inaccuracies. Ask any three eye-witnesses of a routine sequence of events in the street to give a precise account of them, and see how many contradictions are presented. In these circumstances *Private Eye* has managed to bluff its way past many of its own apologies. In the words of Tom Hopkinson, professor of journalism at University College, Cardiff, it has managed

> to establish an impression that to sue *Private Eye* is degrading and absurd, though it is not either absurd or degrading – but on the contrary courageous and idealistic – for *Private Eye* to provide occasion to be sued. This is surely a most valuable protective earthwork to have thrown up.

In March 1966, a further serious libel action was settled. Quintin Hogg agreed to drop his complaints* for a payment of £1000, plus costs of £511. He explained, in passing, that he was 'a generous man'. With hindsight this might have been a much better case to fight. Hogg, like all politicians, might have realised the mixed benefits of re-running a libel through

---

* Concerning the 'Stuff Your Own Quintin Hogg cushion', etc.

the courts. As it was, the two cases caused libel expenses of £9511 in two months, of which £8000 had to be paid on the nail.

In 1968, following a change of solicitors, *Private Eye* actually defeated a libel threat. This was in a case brought by three ex-policemen who ran a firm called Midland County Investigators which specialised in the violent eviction of tinkers in the Birmingham area. It was staffed by ex-policemen. When the writ was issued in February the *Eye* said that it would 'hotly contest' the action. In December *The Guardian* reported that the three ex-policemen were dropping it. *Private Eye*'s costs nevertheless came to £500. The story, 'Tinker's Fuzz', had been a typical 'Footnote', thoroughly researched and offensively written. From *Private Eye*'s point of view the moral victory was of considerable importance.

Two other libel cases, also in the sixties, involved allegations against Glasgow newspaper reporters. Both were lost by *Private Eye*. In the first case the allegation was that two reporters from the *Scottish Daily Express* had taken an old man, John Duddy, out for an interview after which he had fallen down and died. When the reporters sued, *Private Eye* returned to its Glasgow sources (the old fellow's 'outraged' surviving children) and found to its surprise that they were unwilling to swear affidavits about the facts of their father's death. Negotiations were carried on through 'Lawyer Latta', a Glasgow character and a solicitor, who offered to represent *Private Eye*'s interests in the matter. Fourteen months after the story had appeared *Private Eye* agreed to pay 'substantial' damages to the editor and reporters of the *Scottish Daily Express*. The statement acknowledged that the *Express* reporters had written a story claiming to have interviewed Mr Duddy, on the day of his death, but said that 'they had not in fact done so'. 'The defendants,' the statement continued, 'have now checked their sources on which they had relied and realised that they were completely unreliable.' Of that there was no doubt whatever.

Shortly afterwards the *Eye*'s trusted man in Glasgow, Lawyer Latta, was given an eight-year prison sentence for conspiracy.

Nothing daunted, *Private Eye* waded back into Glasgow in 1969. The result was the first case to reach court since the Cesspool débâcle. On the face of it *Private Eye* had its strongest chance ever, but the judge was to decide otherwise. The story which the judge disbelieved alleged that two reporters working for *The People* had purchased a Glasgow prostitute for the use of Stuart Christie, the Scottish anarchist released from a Spanish prison. It was essentially a postscript to a much longer story about how Lord Snowdon and a reporter on *The Sunday Times* had done the same for a released prisoner on behalf of the *Sunday Times Magazine*.

The case was eventually heard by Mr Justice Brabin in January 1969 and *Private Eye* had, apart from Stuart Christie, called four other witnesses. The reporters produced an alibi story that depended on going into a restaurant which both swore they had entered. *Private Eye* showed that this restaurant was shut on the night in question. The judge nonetheless found for the plaintiffs and awarded them £500 each for the libel, which he did 'not consider to be grave'. *Private Eye* had to meet costs for both parties in excess of £10,000 and so the second appeal to readers, 'Gnomefam', was launched. This ran for twenty-nine issues (188–217) and closed at £1932 after sixteen months. During the course of time it became a generalised libel fund rather than an appeal for *The People* case.*

In 1971 *Private Eye* scored another small success, this time before the case came to court and without incurring any costs; an improvement on the £500 it had taken to defeat the Midland County Investigators. The story had taken *Eye* readers back into the murky world of private law enforcement, and suggested that the Granada Group's retail credit manager had been taking a £20-a-month back-hander for employing two unsavoury debt collectors. This allegation led to a letter from the firm of Goodman Derrick & Co.

Dear Sir,

We act for Mr Arkell who is Retail Credit Manager of Granada TV Rental Ltd. His attention has been drawn to an article appearing in the issue of *Private Eye* dated 9th April 1971 on page 4. The statements made about Mr Arkell are entirely untrue and clearly highly defamatory. We are therefore instructed to require from you immediately your proposals for dealing with the matter.

Mr Arkell's first concern is that there should be a full retraction at the earliest possible date in *Private Eye* and he will also want his costs paid. His attitude to damages will be governed by the nature of your reply.

Yours etc.

* In one memorable week readers contributing to 'Gnomefam' included the Corporals' Mess, 4 Guards Brigade Signals Squadron, BFPO 17, and the Junior Common Room of Oriel College, Oxford.

Apologise, and don't give a damn

The reply was as follows:

Dear Sirs,

We acknowledge your letter of 29th April referring to Mr J. Arkell.

We note that Mr Arkell's attitude to damages will be governed by the nature of our reply and would therefore be grateful if you could inform us what his attitude to damages would be, were he to learn that the nature of our reply is as follows: fuck off.

Yours etc.

The intense relief after nine years of grovelling apologies echoed through this merry response. No more was heard from Mr Arkell.

It has often been noted that a disproportionate number of litigants against *Private Eye* are journalists. Various explanations have been advanced. That journalists are not used to 'taking it' or that they cannot resist the chance to try the boot on the other foot. There is a further possibility, that they can indulge all the pleasure of litigation without any of the risk, since their costs are frequently met by their employers. Two memorable legal battles, both against the same journalist, illustrate this point. They marked the end of an epoch and a change of tactics in *Private Eye*'s approach to libel.

The major case, which *Private Eye* won, was in the law of copyright. It arose from a 'Footnote' which revealed the manner in which the lobby system worked to the advantage of politicians. It was headed 'The Ballsoff Memorandum' and gave the background to an obsequious study of Reginald Maudling written by Nora Beloff in *The Observer*.

This story had replaced a rival proposal by the paper's business team for a thorough investigation of Mr Maudling's financial affairs, which were then the subject of many stories in the *Eye*. In order to show how Nora Beloff had substituted her bromide for the business probe, 'Footnotes' quoted the full text of a memorandum sent by Beloff to the editor (and proprietor) of *The Observer*, David Astor. The *Eye* thereby made Miss Beloff look extremely foolish since she claimed to be confronting Maudling with the evidence against his financial probity but had suceeded merely in making it obvious that she was trying to help him.

Since the 'Footnote' was so heavily evidenced, Miss Beloff

could not suggest that it was untrue and could not sue for libel. Instead she chose to bring a case for breach of copyright. This was in itself something of an embarrassment to a national newspaper since it presented the spectacle of an editor and a political correspondent supposedly in the business of public disclosure using the law to prevent disclosure of a political document. *Private Eye* produced various stories in *The Observer* which had been based on leaked information or stolen documents. They also produced the business editor of *The Observer*, Anthony Bambridge, and Anthony Howard, at that time a rival political commentator to Miss Beloff on *The Observer*.

The case before Mr Justice Ungoed Thomas lasted eight days, for four of which Miss Beloff's counsel addressed the judge without interruption. He spoke extremely slowly and had a turn of phrase which, even by the standards of the Bar, was somewhat out of date. His finest pearl, produced at a moment when everyone else in court seemed to have passed into a deep coma, was 'I should have thought that even *the veriest neophyte* would have realised that.' The case was of incidental importance to *Private Eye* since it was the first in which the editor submitted himself to the ordeal of cross-examination. It was heard in July but judgement was reserved until October. There was a nasty moment in September when a rumour circulated that the judge had lost his notes and there was wild speculation that the case might have to be heard again. Finally, in October, judgement was given for *Private Eye*, and costs of £10,000 were awarded against Miss Beloff. These were met by her employer.

The week following the great victory over Beloff her second case opened in the High Court. In contrast to the copyright case this was not provoked by a carefully researched factual story, but by one written by Auberon Waugh. The item, which appeared in the same issue as the 'Ballsoff Memorandum', read as follows: 'Miss Bailiff, a sister of the late Sir Alec Douglas-Home, was frequently to be found in bed with Mr Harold Wilson and senior members of the previous administration, although it is thought that nothing improper occurred.'

This sentence was so obviously intended as a joke that no one on the staff could at first believe that Miss Beloff seriously intended to go through with her case. Her name was not Miss Bailiff; this was an echo of the *Eye*'s nickname for Douglas-Home, whose sister she was notoriously not. The idea that this dry old stick who took herself so toweringly seriously could ever have been found in bed with Wilson was too absurd to need explanation. If it was to be taken at face value it was then explicitly stated that nothing improper had occurred. Presumably half the parliamentary lobby and most of the senior civil service were also to be found in this remarkable bed, perhaps in the hall of the Treasury, attached to a six-cylinder engine for easy movement to the House of Commons. Any libel would have had to have been made to the readers of *Private Eye*. Only experienced readers of the paper would ever have reached this sentence, buried in a column on page 19, and then been able to make any sort of sense out of it. As a libel action, based on Miss Beloff's argument that it was intended to suggest that she had had an affair with Harold Wilson, the thing was an obvious non-starter. The case, which opened in the High Court, lasted two days and ended in £3000 damages for Miss Beloff and £2000 total costs against *Private Eye*. The only lesson (by now familiar) seemed to be that judges and juries could usually be counted on to leave their senses of humour in the street.

Miss Beloff did not make herself popular in Fleet Street with these two actions. *The Sunday Times* and the *Financial Times* both considered that the copyright action had been highly damaging to the press, for the restrictive nature of the arguments deployed by Miss Beloff had found favour with the judge, who had only awarded the case to *Private Eye* on the technical ground that the copyright was owned by *The Observer*, not by Miss Beloff. Bernard Levin, writing in *The Times*, put the general opinion bluntly: 'Neither action should have been brought. Both should have failed.'

Although they had come out of the encounter as winners in both money and prestige, *Private Eye* were sufficiently annoyed to exact a rather cruel revenge on Miss Beloff.

Everyone [said *Private Eye*] will by now be thoroughly sickened and bored by this silly woman, her endless litigation and attempts to justify herself. The fact remains that *Private Eye* will have to pay her £3000 and costs estimated at £2000 as a result of her victory in the libel action. We shall do our best to raise this money from our own coffers. In addition, we are starting a special fund to be called the Ballsoff Fund so that readers may have the chance to help *Private Eye* pay the money and register a public protest against the litigation brought against *Private Eye* by Ballsoff.

This was a novel use of the appeal to readers. (It was clear by now that *Private Eye* could well afford to pay £5000 for a

The Ballsoff Fund

The Fund now stands at £357.15

We would like to thank the following for their donations.

G D Jordan
J Booth
C P Rouse
Nicholas Faith
Celia Haddon
Peter Watson

W C & N Parrett
Graham Cooper
Elaine & Roger Thurgood
G H Tatham
Prof. W B Bon~
Robert F~

libel action. Sales in the first half of 1972 had reached an all-time high of ninety-eight thousand.) This appeal made Miss Beloff look foolish for month after month. Her grim photograph was to appear in issue after issue beside the title 'The Ballsoff Fund', recalling the nickname Nora Ballsoff which had even caused the judge to laugh; and beneath this photograph was the growing list of those who were paying to keep it there. The first list included the Marquess of Londonderry, the Labour Party Research and International Departments, Tom Stoppard and Dr Miriam Stoppard, the Headmaster of Eton and the *King's Cross Whisper*, Sydney. Later there was to be Michael Foot, Brixton Employment Exchange and the Marchioness of Salisbury. The fund ran until the following April and raised £1282.75. Nora Ballsoff became a catchphrase up and down the land. It was a painful demonstration of the disadvantages of suing for libel.

In 1966 *Private Eye* nearly closed because it was faced with libel damages of £5000 to Lord Russell of Liverpool. In 1969 libel actions were costing £5000 a year and this could be managed reasonably comfortably. In 1977 the exceptional circumstances of the Goldsmith case cost £85,000 and readers' donations of £40,000 were essential to keep the paper going. In 1980 libel actions cost £75,000, which was again manageable. In 1981 annual costs and damages were estimated at £100,000. Then in May 1982, a fifteen-day High Court hearing in which Desmond Wilcox recovered £14,000 damages for libel resulted in costs for both sides of £80,000. The annual libel provision had to be doubled. Sue, Grabbit and Runne of Cheapside are still doing very nicely.

Apologise, and don't give a damn

Fluck and Law. Photography by John Lawrence Jones.

6

The gravy train picks up speed
1966–1972

For a few years Private Eye *had the disturbing experience of being praised by judges, politicians and tycoons. It made a new reputation as 'a serious investigative journal'. In 1966 it was very nearly closed by the Lord Russell libel action. By 1972 its finances had been transformed and a company villa in the Dordogne had been purchased. The editorial structure assumed its present form (Mr Richard Ingrams); Andrew Osmond returned as managing director; the paper shed some of its uncomplicated 'student' radicalism; for the first time it successfully resisted libel writs, and it even won a case in the High Court. The magazine's critics began to complain that* Private Eye *was 'philistine'.*

In January 1966 *Private Eye* was edited by a board of two, Ingrams and John Wells. What happened next can be seen from the masthead, and might be described by an ornithologist as a characteristic perch-shuffling stategy. In March Ingrams became 'Editor-in-Chief' and Wells was cast as 'Creative Editor and Literary Influence'. By May Wells's name had disappeared altogether and Ingrams had become 'Editor' – a position he has held until the time of writing. In due course the masthead itself was to go and the authorship of the magazine was to become largely anonymous. And by the end of this period the editor would have fallen out with his most important contributor, who had been taking an increasing share of the limelight. It would be fair to say that in all these developments, except the last, Ingrams had the cheerful support of his staff.

Editing *Private Eye* has never been a full-time job (there was time in February 1966, for instance, for Ingrams and both Rushtons to pose as models for *She* magazine). But in Ingrams's view membership of the board demanded more commitment than Wells was showing. Ever since he was left behind by the *TW3* gravy train, Ingrams had concentrated on *Private Eye*. Meanwhile, Wells was embarked on several other careers, in acting, scriptwriting and straight journalism. He was also becoming 'socially prominent' and was mentioned by the gossip columnists as 'a friend of Princess Margaret'. None of this endeared him to his fellow satirists. *Private Eye* has always been a mixture of an exclusive club and a secret society. When Wells was mentioned there was talk of 'using the *Eye*', one of the most serious breaches of the brotherhood's rules. At one point Princess Margaret took to telephoning the Greek Street office and leaving messages for 'Jawn', a development which his colleagues found it impossible not to parody. Issue 115, the first issue which Wells did not sign, carried a study of Princess Margaret by Gerald Scarfe. So, in what was to become the traditional manner, was the world alerted to the former editor's new position beyond the pale.

The masthead went nine months later, in February 1967. There was some anxiety at the time on the top floor that 'the minions' (that is the non-editorial members of the staff) might be disappointed. So it is interesting to note that of the seventeen names which appeared on the last masthead, nine are still *in situ* or remain regular contributors.

Paul Foot by Fantoni.

The decision to abolish the masthead was taken shortly after Paul Foot had joined the paper and it seemed at first as though he had thereby been deprived of his chance of a by-line. It was subsequently discovered that he had overcome this problem by re-christening his column 'Footnotes'.

The character of *Private Eye* in this period was largely determined by first the arrival and then the departure of Paul Foot.

Foot had been a contributor since coming to London in 1964 after his first job on the *Daily Record* in Glasgow. In London he was with *The Sun* and then with the *Sunday Telegraph*, and he formed the habit of coming round to Greek Street on his day off, Sunday, which was then *Private Eye*'s press day. From there he would phone various contacts, mostly experienced journalists, and talk to them about any stories they had decided, for whatever reason, not to write in their own papers. John Morgan, Alan Brien, and Anthony Howard were among those on his regular list. Recalling it now, Foot says:

> In the summer of 1966 we began to get many more contacts. It was the height of 'Swinging London' and London journalists thought that we had the world at our feet. I remember people on the *Economist*, and people like Nick Harman and Joe Roeber, started to give us informa-

113

tion. In those days if you rang up and said that you were from *Private Eye* people didn't believe you really. But a few journalists saw the potential we had for publishing information. If they didn't get a cheque they didn't complain because they looked on us as a good cause. And if we gave them £5 for something they wrote it was very nice.

Then the stories started getting better. Rhodesia became a big issue. Among the middle classes *Private Eye* was exceedingly popular. There was criticism of some of the jokes – C. P. Snow being blind, that sort of joke, and Katherine Whitehorn being called a lesbian when she wasn't. But it was hard to find a real enemy in our world. It wasn't that the papers printed less than they do now or a desperation to get things published. It was much more an eagerness to be 'in with the *Eye*'.

People felt they could do what they liked in the sixties. There was an atmosphere of disclosure that doesn't exist today. And Richard gave me my head. In those days my column in *Private Eye* was a radical column. I had a partnership with him, and I could shape my own pages.

In February 1970, Auberon Waugh joined the paper, and formed an unlikely partnership with Foot. As John Wells wrote at the time:

> Unlike the fundamentally tolerant gossip at the front of the magazine, from which it would be possible for a stranger to believe that the vital power of the nation was centred in the drawing rooms, in El Vino's and in Kensington Palace, the Foot news at the back, following the Cockburn tradition, is for the most part rigorously researched and written from a point of view of extreme political intolerance, attacking capital and its minions with a single-minded fury.... The combination of political opposites, of classical moderation with romantic extremism, of the Ingrams faction of bald, waspish and amusing Auberon Waugh and the Christian Alliance of Booker and Fantoni, set against Foot and his wild-eyed news gathering fanatics, seems to work extremely well.

The attraction of this combination was that people were interested in what *Private Eye* thought and revealed but they could not predict it. In order to be 'in with the *Eye*' it was necessary to buy it, an obviously successful formula for any magazine. The combination worked until the departure of Foot in October 1972. The final 'Footnotes' was in Issue 282.

From now on the dominant by-line, the alternative, independent view, was to be Waugh's; a more complex, allusive, unpredictable and amusing view – but nothing can make up for 'the Facts'.

When Foot left there was a farewell dinner in a private room at the Terrazza. Ingrams was presented with a cartoon by John Kent entitled 'Dropping the Revolutionary', and Peter Cook made a long and emotional speech. Foot resigned just before his High Court victory over Nora Beloff in a blaze-of-glory situation. Three months later he was made 'Journalist of the Year'.

Auberon Waugh's transfer to *Private Eye* from the *Spectator* had followed his opposition to a libel action brought by the *Spectator* against *Private Eye*, when he had gone so far as to threaten the proprietor Harry Creighton with a strike if he persisted. And his abusive political column had been a source of growing discomfort to a paper which was (in those days) of fairly orthodox Conservative views. Then a parody Waugh wrote of *A Christmas Carol*, showing Wilson behaving like Scrooge over Biafra, was spiked by the *Spectator* and eventually appeared (rather late for Christmas and rather out of place) in *Private Eye*. Waugh's next move was to become bored at the printers and to make a joke in the *Spectator*'s contents box, describing veteran contributor George Gale as 'Lunchtime O'Gale'. At this point Waugh was dismissed* by the editor, Nigel Lawson.

Waugh's column gave *Private Eye* an entirely new range. He was called the paper's political correspondent, the first time *Private Eye* had possessed anything so grand, but his column was a unique mixture of jokes, abuse and accurate political gossip. For two years his alliance with Foot was directed against the moderate Tory government led by Grocer Heath. *Private Eye* is always said to be funniest when there is a Tory government and for this period it was able to vilify its favourite targets from opposite sides at the same time. These four short years of Tory rule always seemed to Ingrams to be an unnatural interregnum in what then seemed an indefinite period of Labour government. *Private Eye*'s response was the 'Heathco' column which did for Heath what the 'Diary' had done for Harold Wilson. It was written by Ingrams and Fantoni. At the same time the cartoonist John Kent started a long-running series on 'Grocer Heath & His

---

* He later won £600 in an action for wrongful dismissal.

Judith Hart in 1967. As a left-wing back bencher joining Wilson's government she was attacked for lack of principle.

Pals'. The paper's stance at the 1970 General Election which returned the Grocer to power remained pro-Labour.

One result of Waugh's arrival was that a number of new targets were chosen, some of them old friends of *Private Eye* who had formerly been able to count on immunity. Both Christopher Booker and John Wells were nibbled by the new dog, and Alan Brien and Bryan Forbes, both loyal supporters of the past, were singled out for attention. Charles Douglas-Home, then features editor (now editor) of *The Times* and therefore Waugh's other employer, was also roughed up. Douglas-Home then fired him – so booking himself a regular appearance as 'Charlie Vass' in the Waugh *oeuvres* for ten years (to date).

The arrival of Waugh also meant a shift in political sympathy away from the Left, but there had been clear signs of a rift between *Private Eye* and the Left for some time before that. It had been sparked off by Wilson's panicky economic policy, known as the 'July measures' of 1966, and was stimulated further by Jim Callaghan's racialist Ugandan Asians bill. At the end of 1966 the socialist journalist D. A. N. Jones remarked that 'the public schoolboys who satirise Harold Wilson in *Private Eye* make great play with words like "Chilprufe" and "Squeezitoy"' (though Mr Jones chose to draw this apparent snobbery to the attention of the egalitarian readers of *Vogue* rather than to his regular readers in the *New Statesman*). Then in 1967 the first of many rivals to *Private Eye* was announced. It was called *Oz* magazine and its editors declared that '*Private Eye* is now an ageing sensation and too occupied with Fleet Street.' (In the event this infant Australian sensation was to expire rather earlier than the ageing British sensation.)

The Left was correct in noticing that *Private Eye* was no longer to be counted on, and the reason was, quite simply, the General Election of 1964. From the start the *Eye* had always been *contre*. By 1966 there was a Labour government beginning to make itself just as ridiculous as the Tories. For a journal of dissent rather than of party, it was simply a question of finding the means with which to attack the new men of power. As usual the paper seized any weapon that came to hand. Leaks about proceedings in the cabinet led naturally to stories about George Brown's extravagant behaviour. It was quite impossible in those days for the press to say that a cabinet minister was drunk. Fleet Street instead used synonyms. *Private Eye* thereupon published a spoof Foreign Office memo giving the translation in French, Italian, German and Russian for the words 'tired, over-

BROWN F.O. Acts

by Our Diplomatic Staff (Maj. (Retd.) B. Sillbint).

Following the appointment of Mr. George Brown as Foreign Secretary I am reliably informed that a special memo has been dispatched by the F.O. to embassies and consulates abroad.

The memo (see below) is intended as a guide to ambassadors and embassy spokesmen when dealing with the Foreign press.

ENGLISH	FRENCH	ITALIAN
TIRED	FATIGUÉ	STANCO
OVERWROUGHT	ENNERVÉ	VIVACE
EXPANSIVE	GENEREUX	ESPANSIVO
OVERWORKED	CREVÉ	TROPPO LAVORATO
COLOURFUL	BIZARRE	CON MOLTO COLORE
EMOTIONAL	EMÛ	EMOTIVO

ENGLISH	GERMAN	RUSSIAN
TIRED	MÜDE	надоёджимвбій
OVERWROUGHT	ÜBERANGESTRENGT	надобоѣот
EXPANSIVE	GROSSZÜGIG	обшйрнбій
OVERWORKED	ÜBERARBEITET	обрбсшпй
COLOURFUL	FARBIG	бецизéтнин
EMOTIONAL	EMOTIONELL	птбіјінкий

PRIVATE EYE

No. 134 Friday 3 Feb. 67 1/6

NON!

Georges est un peu fatigué, Votre Majesté.

You do the Hokey Cokey and you shake it all about..

L'œil Privé

Le seul Journal satirique du Monde

wrought, expansive, overworked, colourful and emotional'. One of the most famous *Eye* phrases, 'tired and emotional', had been born.

It was this propensity to reduce the great issues of the political day to a homelier level that really upset commentators such as D. A. N. Jones. Those who want to rebuild the world and those who want to laugh at it are frequently at odds. Under the Tory government *Private Eye* had been able to ignore this division, now it had to choose; and those of its readers who found Labour politics more important than jokes became increasingly critical.

The natural response was to tease those who defended the government. The *New Statesman* was prominent among them, and in February 1967 *Private Eye* succeeded in getting its managing director to sue for libel. The outcome of any such action was not the point. For *Private Eye* the whole incident had a built-in advantage. Here was the *New Statesman*, a paper that was symbolic of the Left and of dissent, yet apparently what *Private Eye* had to say about its managing director was so outrageous that he was reduced to taking legal action. *Private Eye* had therefore become the paper of dissent and the paper for outsiders. In failing to realise the truth of this assertion the *New Statesman* was confirming it.

The Vietnam war provided another opportunity for *Private Eye* not to take 'a line'. So the cover of Issue 161 took a fairly orthodox left-wing view of the brutality of the war, and in Issue 165 there was a story exposing the Fleet Street myth of extensive injuries to the police during the great Grosvenor Square demonstration against the war. On the other hand, *Private Eye* generally refused to take the protest movement against the war at all seriously. This now seems a perceptive attitude. Contrary to the heady expectations of 1968, the only permanent effect of the student riots was the increase in the numbers of the police Special Branch, as prophesied at the time.

The paper's refusal to identify itself with a fashionable student viewpoint was more remarkable in view of the readership survey of September 1968, which showed that 84% of the readers were under thirty-four, and 59% had had a higher education.

Meanwhile the ill-fated *Oz*, in contrast, was party-lining with the young Left on every issue, and struggling with its self-appointed task of 'supplying the revolutionaries with satire'.

Although the dominant influences on *Private Eye* throughout this period were Ingrams and Foot, there were occasionally other editors who introduced a marked change of style. While Ingrams was in the Dordogne in the summer of 1966 brooding over the remains of Cro-Magnon man, Christopher Booker and William Rushton produced an issue that was slightly reminiscent of the old days of the satire boom.

So, the 'Gnome' column denounced Ingrams as 'a leftie' and welcomed the return of two men who had 'toiled selflessly in defence of the old values'. Eric Buttock made a guest reappearance. Inside the Booker issue there was a lengthy attack on the sexual permissiveness of 'Swinging London' which must have puzzled regular readers, who would not have realised that the founding editor of *Private Eye* was by then an altered man. He had rediscovered a belief in Christianity. He had also developed an interest in the ideas of Jung. And he had started to write about ecology.

Booker was in 1966 only three years short of producing *The Neophiliacs* and was living in a flat in Victoria largely furnished with old newspapers. Years later he was to tell a gathering of Billericay Baptists of his re-conversion. 'I was given an unmistakable assurance,' he said. 'I began to pray.

PRIVATE EYE

No. 161
Friday
16 Feb. 68

1/6

Opposite: *The issue edited by Booker on his return from exile. This cover drew the first complaint to the Press Council.*

... I went down the road to my nearest Anglican church, St Margaret's in Westminster.' His new intellectual interests, religious belief, Jung and ecology, were none of them fashionable in the mid-sixties; and his new position was very much more lonely than his previous one, at the heart of Swinging London, had been.

A year later, in 1967, while Ingrams was taking another summer holiday, Booker was to repeat the trick. Where readers may have been puzzled before they must now have been quite baffled by a copy of *Private Eye* that carried as a front cover an editorial attack on Anthony Wedgwood Benn, then Minister of Technology and described as 'The Most Dangerous Man in Britain'. Where there were usually jokes there was now a sermon about the old enemy (Macmillan) and the infinitely more dangerous new one (Benn).

However, the inside pages included 'The Young Person's Guide to the Modern World' with its descriptions of the old and new versions of figures such as the Parent, the Teacher, the Farmer and the Priest, a reminder of Booker's facility with the formal satirical attack. Although Booker has guest-edited subsequent issues of the paper he has never transmogrified is appearance to the same extent.

PRIVATE EYE

No. 120
Friday
22 July 66

1/6

Bloody Harold can pose for the next one himself

YOURS FOR 5/-

(in three months time)

A YOUNG PERSON'S GUIDE TO THE MODERN WORLD

1. Parents

*I*n the Bad Old Days a PARENT was a horrid stern figure who was always telling children NOT to do what they called NAUGHTY things, like saying rude words and dropping sweet papers on the floor and being late for meals. Life was terribly BORING in those days. Mummies had to spend the whole day cleaning the house and then you went to bed at six o'clock and they told you soppy stories about magic and fairies and everyone tried to be what they called GOOD. Now all that is changed. Now children can do what they like, and parents are much more sensible because they have realised that children know much better than they do what is good for them. Nowadays parents don't have to bother to stop their children saying rude words because they say them all the time themselves. And they don't have to fuss around any more in the evenings because they can leave their children looking at TELEVISION and go out every evening if they want. Another thing is that in the old days parents had to put up with each other sometimes all their lives. Now they have a much better idea so that Mummies and Daddies can change each other as much as they want. Life is much more fun nowadays, isn't it?

Another contributor, Barry Fantoni, then much under Booker's influence, also experienced a religious conversion in February 1969. In Fantoni's case this resulted in feelings of regret that he had 'guyed the royal family'. Now, he said, he prayed for them each week when he went to church. 'I was in the hands of the Devil,' Fantoni told a reporter from *The Sunday Times*. 'Whenever you come out on top the Devil is at his nearest.' He added that he was dead-scared that his friends would think that this was 'another Fantoni gimmick'.

But despite these novel enthusiasms the usual *Private Eye* line on God remained that of the conventionally bored young agnostic. Booker may have told the readers of the *Weekend*

"I've fought the church for years to have squash racquets included in Exorcism Kits!"

"Now, now, Mrs O'Grady, you know I'm not supposed to . . . . ."

"In a moment, my child, we'll see what the computer comes up with in the way of penance."

Opposite: *Peter Cook's cover for the week of the Oz trial.*

Telegraph in 1966 that the mini-skirt was different in kind to (and much worse than) 'the over-exposure of the breast which Tolstoy abominated'. But for the readers of *Private Eye* the existence of Christianity was usually only acknowledged through the work of cartoonists such as Larry, Tidy, Scully and Lowry.

Another discernible change in the editorial line occurred in August 1971 when Peter Cook took charge. The nearest Cook will come to criticising Ingrams is to say that if he were editor 'the paper would be rather different'. The Cook issue suggested some of the ways in which this might be so. This was the time of the *Oz* obscene libel trial and Cook's cover was a straightforward piece of abuse against the judge, Argyle, who had played an interventionist role in the proceedings. Inside there was a weight of information sympathetic to the cause of Richard Neville, the imprisoned editor, which was mostly provided by Cook and Foot. Since the more cynical Ingrams–Booker line was also included in the form of various paragraphs suggesting that the whole thing was a publicity stunt intended to assist the youthful sensation's flagging circulation, the overall impression of *Private Eye*'s reaction to this official attack on a fellow editor was at least as ambiguous as ever. In fact the Cook issue, while showing welcome signs of a fresh hand at the helm, must be counted one of the most editorially muddled ever to have been produced.

The period 1966–1972 contained many notable innovations, among them the 'Grovel' column. This was some time in gestation. In 1970 a fictional character called Anthony Haden-Guest was invented.* He was an implausible, drunken socialite – always described as 'a gifted magazine writer'. Guest, who had unstable political opinions and a torrid emotional life, was supposed to hobnob with various real-life socialites and thereby to show them up.

In the months following the invention of this impossible man, more and more gossip began to appear in the 'Colour Section', some of it inspired by a reporter on the *Daily Express*'s 'William Hickey' column, Nigel Dempster. Many of these stories were attacks on Hickey's rival column 'Charles Greville' in the *Daily Mail*. So successful was Dempster at discrediting the Greville team of reporters that

Mr Anthony Haden-Guest.

* He was based on a real-life journalist, also called Anthony Haden-Guest.

PRIVATE EYE

No. 252
Friday
13 Aug. '71

10p

Inside SPECIAL JUDGES issue

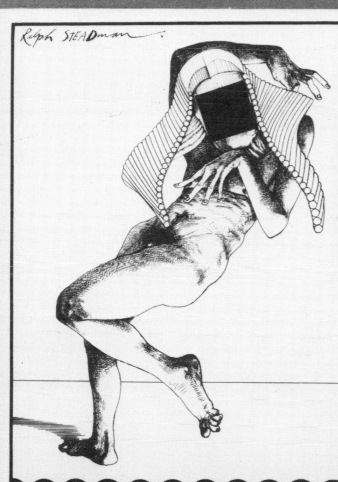

THIS JUSTICE SHOULD BE SEEN TO BE DONE

Judge
Michael Argyle
A recent portrait

To avoid prosecution under the Obscene Publications
Act, the obscene parts have been blacked out.

The Private Eye Story

he was eventually offered their job, and he began his career as the *Mail*'s gossip columnist. Meanwhile *Private Eye* had launched 'Grovel'. 'Grovel', which I then wrote, was intended as a way of telling amusing stories about complete nonentities such as Kenneth Rose, Lord Brocas or Richard Branson. It was the existing *Private Eye* convention that the activities of such people were of no conceivable interest to an intelligent readership but – on the 'Haden-Guest principle' – it became apparent that self-important people could if ridiculed become just as interesting or amusing as genuinely important people.

So 'Grovel', a gossip column, was born in January 1971 and of the early 'Grovel' it could be said that it was unusual among gossip columns in carrying very few references to 'the leg-over question'. Of the stories of 1971 none at all seem to be concerned with this aspect of human behaviour; instead there was a sequence of anecdotes about other matters: the tendency of an elderly millionaire (Getty) to check under the beds of his friends in a tireless search for burglars; the gambling habits of a Labour cabinet minister (Lever); the propensity of the son of a US ambassador (Angier Biddle Duke) to piddle over the limousines of his father's fashionable neighbours. Of course, in the seventies the national gossip columns were not so preoccupied with sex either. To some extent they still observed Lord Beaverbrook's enigmatic adage – 'Always remember, fucking is free.' And they, too, still had room for curiosity about other matters.

THE REGISTER OF FILIPPINO FANCIERS

This has been flagging lately. The only name I can add to the list is that of

BERNARD DELFONT

who keeps a very lively pair at his Sussex residence. Readers should wake up and send in more names.

Unfortunately Lord Boyle of Handsworth, the Vice-Chancellor of Leeds University, will have to be removed from the register. He has issued an official denial to *Leeds Student*.

An article in *Private Eye*, a scurrilous fortnightly magazine, listed Lord Boyle as a "Filipino Fancier"—someone who employs Filipino servants at low rates of pay in the knowledge that if they leave their contracted employment, their work permit is automatically rescinded and they are repatriated.

"It just isn't true," he told a *Leeds Student* reporter, "I don't have any living-in staff, and I never in my life employed a Filipino servant."

No-one from *Private Eye* was available for comment.

The Vice-Chancellor does not intend to take any action on the matter: "I shan't bother with *Private Eye*; and that isn't justs wank," he said, "it's just that one has better things to do."

There were at least five other notable innovations in this period: 'Pseud's Corner', the Crossword, 'Nooks and Corners', 'In the Courts' and 'In the City'.

'Pseud's Corner' was launched in November 1968 with an extract from the works of Ken Tynan. It was suggested by Christopher Booker, and was an offshoot of *The Neophiliacs*. Three of the first entries came from the cuttings Booker had gathered during his research. It was to be one of the most successful items in the paper, attracting a readership of its own. This readership relished seeing their rivals discomfited and appreciated this new method of hitting back at the growing army of cultural placemen. The noun 'pseud', coined at Shrewsbury, was derived from the term 'pseudo-intellectual'.

The Crossword was started in 1969. For some years the identity of the compiler was a secret and he was always described as 'a distinguished academic churchman', a description made more interesting by the competition's reputation as being by far the filthiest, as well as one of the hardest, available. The 'distinguished academic churchman' adopted the pseudonym 'Tiresias' in 1972. He was himself at that time going blind, and he named himself after the blind seer of Athens who, in Tennyson's words, when he was doomed by the gods was told: 'henceforth be blind for thou hast seen too much.' This was no doubt true in the case of Tom Driberg, for it was he, as was revealed after his death in 1976.* After Crossword 98 *The Sunday People* noted that the winner 'R. Runcie of St Alban's' must be Bishop Runcie. The bishop denied this and it transpired that the solution had been sent off in his name by his wife, Rosalind, and his niece, Deborah. In order to win their £2 prize the bishop's ladies had mastered such clues as: 'Seamen mop up anal infusions (6)',† and 'Sounds as if you must look behind for this personal lubricant (5)'.‡ Driberg also contributed a strip called 'Focus on Fact', devoted to the Astor family.

'Nooks and Corners' ('of the New Barbarism') was launched in 1971, and its first genius was Sir John Betjeman who set its gentle but deadly tone. He was succeeded by his daughter, Candida (now Lycett-Green), who developed an unsuspected talent for investigative reporting of the most rigorous kind, to the point that she was eventually threatened with physical violence by one of her shady building contractors. She was the first woman to become a regular *Eye* contributor.

'In the Courts', another column with a very high standard of accuracy, was based on reports of cases that had escaped general attention because the regular court reporters had not been present or because they no longer noticed the interesting aspects of a case. It was compiled by two barristers.

'In the City' was started in 1970. It soon became clear that this was going to last, if only because of its high standard of accuracy.

In the first half of 1966, sales were 39,868. In the first half of 1972, when Paul Foot left, they were 98,047. Not all the readers were equally pleased about this success. Among the least enchanted were Zionist sympathisers who objected to

---

* Crosswords had been among Driberg's lifelong passions, and he once came second in *The Times* National Crossword Competition.
† 'Enemas'.
‡ 'Sebum'.

Nooks and Corners

of the New Barbarism:1. Hillgate House, Ludgate Hill

"... a large modern group by Theo Birks ... It looks promising at the time of writing" - Professor Doctor Nikolaus Pevsner. Buildings of Britain (City and Westminster, 1962).

No. We did not get Reynolds Stone to design the lettering over the front door in Old Bailey. The Board of Trade which took over the building when we couldn't let it to anyone else chose this. To compensate we have emphasized to the outside public the essentially upward line of the staircase to the first floor. A plank of wood in the form of an ungrippable bannister rail continues the upward line and is itself a forward-looking feature of its time.

To show that this is a modern building we have deliberately off-centred the prominent features on an otherwise restrained facade. This has been skillfully done by the introduction of a concrete projection which, though affording no shelter, performs the function of drawing the eye down to the door and window which are themselves off centre with the projection. The effect of weather further emphasises the downward line and contrasts with the plain serenity of the facade in a happy way. We had not, of course, calculated on the demands of the London Fire Service, but I think the fire hydrant notice and the triple fire alarms are rather fun. To add to them is the exciting intrusion of the street name "Old Bailey" kindly awarded by the Corporation of the City of London. To bind the whole composition together and to suggest a vertical motif the strips either side of this facade are of purple mosaic.

John Betjeman

Private Eye reporting Israeli atrocities after the 1967 war.

In fact that war found *Private Eye*, with the rest of the press, generally sympathetic to Israel. But the balance quickly shifted as news of events behind the Israeli publicity screen began to reach Greek Street. An article about Moshe Dayan's political ambitions ('One Eyed Man for King') in July 1967 led to many cancelled subscriptions. By November the novelist Mordecai Richler had become so offended by *Private Eye*'s line that he complained in *The Observer* that the paper was making jokes worthy of the *Storm Trooper*, the organ of the American Nazi party. Shortly afterwards two Labour MPs who were ardent Zionists followed this up by likening *Private Eye* to *Der Sturmer*, the organ of the German Nazi party in the thirties. Unlike *Der Sturmer*, *Private Eye* published these letters, although at that time it had no regular readers' letters column.

In 1972 *Private Eye* was able to show how Zionists brought pressure on more orthodox publications. It revealed that Lord Sieff, then president of the Zionist Federation of Great Britain and chairman of Marks and Spencer, had written to *The Guardian* in 1967 to protest against reports of the Middle East war, while threatening to withdraw all Marks and Spencer advertising unless there was an improvement. After the editor of *The Guardian* had been confronted by the source of the *Eye*'s story, he agreed that the letter had indeed been written.

The 'fascist' tag was also applied to *Private Eye* by elements of the doctrinaire Left. In November 1972, *Workers' Press* described *Private Eye* as 'fascist' for equating the jailed dock strikers with the Kray twins. Six weeks later it was revealed, apparently by the Monday Club's 'anti-subversion unit', that *Private Eye* was 'Marxist'. A confidential document was circulated which identified *Private Eye* as a front for the International Socialist Party. 'It has been learnt that International Socialism is to make a determined challenge to take over the editorial side of the magazine in 1972,' wrote the anonymous analyst. The truth about Paul Foot's departure was out at last.

Cartoon presented by Paul Foot on his departure. In the pulpit are Fantoni, Ingrams and Booker.

DROPPING THE REVOLUTIONARY.

7 'We've *really* got them this time'

To hear people talking about the facts you would think that they lay about like pieces of gold ore in the Yukon days waiting to be picked up.   Claud Cockburn

I want a strong libel law. It adds credibility to what we print.
Paul Foot, in evidence to the Faulks Committee on Defamation

Private Eye was presented with what the editor of *Le Canard Enchaîné* had termed 'the hot potatoes' within five years of getting started, rather than within the twenty years he had suggested, because it secured friends in government almost at once. Paul Foot, who started the investigative side of the paper in 1966, remembers that no one else was trying to do the same. 'Insight' had first appeared in *The Sunday Times* in 1963, but after a strong start with the Profumo story it degenerated into

> fringe stuff about antique dealers' rings and that sort of thing. It was no longer about politics. We were the only people who would write in that way about political news. The other thing that helped us was Wilson's intriguing. It played right into the hands of our journalism because we had channels going deep into the government. For example, two of our best sources were the head of a government publicity office and a junior government minister. We also had friends in the Treasury, and we had several personal links with members of the cabinet.

The result was that right from the start *Private Eye* was able to provide reliable and confidential information about cabinet in-fighting and the battle between the Treasury and the new Department of Economic Affairs. This encouraged sources in other ministries to come forward. Jim Callaghan's relationship with the Cardiff businessman Julian Hodge attracted attention after a clause in Callaghan's budget benefitted three-wheeled vehicles (of which Hodge manufactured one type). And Callaghan's manoeuvrings to secure the party treasurership, and ultimately the leadership, were accurately reported.

Apart from the excellence of the early sources, there was also the freedom given to Foot and other contributors to write what they wished.

Writing for *Private Eye* [says Foot] is a completely different experience. It is amazingly liberating. There isn't any sense of responsibility and this means that you can write with extraordinary freedom. I still have that feeling when I write for it occasionally today. There is no one on your back. You aren't out to impress the boss. It's not all good because there are no checks and balances. The only problem used to be getting round the lawyer and there were stylistic devices for that. Also there were no subeditors. It is very good for a writer to know before he starts that nobody is going to bugger it around. It's still like that. It retains its freedom from proprietorial control and it's not a big machine. It's a little bit to do with not signing the article, but not much. It's more to do with the nature of the publication. It's in the old tradition of the lampoon and the street paper, where people blasted off and didn't worry about libel and bad taste. It's not like the *Poor Man's Guardian*, for instance [a Victorian workers' paper], because *Private Eye* is middle class, but the fact is it is still really a lampoon.

There are two views about news reporting. One is the Muggeridge-Cockburn view – also favoured by Auberon Waugh – that 'facts' and 'the truth' have very little in common, that the facts can actually obscure the truth because there are so few of them, or, if there are many facts, that they are frequently contradictory and of uncertain validity until their moment has passed. From this point of view the journalist decides what the story is and then 'shepherds the facts' or such of them as are convenient, carefully towards the story. In Cockburn's words: 'All stories are written backwards – they are supposed to begin with the facts and develop from there, but in reality they begin with a journalist's point of view . . . from which the facts are subsequently organised.' The opposite view is that there are a limited number of facts, that with a great deal of hard work they can be discovered, that they will then reveal the truth and that this can then be published, backed up by meticulous research. This is the view adopted by Foot and by the *Eye*'s other outstanding investigator, Michael Gillard.

131

The Private Eye Story

Many of the early 'Footnotes' did not become 'official' until years later. A piece in July 1967 drew attention to the forthcoming disturbances in Derry on July 12 and predicted the rise to power of an obscure Protestant clergyman, 'Dr' Ian Paisley. The story was provided by a Catholic schoolteacher from Derry who realised even then that his best hope of drawing attention to what was about to happen in the province lay not with Fleet Street, but with this 'joke magazine banned by the two biggest newsagents in Britain', as Richard West once described it.

In June 1969 'Footnotes' had the first corruption stories following the sacking of the chief executive of Wandsworth Council after he had called in Scotland Yard to investigate certain irregularities in council building contracts. Some of those involved in these irregularities were eventually to go to prison, but at this early stage in the game it was the honest men who were being penalised and the situation was ideal for *Private Eye* to exploit.

Foot remembers that,

Ronan Point by Steadman.

Teamability

The ability to work closely together, within themselves and with others smoothly, speedily, skilfully. Taylor Woodrow have it. They call it teamwork. They are frequently asked to undertake a job from concept to conclusion, including the design and planning. Taylor Woodrow are geared to do this.

In 1968 the material we were getting suddenly changed. The stories about Dr Christiaan Barnard's heart transplants were the watershed. They were taken seriously and started an argument. I really worked on them. We put out a pamphlet of reprints which sold fifteen thousand, when magazine sales were less than fifty thousand. Then there was Ronan Point. This was the year when we put ourselves on the map. People started to take things seriously when we printed them. There was no register of interests in those days. People could still laugh at you when you made these outrageous revelations. Poulson has changed people's attitude to that, and the Salmon commission. That was largely started by *Private Eye* I think.

There was also regular coverage of Northern Ireland and the Israeli occupation of the West Bank.

The characteristic mark of 'Footnotes' was its energy and enthusiasm. Every fortnight there were three more pages of original information, the completion of which was announced by Foot with the cry of the true believer: 'We've *really* got them this time.' The year 1970 was a high point. Stories about Dan Smith and Poulson were, as usual, ignored by Fleet Steet though they have since become famous, but there was also the story of BP's sanctions busting in Rhodesia, eight years before any other paper mentioned it.

Then there was a story from Ireland about the involvement in illegal gun-running for the IRA of various prominent politicians, eventually to lead to a trial in which a subsequent Irish premier, Charles Haughey, was acquitted of these charges. The original story was censored in Dublin. The return of the Heath government was celebrated with a spirited series of stories about his expensive boat, and Mr Maudling's relationship with Jerome Hoffman was thoroughly explored.

The justification of muck-raking journalism, as defined by Claud Cockburn, is that serious news tends to start as a rumour and the best way to establish the truth of a rumour is to make it public. This may have been ideal for a penniless broadsheet like *The Week*, which was circulated privately to a select group of elite subscribers, but a magazine that hopes to appeal to the intelligent public-at-large needs to acquire a reputation for prescience and reliability. It has to be more selective with its rumours, and to take them beyond the area of hearsay.

Private Eye's reputation as a muck-raker was sufficiently advanced by July 1971 for the BBC TV team who were researching *Yesterday's Men*, and who wanted to 'dig up some dirt', to apply to *Private Eye* for assistance. They needed someone 'outside the Corp.' to do their digging. The potential raker declined this offer on the grounds that the BBC, as all too frequently, were not offering sufficient money to attract a top-quality raker of muck.

Other stories in this year were 'The Ballsoff Memorandum', the connections between Israel and the Mafia's Meyer Lansky and the bribing of BBC radio disc jockeys.

Lord Goodman approached Paul Foot after a long story had appeared in 'Footnotes' about the way in which Goodman was stifling press criticism of the British Lion film company. Goodman phoned Foot and expressed a warm interest in the campaign to get a pardon for James Hanratty, who had been hanged for murder. Goodman went so far as to put down a question on the subject in the House of Lords before losing interest in the campaign when Foot continued to investigate British Lion.

In 1972, Foot's last year, there were stories about Andy Cunningham, Tory government talks with the IRA (again *Private Eye* was the choice of the IRA for this leak), Lord Carrington's property deals, Desmond Plummer's property deals, the fire at Odhams Press, Jim Slater's land deals, and Rio Tinto Zinc and the Avonmouth smelter. At times it almost seemed as though *Private Eye* was becoming a one-

The *Eye* was interested to see that Mr Michael ("Lunchtime") O'Halloran, the ebullient MP for North Islington, had signed statements both for and against the Common Market. Lunchtime explained that the declaration in favour of the Common Market was presented to him in the House, "and quite frankly, I never read it. It is no good blinking it - it is my fault. The first thing I knew was when I saw my name in the *Guardian* advert."

Readers will remember Mr O'Halloran's previous explanation when he was asked by a Labour Party committee of enquiry if he had received money from a local sympathiser. Lunchtime made the immortal reply: "Categorically - er - no. Unless I was drunk at the time."

One of the most celebrated stories to have appeared in the Colour Section.

Lord Goodman by Scarfe.

133

man alternative Fleet Street. This was partly because of the stories that were then appearing, but also because the Poulson affair had become 'official' news. The bankruptcy hearings started in July and the national press suddenly woke up. It was the biggest political scandal since the days of Profumo and, when linked to Maudling, of far more genuine significance, for it showed the extent of incompetence linked to corruption with which the country had been governed in the Labour interest and was still being governed in the Tory one.

For *Private Eye* readers that July, it was as though a list of characters from some private world had come to life. Never before or since had their status as insiders been so apparent. In the case of the Poulson story the rest of the press were unstinting in their recognition of *Private Eye*'s contribution. On the first day of the court hearings the headline in the *Yorkshire Evening Post* was 'Architect Blames *Private Eye*'. The programme *What the Papers Say* duly credited the *Bradford Telegraph and Argus* with first breaking the story and then said: 'Fleet Street's record on the Poulson story stinks . . . [but] . . . the significance of the story did not escape that extraordinary magazine which is more important to journalism than half the Fleet Street papers.' In August Maudling was forced to resign. 'Footnotes's' last hour was certainly its finest.

Michael Gillard was first introduced to the *Eye* in 1969 when he was working on the City desk of the *Daily Express*. He was attracted by the idea of writing for a paper which would give him the freedom to print what he knew, which was very far from his experience of Fleet Street. He remembers 'the dirty dealings among the hacks, and the lack of space for detailed investigations due to the pressure of daily news. Some of the information I could not use was about big people who were difficult to attack legally, or it was about little people the *Daily Express* would not bother with.' As the Stock Exchange boom of the late sixties and early seventies got under way, Gillard began to enjoy himself. As he now recalls:

'Slicker' was first widely read in the City because it was so rude. That was a novelty. It was the days of the Slater Walker miracle. We were the first not to believe in that. Also we were the first to be sceptical about fringe banks, and a lot of the so-called City whizz kids, as well as Edward du Cann and the other directors of Keyser

Ullmann. These were all stories about big people. The biggest coup was about a Bank of England employee being involved in a dollar premium scandal. The Bank issued a statement on the afternoon of the day the *Eye* came out, and our story was followed up by every national paper next day.

The normal *Private Eye* scattershot approach would not work in the City because you would very quickly lose your credibility. My strength is in detail, a crushing weight of detail. If there are that many facts, it must be true. And there is no concession made to the layman. The column is aimed at professional readers. Others can understand it, it is not written in jargon. But the layman must make an effort.* It is better to have it this way round than bore the experts by spelling it out. By writing it in City terms it makes it more of a column for insiders; this is a further encouragement to influential readers.

It is untrue to say that City people do not sue as much as others. They do, but the defence is accuracy. I have always applied the same standards to the accuracy of my work wherever it was going to be printed. We have only three times had to make an apology. Once to a Unit Trust, once over one of several stories we carried about Patrick Sergeant. The last one was over ten years ago. There were also three civil libel writs from Goldsmith, but we did not have to apologise about any of them.

In the last five years the column has become very influential. It is read by the police, the Bank of England and the Security Exchange Commission in Washington. It has fired City editors to be more hostile. In order to keep our reputation for being ahead we have to push the boat out further and further. That is one of *Private Eye*'s achievements. Also they now follow up our stories much more than they used to. 'Pretty Boy' Bentley, 'Black Jack' Dellal and Rowe 'Dudd' – all nicknames we invented – have now been taken up by Fleet Street. Even the *Financial Times* takes a more positive line than it used to.

The only remark made about 'Slicker' by Richard which I really object to is his line over Jews. When he is asked why people say *Private Eye* is anti-semitic he usually says that there just happen to be a lot of Jews in the City and so we happen to expose a lot of Jewish crooks. In fact 'Slicker' has attacked more non-Jews than Jews. If Jews *are* there it

'We've *really* got them this time'

* One layman who does not make this effort is Ingrams. He has said that he rarely understands a Slicker story.

is because they are crooks, not Jews. And we have twice run stories in 'Slicker' attacking the city for being anti-semitic.

Foot considers Gillard to be 'one of the great phenomena of *Private Eye*'.

The level of his accuracy is uncanny. When he wrote the piece about the PR men working for Rossminster he took on the biggest tax evasion operation since the Vesteys. It was a brilliant operation and very well defended in the media. Gillard destroyed them. They appointed a PR man and Gillard went for him too. How does he get his stuff? He is read in every merchant bank and pension fund and stock brokers and jobbers office. Quires come into the *Daily Mirror* and get distributed round the building. It is the same in the City. The Slicker index of stories is one of the most valuable documents the *Eye* has produced. In his way he is a genius. He has a memory like a filing cabinet. He seems to rely on two or three rather shady little men. He is an interesting contrast with Oliver Marriott. Marriott was a brilliant journalist but he took the familiar road. He wrote an excellent book about the property boom and then he became a property developer. Gillard could have done that and made a fortune in the City. But he sticks to his last. He has been lucky in the sense that he could never have got his stuff published anywhere else if Richard had not published it.

Not even Ingrams knows how Gillard operates. Unlike most of his contributors, Ingrams has never asked Gillard for his sources. He says that there is no point in inquiring because he would not know the names if he was told them.

Gillard's confidence in the high reputation of 'In the City' was confirmed by an article in the *Institutional Investor* (18 November 1981) by John Dizard.

Once disdained as a sophomoric, reflexively anti-establish-ment rag, *Private Eye* has become a significant force among important members of what might still be called the British ruling class. In a country where few economic statistics beyond the unemployment rate show increases lately, the magazine has doubled its circulation over the last three years to more than 160,000 readers – many of them the bankers, stockbrokers and investment managers who work in the City. Indeed, according to a market survey done last year for the *Financial Times*, 42 per cent of a sample of 3,700 British stockholders and fund managers read *Private Eye* regularly, nearly twice the proportion who read *Institutional Investor* (23 per cent) and more than three times the proportion who read *Euromoney* (13 per cent). 'Nobody here wants to admit they read the bloody thing,' says one National Westminster Bank spokesman, 'but of course they all do. We get several copies in the bank's name.' Adds a Bank of England official: '*Private Eye* is a sort of awkwardish subject around here, but yes, we do read it.' . . .

. . . Among other readers are detectives in the City's company and fraud departments who, according to one, 'read it religiously', as well as top London lawyer David Freeman, who says the magazine's 'amazingly accurate articles in the "City Slicker" section read as though written by someone with a lawyer's knowledge of company law'. One very senior director of Lazard Brothers & Co goes so far as to say that *Private Eye* should be 'Required reading' for the bank's credit committee. 'There's no question that it can give you pointers about where to expect trouble,' he says. And a senior S. G. Warburg man echoes this sentiment, praising the magazine for the way it 'latches on to flamboyant or raw characters and then pursues them to the end'.

. . . As one portfolio manager says, 'One problem with the City is that many of us turn over every five or ten years, and there isn't enough institutional memory of who did what to whom ten years ago. *Private Eye* follows these people to their graves.

One area which *Private Eye* has usually been wary of, even at the height of its investigations, is national security. The paper got off to a bad start with the spies. Commander Courtney was a Conservative MP who was the victim of a KGB smear campaign in 1965. *Private Eye* printed the allegations against him although it realised who was behind them. In 1968 the *Sunday Telegraph* wrote that Courtney 'never had a single complaint about his treatment by newspapers, apart from one nasty little breach of confidence by someone supplying information to *Private Eye*'. The *Western Mail* wrote at the same time that 'Courtney leaked an angled story to the *Sunday Telegraph* to gather popular support. *Private Eye* filled in the more sensational details.' In fact Ingrams has since accepted that *Private Eye* was wrong to breach the general silence about Courtney. The problem with spy stories is that it is more than usually difficult to work out who is leaking the information and to what purpose. But this detachment did not prevent *Private Eye* and the security services from keeping each other under somewhat bleary observation.

In November 1966 *Private Eye* suggested that George Wigg, then Wilson's head of government security, was snooping on the *Eye*'s weekly lunch in an attempt to discover who was supplying the paper with its accurate stories about cabinet disagreements. This suggestion was first made by a regular luncher with influential connections in the Labour party who insisted on being announced at lunch as 'Mr Richmond', although his identity was well known to most of his fellow guests. Mr Richmond would peer from behind the fly-blown curtains on the first floor of the Coach and Horses and announce that he could see Wigg's man in a car outside. Since it has subsequently been suggested that 'Mr Richmond', alias Tom Driberg, was at that time supplying information to both the KGB and MI5 there would have been little need for another official snooper to lurk outside the Coach and Horses – unless the agencies were checking up on Driberg's time-sheet.

One of Driberg's first stories for *Private Eye* had been of how he was himself excluded from the Wilson cabinet because he was homosexual and therefore a possible source of future embarrassment. He claimed that he had been more or less promised the position of first Minister of the Arts, and *Private Eye* loyally reported this as an early failure of Wilson's nerve. With hindsight it seems most unlikely that an MI5 agent who was also suspected of working for the KGB would have been offered any sort of ministry, and Driberg may have cooked the whole story up to explain to *Private Eye* his apparent disillusionment with Wilson, his availability as a source and his presence at the lunch. In any event he provided remarkably little information even about the national executive of the Labour party, of which he was a member, though he may well have inserted himself sufficiently into the confidence of *Private Eye* to be able to speculate about several of their sources of information.

Two stories in particular would have attracted official attention. At the time of the Philby affair in the autumn of 1967, *Private Eye* printed a certain amount of information, supplied by the spy's son, which was generally hostile to the more outspoken critics of Philby *père* and which suggested (accurately) that there were other spies at large who were yet to be revealed. (It was at this time that General Kim Philby, KGB, became a subscriber to the magazine.)*

At the same time *Private Eye* was running stories about Jack Dash and the seamen's and dockers' strikes (Wilson's 'tightly knit group of politically motivated men') which were written by Foot and were very different in tone to the subsequent 'Pentonville Martyr' jokes. At this time *The Observer* described Foot for the first time as 'a Trot'.

Another security story which *Private Eye* covered was the dismissal of Colonel Sammy Lohan of the 'D' Notice Committee. It had been the Colonel who summoned the editors around originally in 1963 and asked them to accept his 'D' Notices, later thinking better of it and not sending any. At the time of his dismissal he took to dropping in at Greek Street and drinking a good deal of whisky. His genial manner ensured that he got the paper on his side, and the editorial staff would spend many hours pumping him about his work. His astonishing frankness and abrupt changes of subject did nothing to harm our national defences but they did show the inner world of security in a rather ludicrous light.

This may have prompted MI5 to replace 'Mr Richmond' with someone even more reliable. One of those receiving adverse mention in the *Eye*'s Philby stories had been Captain Henry Kerby, MP, who was a fluent Russian speaker working for MI5. After a suitable interval the Captain wrote an adulatory letter to Lord Gnome, praising a recent story about Peter Masefield's business affairs and enclosing a £5 note, half of which was to renew his subscription and the other half to go into the libel fund. 'PS,' he added, in case the possibility had been overlooked, 'I am a staunch supporter of His Lordship.' Sure enough, it was not long before Kerby was also a regular attender at the *Eye* lunches, Mr Richmond by this time having disappeared to Malta on an extended 'rest cure' (in fact on the advice of his lawyer, David Jacobs, in order to avoid involvement in the current 'guardsmen in the park' scandal).

*I had intended to reproduce Kim Philby's subscription card among the illustrations of this book. However Ena McEwan, the magazine's subscription manager, firmly rejected this proposal on the grounds that it would be an outrageous breach of her department's security. Things must be very different from those days, in the early 70's, when troublesome subscription cards were filed under the carpet.

PRIVATE SPY

No. 468
Friday
23 Nov. '79

25p

I hear the Queen is terribly upset

I most certainly am

BLUNT LASHES OUT

Unfortunately Kerby died after only one year on lunch-duty and was obituarised by Auberon Waugh. Under the heading 'Man of a Thousand Secrets', Waugh recorded,

> ... with sorrow the death of Captain Henry Kerby, the member of Parliament for Arundel and Shoreham, Sussex. ... Beneath the pose of a half-witted, extreme Right-wing Tory MP, Kerby concealed a ready wit and a staunch admiration for *Private Eye*. His early career remains shrouded in mystery ... [he became] an orphan of the struggle between various branches of British secret intelligence. While continuing to be employed for assignments both in England and abroad by one branch, he was soon to be denounced to the Conservative Chief Whip as a suspected Russian agent by another.

So perhaps both MI5 and the KGB were as well informed as ever on the fascinating topic of the *Eye* lunch.

Eventually, in 1979, *Private Eye* did score a hit with a spy story, that of Anthony Blunt. The truth of this was of course established by Andrew Boyle in his book *The Climate of Treason*, but he called Blunt 'Maurice'. *Private Eye* had heard allegations about Blunt for years but had not pursued them. But the month before *The Climate of Treason* was published Ingrams read the proofs of Boyle's book while visiting Malcolm Muggeridge. The *Eye* then revealed that Michael Rubinstein (a well-known libel lawyer and once *Private Eye*'s lawyer) had phoned the publishers and said that he wished to read the book lest it contain defamatory references to 'his client'. Rubinstein was then forced to admit that his client was Sir Anthony Blunt. *Private Eye* made it plain that it was 'Maurice' Rubinstein was thinking of. It pursued this matter with some success. Because Blunt was named by *Private Eye*, questions were asked in Parliament and Mrs Thatcher responded by telling the full story. *Private Eye*'s coverage was also very funny. The blundering involvement of Rubinstein and then of his brother Hilary, Blunt's literary agent, would not have been pointed out elsewhere.

With regard to the police *Private Eye*'s investigations had a rather more impressive record. The most striking example of this was the succession of stories that started with one about Patrick Murphy, a convicted murderer. In 1971 the position was that Mr Murphy was serving a life sentence for the murder of a postmaster in Luton. His father, Stephen, came to *Private Eye* with evidence that his son had never received a fair trial. One of the policemen responsible for his conviction was Commander Drury, then head of the Flying Squad who, incidentally, Mr Stephen Murphy suggested, was not all that he should be for a man in such a position. *Private Eye* accordingly printed several stories raising the question whether or not Patrick Murphy had been rightly convicted. A petition for his case to be reopened was started. An investigation was then launched into Commander Drury and his connections with leading gangsters, and into Commander Virgo, the head of the obscene publications squad, who were between them supposed to police the magazine's close neighbours, the Soho porn merchants. The story about Commander Drury never appeared in *Private Eye* because the freelance reporter who had undertaken to write it sold it to *The People* instead, after a week on the *Eye*'s telephone. But the eventual consequence of all this was a widespread press campaign. And in November 1973, Patrick Murphy's murder conviction was quashed by the Court of Appeal. New evidence was provided by a witness who had responded to the publicity started by the *Eye*. Then in 1977 Commander Virgo was jailed for twelve years for corruption, after a trial in which the *Eye* article had been produced as evidence,* and Commander Drury was also jailed for eight years for corruption. Both police officers had associated with the same Soho porn baron.

Although *Private Eye* remains an investigative journal, and still covers important stories which no other paper will tackle, there is no doubt that it used to do this more effectively in the past than it does at present. In Christopher Logue's view this is a pity. He considers the paper

> ... at its best when it is most politically active and most dangerous. It should be a threat to those in power. The nearest we came to that was with Poulson and Maudling. And there are the hundreds of people that Gillard keeps in line because they're afraid of him. But we've never really caused the government to tremble, and that should be our job. I don't know half the people in 'Grovel'. Who *is* Bubble (sic) Harmsworth? I haven't the faintest idea.
>
> I don't know that we've ever been as strong as *Le Canard*. We've cultivated too many journalists and not

* Commander Virgo's conviction was subsequently quashed.

enough bureaucrats, and the paper is too personal. For a few years the young civil servants came in with information. Then they stopped coming, and I think we've let them down. Footy was the only real frightener, and he's not been replaced. The reason is that Richard does not care about politics. He is a gent.

Candida Lycett-Green is less critical. 'If you suspect something really underhand, there's no one else who would take you seriously apart from *Private Eye*,' she says.

'We've *really* got them this time'

8 A lurch to the right 1972–1977

This was a period of departures. Foot and Osmond both left. Martin Tomkinson and Michael Gillard took over most of the reporting. David Cash became managing director. Two columnists from Fleet Street, Nigel Dempster and Peter McKay, were imported to cover gossip. Private Eye *became more of a Fleet Street paper. Its values changed and its reactions were more predictable. In 1974 Harold Wilson returned as Prime Minister, and this resulted in numerous stories about the influence of his advisers. 'Mrs Wilson's Diary' was revived.*

At the beginning of 1973, when Foot was named 'Journalist of the Year' for his work at *Private Eye* over the previous six years, Fleet Street was still echoing to his stories. But in Greek Street it was a question of rearranging the news section to take account of his absence. The three-page 'Footnotes' became the two-page 'Notes', later 'Business News', and two other columns ('In the Courts' and 'In the City') were moved to the back. The main burden of filling the remaining space fell first on myself and then on Martin Tomkinson who had recently joined as a reporter. Despite the greatly reduced length of the news section the Foot-touch was missing. Good stories continued to appear regularly, but there was no equivalent view of the world as a great conspiracy of the governors against the governed.

Financially this was a prosperous period. In May 1973, *Private Eye* raised the cover price from 10p to 12p. This was the first price rise since October 1965. It was justified on general grounds, but the decision was taken at a time when the sales had doubled in two years to ninety-eight thousand (including fifteen thousand subscriptions), so the resulting increase in profit was considerable. Sure enough, it was reported in the *Daily Mirror* of 29 June 1973 that *Private Eye* had purchased a villa in the Dordogne for £11,000. Earlier in the year *The Guardian*'s consumer correspondent had accused the *Eye*'s small ads column of including advertisements from a shady enterprise. Subsequently *The Guardian* had to retract this suggestion as it transpired that *Private Eye* had refused the offending ad some time before *The Guardian* printed its story. The small ads columns were also the subject of a question in the House of Commons in September 1973, when they became popular with people trying to arrange marriages with British citizens in order to obtain citizenship. This fashion eventually led to a change in the citizenship laws.

Although the libel lawyers were relatively inactive, a claim was made by Chapman Pincher, who received £1000 for the untruthful suggestion that he had telephoned the *Daily Mail* (353–6000) rather than his own paper the *Daily Express* (353–8000), in order to read out a story. This was one of the most self-important libel claims ever made against *Private Eye*. The Goldsmith case was to liven things up in 1977, at which time Jeremy Thorpe also tried to bring a case of criminal libel against *Private Eye*, when it looked as if nothing less might divert public attention from police investigations into his behaviour (27 April 1976). Harold Evans, then editor of *The Sunday Times*, issued one of his writs almost at the climax of the Goldsmith case, a bad psychological moment for *Private Eye*.

There were signs of a novel defence being raised against libel actions in Auberon Waugh's column in January 1975. Waugh developed the idea of a curse which worked against those who sued Lord Gnome. An early victim of 'The Curse of Gnome' was considered to be John Stonehouse, MP, who issued a writ for libel on the eve of his disappearance off a Miami beach. This poor-taste joke was then thoroughly developed by Waugh with reference to Aristotle Onassis. The Onassis writ had been issued after a story in 'Grovel' that he intended to divorce his wife, Jackie. After his death it was confirmed that the story had in any event been true. It was one of the features of the Onassis case that, because he was resident outside the jurisdiction, *Private Eye* had planned to ask the court to require the richest man in the world to lodge a bond, lest he be unable to meet any costs that he might incur. Because of his death, this move was never implemented.

The other unusual litigation of this period arose not from the magazine but from a book published by *Private Eye*, written by Richard West and entitled *Victory in Vietnam*.

West had been contributing steadily to the paper since 1965 and many of his best pieces had been from abroad. He was one of the first national press reporters to see how this

The bookjacket of Victory in Vietnam *drawn by Heath. The author Richard West appears centre in glasses.*

apparently obscure little magazine could be made useful and achieve an important role as a publisher of 'alternative' news; that is of stories from around the world which offended – for whatever reason – the prevailing pieties of Fleet Street and which it was therefore impossible to publish in the national press. West sent much of his best reporting from Vietnam to *Private Eye*. And *Victory in Vietnam*, the book which he eventually wrote about his experiences there, has since become something of a classic. The book opens with a description of the death of an English journalist named Peter Duval-Smith, by all accounts a most engaging man. Duval-Smith left a young daughter and she had acquired a stepfather in the person of *The Sunday Times* journalist David Leitch. Leitch decided that the description of Duval-Smith's death was so unedifying that his infant charge must for ever be protected from it. He accordingly sought and won an injunction from a judge in the Family Division preventing the publication of the book, even though it was ready to go into the shops. This ruling was overturned on appeal, in a rather important decision for free publication of books. Following the case there was a spirited correspondence, launched in *The Times* by Tony Howard, as to whether *Private Eye* was right to pursue David Leitch with garnishee orders in order to recover its costs. The *Eye*'s position so outraged Booker, a friend of Leitch, that he wrote a fierce attack on his former paper in the *Spectator*.

The legal profession scored a victory when 'Justinian Forthemoney', the author of 'In the Courts', ran into difficulties. Issue 320 in March 1974 carried a note at the foot of the column: 'Following a vindictive and treacherous counter-attack by the legal profession, Justinian Forthemoney is in severe danger of death by starvation. His survival depends on steady supplies of information from readers.' Brian Sedgemore, the barrister who wrote half the column, had been shopped by his fellow contributor to the head of their chambers. The fink who did this had been threatened by the criminal solicitors who gave him most of his work with future loss of earnings if the revelations did not cease. While this may have been an excellent reason for the fink to stop writing the column it was hardly a good reason for shopping Sedgemore. The column continued with some success, but a replacement for Sedgemore proved hard to find. It was not for nothing that he had chosen his soubriquet, even if he was one barrister who did not deserve it.

Other contributors fared better. Tom Driberg was awarded a peerage in 1975. For Tiresias it was nearly the end of a long haul. He had retired from the House of Commons at the previous General Election, to be succeeded by Ian Mikardo's extreme leftist secretary, so handing on the torch of his own more youthful convictions. Driberg is the only *Private Eye* contributor to have been ennobled. Dr Germaine Greer became a contributor following several attacks, mostly in the 'Grovel' column, about which she was most forbearing. Her response to the suggestion that she was about to buy a house and evict eight tenants was a sunny and mildly informative letter, a fine example of the non-suers' response to attack. Her 'Gardening Notes', later 'The Revolting Garden', started in May 1977 when a racing column by 'Colonel Mad' (Jeffrey Bernard) was also started.

Another sunny response was evoked from an occasional contributor, Nicholas Tomalin, who had written an article advocating holidays in fascist Greece. Earlier he had written an article condemning the same. What was not revealed at the time was that, when he was telephoned about this contradiction, Tomalin actually agreed to go to his cuttings file and read out his own earlier story in order to document the inconsistencies. 'It's *Private Eye*,' he said to his wife. 'They want me to read out my own cuttings so that they can attack me.' And this, under gentle protest, he then did. He died in October 1973, while reporting the Arab–Israeli war.

The editors increased in respectability during this period. Ingrams was included in *Who's Who* in 1973 for the first time. Booker's interest in investigative journalism, which he had briefly indulged years before on *Time & Tide*, was re-awakened by a four-page feature which he wrote for the magazine in the summer of 1972 in collaboration with Candida Lycett-Green. In partnership with Benny Grey, Booker wrote a series of articles about property deals, some in *Private Eye*, others in *The Sunday Times* and *The Observer*. They were eventually declared to be 'Campaigning Journalists of the Year'. Booker then tried to turn himself into an altruistic property developer in a forlorn attempt to save a corner of nineteenth-century London from destruction. This caused *Municipal Engineer* to print the memorable headline 'Former Editor of *Private Eye* offers to take over Joe Levy's Huge Tolmers Square Office Development for Camden Council'. The scheme was actually backed by two banks and was non-profit making, but was turned down by the council. Later, while Ingrams was on holiday, a story appeared written by Gillard and Tomkinson concerning

Germaine Greer, alias Rose Blight, by ffolkes.

Benny Grey's early career as a property developer. This story was withdrawn. It brought to mind Ingrams's remark on an earlier occasion, 'We like to attack our friends as much as possible.'

The most serious loss, apart from Foot, was the Barry McKenzie strip. This was killed in March 1974 at a time when it was getting filthier (if that was possible) but also funnier. In the penultimate strip there were promises of the 'next oral episode'. This was ambiguous since Barry had become involved with an Aussie dentist who was also running an abortion clinic along suspectedly intimate lines. Then ... silence. It was left to *The Times* (March 1974) to reveal that the banned episode had contained scenes of lesbianism, which, even when modified, had proved too much for the editor. When asked to explain this Ingrams said: 'I am the editor. Nobody has a free hand.' There was one further strip, but honour was not satisfied. Both Nicholas Garland and Barry Humphries took strong exception to the interruption, and the series has not appeared since. There was also a somewhat plaintive interview with Peter Cook (who had been a great fan of McKenzie's) in *The Times*. Cook had been overworking. 'I should have a year's financial security to do what I really enjoy and that is writing for *Private Eye*,' he said. 'Although I'm Lord Gnome I don't contribute much at present.'

Paul Foot's departure did not go unremarked. Ingrams decided that if International Socialism was going to attract his attention in this way it should pay the price, and there was a story about IS attempting to make a quick profit on the sale of its Liverpool headquarters.

Foot's departure was also followed by trouble with the printers. While Foot had worked at *Private Eye* he had expressed some anxiety over the fact that the paper was printed by Leo Thorpe & Son, a non-union firm. The difficulties with Thorpe grew but they were technical, not political. The print run was getting too long for his machines, and the magazine started to appear late. When the time came for a change in 1974 (Issue 333 was the first not to bear the Thorpe imprint since 1962), the chosen successors were FebEdge, or SW Litho Ltd, the printers of *Socialist Worker*, a firm run by Jim Nichol who was a member of IS. This change occurred in September. In December Tony Rushton received a visit from the assistant secretary of the National Graphical Association. This person, B. W. Coppock, inquired whether Mr Rushton, who laid the paper out, and his assistant Steve Mann, who typed it, were members of the NGA. When he was told that they were not he invited them to join. The following correspondence then ensued.

20 December 1974

Mr T. Rushton

Dear Mr Rushton,
You will no doubt recall our meeting in your offices when I spoke to you and your colleague Mr Mann regarding union membership.

I would be obliged if you would kindly let me know whether or not both of you are interested in joining this association.

Your cooperation is appreciated.
Yours sincerely,

B. W. Coppock
Assistant Secretary

30 December 1974

B. W. Coppock Esq.

Dear Mr Coppock,
I regret I was unable to reply to your letter before Christmas. Mr Mann and I both appreciate the personal interest you have shown in us but feel that your Association would not benefit from our membership and contrariwise. We just aren't 'joiners'.

Best wishes for the New Year.

A. P. Rushton.

7 January 1975

Mr T. Rushton

Dear Mr Rushton,
I am in receipt of your letter dated 30th December and I regret to note that you and Mr Mann are not interested in joining this Association.

This is to advise you that I have today written to our chapel at FebEdge Ltd. advising them of the position reached to date and drawing their attention to the Rules of this Association which prohibit them from handling work from a non-union source. Whilst I personally regret having to undertake this course of action, you will appreciate that in the protection of my members, I am left with no alternative other than to ensure that only those who are in membership of this Association undertake duties appropriate to the NGA.

Yours sincerely,

B. W. Coppock
Assistant Secretary

BY HAND

9 January 1975

B. W. Coppock Esq.

Dear Mr Coppock,
Mr Mann and I feel on due reflection that our decision conveyed to you on December 30th was hasty and unconsidered. Therefore we would like to take this opportunity to apply for membership of the N.G.A. forthwith.
Yours etc.

A. P. Rushton

9 January 1975

A. P. Rushton Esq.

Dear Mr Rushton,
Thank you for your letter dated 9th January. I am pleased to note that Mr Mann and yourself wish to join the NGA. Consequently, I am taking this opportunity of enclosing herewith two sets of application forms etc, etc . . .

This seemed to be a 'game, set and match' situation. A reference was made to this matter in Issue 340.

Private Eye's coverage of the affairs of another print leader had started some time before this. In June 1973, there was a report of the curious business arrangements made by Richard Briginshaw, the general secretary of NATSOPA, whereby he became the employer, as well as the union leader, of many of Fleet Street's clerical staff. The *Evening Standard* attempted to follow this story up, and its abject failure was reported in July. In order to silence the *Standard*'s reporter, Briginshaw had merely said, 'I would not like to put you into a position whereby the production of your newspaper this evening could be affected.' The next national paper to try to write about Briginshaw and fail was *The Observer*, so in September *Private Eye* devoted a full page to the matter under the headline 'The Knuckle Sandwich Man'. At the time Claud Cockburn was critical of this piece, saying that it 'reeked of

**Private Eye
An Apology**

We regrit that owing to an Industrial Dispote, this poge of Private Eye is only being pronted in one editin.

The dispote arosed fillowing some very reasonable propisols mad by the membrs of the Notinal Graphical Astociaton who are osking for more dibs to bring them into line with Paul Getty.

Issue 340.

the *Daily Express*', mainly because it drew attention to the general secretary's personal opulence. But, as subsequent events proved, this was the essential clue to Briginshaw's form of corruption. The final result was not 'Union Chief Sues *Private Eye*' but 'Print Union Sues Chief' (*The Daily Telegraph*, 7 July 1979).

It was at this time, too, that another contributor, Nigel Dempster, began to acquire national notoriety. Dempster had taken over the 'Grovel' column towards the end of 1972 and immediately used it to attack his former employers at Beaverbrook Newspapers. Jocelyn 'Piranha Teeth' Stevens, then managing director of that company, was most put out by this steady supply of accurate information. He described Dempster as 'a paid hypocrite', suggesting that he was allowed by the *Daily Mail* to write in *Private Eye* provided he kept the owners of the *Mail*, the Harmsworth family, out of 'Grovel'. To the readers of *Private Eye* this must have seemed a rather inoffensive form of hypocrisy since they were at least getting information about 'Piranha Teeth' and his shoal which would not otherwise have been available in either the *Mail* or the *Express*. Stevens's own hypocrisy was perfectly clear. In any case it was not long before stories about the *Mail*'s ruling group also began to appear.

Dempster's ability to write about Fleet Street in this uninhibited way, while remaining one of its more prominent figures, gave him considerable prestige among his Fleet Street colleagues. Then in April 1975, in the *Daily Mail*, Dempster revealed that Harold Pinter and Lady Antonia Fraser were having an affair. Nothing new in that, but during the summer Mrs Pinter sued for divorce, naming Antonia, and Dempster printed the story under beaming pictures of six of Antonia's previous lovers. The resulting furore, with Mrs Pinter making several immortal remarks about Antonia ('He says he's coming back to get his shoes. He could always wear hers'), seemed in some way to rebound upon poor Dempster, on the ancient principle of 'shoot the messenger'. There was a savage attack on him in *The Observer*. As a result he became a hate-object among the upper classes, which was, in a way, the making of him.

In 1975 Dempster was joined on 'Grovel' by Peter McKay, then of the *Sunday Express*. For a time their position was difficult. Both were supplying information about each other's papers to 'Grovel', and neither could prevent the other's stuff from getting in. Accordingly, when the *Spectator* reported

A lurch to the right 1972–1977

The Man Who Admitted He Hadn't Been To Bed With Lady Antonia Fraser.

that they were the joint editors of the 'Grovel' column, they wrote to that paper to deny it (26 July 1975). This was true since Ingrams was essentially the 'editor' of the column, but they were nonetheless the principal contributors to it. Oddly enough at the time Dempster was under general attack *Private Eye* also attacked him, for sanctimoniousness in his attempts to defend himself, and then for triviality and obsessive interest in 'leg-over' stories. The way of a *Private Eye* contributor is indeed hard. In 1976 'Grovel' started offering £5 bribes for further information.

Not that any kind of filth could be printed. In June 1973 a Dutch 'sailor' turned up one day in the office saying that he had photographs of a prominent British politician and bachelor which showed that he was homosexual. The Dutchman asked how much *Private Eye* would purchase these for, and was told that it was unlikely to be much money but that all further discussions would have to follow a sight of the pictures. No further discussions took place because he never returned, although from subsequent information (provided by Tom Driberg) it seemed likely that he *had* been in possession of the photographs. Ingrams has since said that he would not have used the information even if it had been provided free.

During all this time the *Eye*'s fortnightly Wednesday lunch was an important source of information. This lunch has become quite a celebrated occasion and invitations to it are at a premium, though why this should be so is not entirely clear. It is held in an upper room of the Coach and Horses in Greek Street where the atmosphere is indelibly stained by the personality of the landlord, Mr Norman Balon. Mr Balon bills himself as 'London's rudest landlord'. He is a tall, thin, stooped figure, bearing some resemblance to Walter Mathau's gloomier kid brother, but rather lacking Mathau's old-world charm. Tina Brown wrote of Norm 'dropping steak and chips' in front of the lunch guests 'from a height of ten feet', which is a fair first impression, and a fair last impression as well. The only lunch guests who impressed Norm were Jim Slater and Arnold Weinstock. To see Norm smile you have to tell him that one of the guests is incredibly rich; the disadvantage being that no one else then gets any attention at all. He also smiled once, very happily, when he hauled a desperate student shoplifter out of the pub's Gents, where the little fellow had taken refuge, and introduced him to a panting store detective from Foyle's who was about to give up the chase. Ingrams looks on Norm as a close friend and deploys him to great effect as umpire at the annual cricket match between *Private Eye* and Aldworth, Ingrams's home village. After sixteen years Norm is even beginning to grasp some of the rules of cricket.

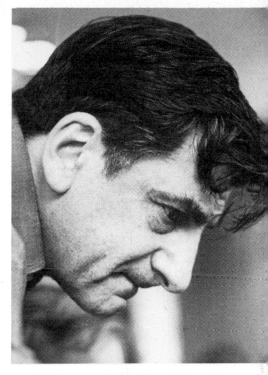

Mr Norman Balon, 'London's rudest landlord'.

In the upstairs room the mood becomes increasingly inquisitorial as the lunch progresses. New guests are usually disconcerted from the moment they arrive. They have to identify themselves to Norm and then walk behind the bar past a line of curious glances. Then, when they reach the upper room, their hosts, Ingrams or Waugh, have usually forgotten that they were asked. Ingrams takes positive steps to avoid being introduced to everyone in the room. Waugh introduces himself to everyone but generally only to insult them in a mock-genial fashion. By the time the unspeakable food arrives, and Ingrams is tucking in happily, the newcomers are in no condition to resist questioning.

Notable first arrivals have included Peter Jenkins of *The Guardian* who actually fell into the room backwards while engaged in a violent argument with Norm as to whether he had been invited. (He had.) Willy Hamilton, MP, was once invited and arrived when Norm was on the phone. 'Please could you tell me where the *Private Eye* lunch is?' said the noted legislator. Norm glanced over his shoulder and replied, 'Fuck off. I'm on the phone.' Mr Hamilton left the pub and has not been back since. Mrs Thatcher and Jo Grimond have been among the guests. It was at an *Eye* lunch that Mr Grimond first heard the allegations against Jeremy Thorpe, Waugh being the only person there with the face to tell the story. Richard Crossman came and as good as admitted that he, Nye Bevan and Morgan Phillips had all perjured themselves in a notorious libel action against the *Spectator*. After Tina Brown's visit, made when she was still an Oxford undergraduate in 1973, she wrote an amusing and highly flattering piece about the occasion in *Isis*. At least two of the men present were in love by the time Norm threw everyone out, and for her it was the start of a brilliant journalistic career. Not many girls can say, as Tina can, 'My life changed the day I went to lunch with ... Norman Balon.' Harold Evans once tried to sabotage the lunch by printing the names of those invited. His agent was Ron Hall, and it was in retaliation for this behaviour that Mr Hall acquired his celebrated nickname, 'the Badger'.

Meanwhile the 'Business News' section, which from December 1973 was written by Michael Gillard and Martin Tomkinson, was again providing some excellent stories. Some of them were entirely in the 'Footnotes' tradition, and occasionally were provided by Foot who continues to contribute to the paper even today. There were more revelations about Poulson and Dan Smith, and pieces about Scottish oil deals, secretive property developments in London, the murder with the help of MI6 of dissident Sudanese politicians, and police corruption.

Other stories showed a slightly different point of view. The Briginshaw story could probably not have been written with any enthusiasm by the new editor of *Socialist Worker*. A story about a dodgy Bible smuggler in Czechoslovakia might never have engaged Foot's attention. It was succeeded by mention of Wilson's associate Rudi Sternberg ('Lord Plurenden'), suspected by some of KGB connections. Finally a story about Grants of St James's, showing that that firm had been selling wine which was incorrectly labelled, a fact for which they were unable to provide any satisfactory explanation, was written in a somewhat gentler and more teasing style than the classic, 'We've *really* got them this time' approach. Possibly that was because no one any longer believed that we had *really* got them this time. It was enough simply to leave 'them' with egg all over their faces.

One of the financial stories about a Manchester man called Richard Murtagh ('Murtagh Most Foul') evoked an unusual response. All 3000 copies of the Manchester consignment of the relevant issue were bought up. The *Eye*'s answer was to repeat the story in the next issue and to double the number of copies available in Manchester. Fortunately Mr Murtagh's purse was exhausted first.

One consequence of the editorial rearrangement was that Auberon Waugh also started to take more of an interest, somewhat disguised, in investigative journalism. Waugh's technique was to cut out the balls-aching business of gathering 'facts', and to go straight to the underlying suspicion. For instance he declared that he did not trust Jeremy Thorpe, who leads 'the small troupe of Exhibitionists, failed vaudeville artists, juicy young Boy Scouts and degenerate old voluptuaries which is the Liberal Party'. This distrust had nothing to do with the allegations made by Norman Scott, which had not then reached Waugh's ears, but was entirely based on the fact that when Waugh was on the *Mirror* Thorpe had once fed him a bum story. By use of this technique Waugh established a kind of 'existential' or 'Waugh' fact, a fact of an alternative nature to the investigated or 'Foot' fact.

The third Wilson administration was an extraordinary period, tailor-made for *Private Eye*. It started with the 'Slagheaps' scandal* and ended with the first rumours about Jeremy Thorpe. And throughout it all Wilson kept up a serene appearance which suggested more the lotus-eater than the man in charge of the shop. His return as Prime Minister in March 1974 was followed by a barrage of anonymous information concerning his activities since the 1940s. Where this came from was never discovered, but it was extremely detailed and convincing, and as much of it as could be checked proved generally reliable. In retrospect, and in the light of Wilson's belief that his own office was at this time being bugged by MI5, it seems likely to have been supplied by someone with connections in the security service. Certainly MI5 was seriously worried about the risk of having Joe Kagan constantly in and out of No. 10 at most hours of the day and night, since he was at the same time hobnobbing with

---

*The name given to the attempt made by members of Marcia Williams's family to develop land in Liverpool. Much of the negotiation was carried on from the Leader of the Opposition's office.

PRIVATE EYE

No. 325
Friday
31 May '74

12p

IT'S LADY SLAGHEAP!

WILSON'S SHOCKER

the head of the KGB in London, a man he had known since the Russian invasion of Lithuania when Kagan first made friends with the KGB there. Naturally none of this could appear in the press until many years later, when Mr Wilson's crony was convicted of theft and false accounting.

This torrent of 'black propaganda' about Wilson and his circle was not thoroughly exploited until the national press had dealt with the Milhench story, which also concerned the financial interests of Marcia Williams and her family, and which also dated back to Wilson's period as Leader of the Opposition between 1970 and 1974. Then in April 1974 *Private Eye* told the story of Mrs Halls, the widow of the civil servant Michael Halls who, as Wilson's Principal Private Secretary, had more to do with Marcia Williams than any one else in the civil service – and who had eventually died from a heart attack caused by overwork. His widow was now suing the civil service on those grounds, stating that much of the overwork had been caused by Mrs Williams. This was the first confirmation that something had gone seriously wrong with the last Wilson administration, as well as with his time as Leader of the Opposition. The Halls story had first appeared in the German magazine *Stern* but no other British paper had followed it up. Paul Foot at *Socialist Worker* chose this time to trace the extraordinary connections between the men who paid for Wilson's political office in Opposition, Israel and Iron Curtain trade. He had originally got the story from a senior correspondent on *The Observer* who was unable to use it in his own paper.

Private Eye took this story up and developed it with the assistance of the anonymous information that was then coming in. In April 1974 this led to a full-page examination of Marcia's influence over Wilson which illustrated for the first time the extent of the Prime Minister's helplessness when faced with his forceful secretary and his highly organised band of 'socialist' supporters. Succeeding issues continued the story of the Field family where the national press had left it – at the most interesting point – and also dug out more about Mrs Williams's frosty relations with another of Wilson's former colleagues, George Wigg.

At this point the whole thing became too much for Wilson and he made his secretary a life peeress, a touching token of support but one which gave the entire press the opportunity to write about her far more freely. From that day to this she has maintained an untypical silence in the House of Lords. *Private Eye*'s response to the peerage was predictably high-spirited. In one issue there were stories about Marcia, Lord

Marcia Williams, now Lady Falkender, by John Kent.

Brayley (Wilson's dodgy Minister for the Army), and Wilson's new solicitor, David Freeman; Lord Goodman having by now apparently washed his hands of the whole business.

Later that year Wilson chose to ennoble the one trade union leader, Richard Briginshaw, who had been under attack in *Private Eye* for over a year. It was almost as if, at this stage in their career, Wilson and Marcia were reading the *Eye* to find 'their kind of people'. To be attacked in *Private Eye* became almost a *sine qua non* of a Wilson Honours list. It was a policy which enabled Wilson to honour a subsequently convicted criminal (Lord Kagan) and two others who died (one by suicide) while police investigations were in progress (Lord Brayley and Sir Eric Miller).*

The Marcia Williams story was one of the great *Private Eye* somersaults. The paper had been either friendly or noncommittal about her since 1964, on at least six occasions going out of its way to deny rumours about her relationship with Wilson. The Marcia story, like the Briginshaw story, would probably not have been written in the same way had the political basis of *Private Eye* not shifted.

The readers themselves played a considerable part in the success of the paper. One of the all-time classic letters was supplied by A. J. P. Taylor, who corrected a story of how Lord Longford had been shot in the bottom while parading a detachment of the Home Guard in Oxford in 1940. Another reader, M. I. Webster, was alert enough to give the come-uppance to one of his fellows who had written the traditional 'I cancel my order' letter, pointing out that she had first done this fifty-seven issues earlier. Finally, W. Sadler scored a highly unlikely first by actually launching a long-running feature, 'Colemanballs', in the readers' letters column.

Wilson's mysterious resignation in March 1976 brought to an end 'Mrs Wilson's Diary'. The last episode suggested that he had resigned because Lady Forkbender had thrown one teapot too many. Mrs Wilson (the real Mrs Wilson) told *Woman's Own* that, after twelve years of reading her 'Diary', if she ever met John Wells she 'would like to bite him'.

Tom Driberg died in August 1976. The Crossword was accordingly terminated. He had enjoyed the dignity of his title for less than a year.

*A case brought against Lord Briginshaw by his union, NATSOPA, for damages for conspiracy to defraud was eventually settled in the High Court.

Although the story of Marcia Williams was the most important series of this period it was by no means the only one to make an impact. In May 1975, Michael Gillard published his book *A Little Pot of Money*, which was a detailed account, based on his stories in *Private Eye*, of Maudling's involvement with two entirely separate crooks, Poulson and Jerome Hoffmann. The *Daily Mail* reported the publication under the headline 'New Book a Plot Against Me, Says Maudling'. It was also in 1975 that Auberon Waugh took up the story, first reported in the *West Somerset Free Press*, about the mysterious shooting of a Great Dane bitch named Rinka on Exmoor. Waugh was to pursue the trail leading from the body of Rinka like some inconsolable Hound of Heaven, until Jeremy Thorpe was acquitted at the Old Bailey of conspiracy to murder and incitement to murder.

And in 1976 the continuing strength of *Private Eye*'s news reporting was shown during the lobbying among Labour MPs to elect a successor to Harold Wilson as party leader. In April *Private Eye* published a detailed account of Jim Callaghan's relationship with the Cardiff businessman, Julian (now 'Sir Julian') Hodge, a beautiful friendship which had first been noted in 1967. The article was immediately offset by some of Callaghan's opponents and circulated among Labour MPs. On April 14th John Stonehouse, MP, already awaiting trial for fraud, was ejected from the House of Commons after insisting on referring to this *Private Eye* profile in the chamber. There was also the Eric Miller saga which culminated in 1977 with Miller's resignation from his own group of companies. Once again *Private Eye* readers, who had been learning about Miller for years, must have felt like insiders.

But all this was to be overshadowed by another time bomb, left ticking in Issue 365. It was an article entitled 'All's Well That Ends Elwes' and it told the story behind the disappearance of Lord Lucan following the murder of his children's nanny. The article was illustrated by a photograph of a millionaire financier, Jimmy Goldsmith.

A BETTER DEAL FOR YOUR DOG

VOTE WAUGH

Auberon Waugh stood against Jeremy Thorpe in the general election as a candidate for the Dog Lovers' Party. This was Mr Waugh's election poster.

9 Jaws

The eighteen months which it took for 'the Goldsmith affair' to work its way through various courts were the most extraordinary in *Private Eye*'s history. The article about Dominic Elwes had appeared on 12 December 1975. In the two succeeding issues of *Private Eye* there were articles about Goldsmith's business activities. The second of these mentioned his solicitor, Eric Levine. Within three days of this last piece appearing, Goldsmith had issued three civil libel writs in respect of all three of the articles. The subsequent legal manoeuvres were as follows.

On January 15, Goldsmith obtained an originating summons for a criminal defamatory libel prosecution against *Private Eye*, on the basis of the Elwes article.

Between January 15 and February 2, Goldsmith issued eighty civil libel writs against forty of *Private Eye*'s local distributors, retailers and wholesalers. Four of these actions were dropped. Nineteen were settled by the firms apologising and agreeing never to distribute the magazine again. Seventeen firms resisted Goldsmith.

On April 14, Mr Justice Wien gave Goldsmith leave to bring a criminal libel prosecution against *Private Eye* and its editor.

On May 18, a statement in the House of Commons said that the Director of Public Prosecutions did not intend to intervene in the criminal libel case.

On May 22, *Private Eye* undertook in the High Court not to publish anything about Goldsmith or his solicitor Eric Levine until Goldsmith had applied for an injunction to prevent such publication pending the criminal libel proceedings. The undertaking bound *Private Eye*, Ingrams and two freelance journalists, Michael Gillard and myself.

On May 26, Goldsmith was knighted by Harold Wilson.

On June 25, Master Warren, on the application of the seventeen remaining independent newsagents, ordered the libel actions against them to be stayed on the grounds that they were 'vexatious', being predominantly intended to

Great Bores of Today. *50.*

". . . and I now ask your Lordships to turn for a moment if you will to the cartoon on page 4 of *Private Eye* Issue 389 that's exhibit JMG 586 in your Lordships' bundle and there can be no doubt in our submission that this cartoon constitutes a clear and undoubted referenc to myself in the light of which I crave leave to refer your Lordships for a moment to *Rex v Aspinall Steam Laundry* where it was stated by Mr Justice Cocklecarrot Times Law Report 1936 that to hold up the Learned Counsel of a party to litigation to obloquy thereby subjecting him to public contumely and opprobrium constitutes and this is our submission in this case my lord a clear case of *scandalum magnatum* for which the defendant should be imprisoned. . . "

obstruct *Private Eye*'s business. Goldsmith appealed to a judge in chambers.

On July 5, Goldsmith applied to Mr Justice Donaldson in chambers for an injunction to restrain *Private Eye* and five freelance journalists (Richard West, Michael Gillard, Nigel Dempster, Auberon Waugh and myself) from writing about him or his solicitor Eric Levine pending the criminal libel trial. Two prominent London figures, the PR man John Addey and a solicitor, Leslie Paisner, failed to attend court to give evidence for Goldsmith. This was the first occasion on which Ingrams and Goldsmith came face to face. Ingrams later described it as 'like the first sight of the shark in *Jaws*'. On July 16, Goldsmith's application was refused in open court. Goldsmith appealed to the Court of Appeal.

On July 12, Michael Gillard issued a writ for slander against Goldsmith and John Addey.

On July 19, Goldsmith issued a libel writ against *Private*

Lewis Hawser QC casting his spell over the courtroom; in the background is the editor of Private Eye. *By Heath.*

Eye for an article it had published on June 25 concerning Slater Walker.

On July 24, Philip Knightley, a *Sunday Times* journalist, issued a writ for libel against Goldsmith. This concerned an open letter Goldsmith had circulated to editors following an article Knightley had written about the state of play between the parties.

On July 30, Richard Ingrams was committed for trial at the Old Bailey on a criminal charge of defamatory libel.

On August 9, Mr Justice Goff in the High Court refused Goldsmith's motion to commit to prison Ingrams and Gillard for breach of their undertaking not to mention him, given on May 22. Instead Ingrams, Gillard and *Private Eye* were fined a total of £1000 for contempt of court. During the case it emerged that private detectives employed by Sir James had been raking through *Private Eye*'s dustbins in order to peruse the contents.

On October 15, Mr Justice Stocker allowed Goldsmith's appeal asking for liberty to proceed with the libel actions against the seventeen newsagents. *Private Eye* and the newsagents appealed to the Court of Appeal.

On October 29, the Lord Chief Justice and two other judges, in the Divisional Court, refused Goldsmith's second application to commit Ingrams to prison, and to sequester *Private Eye*'s assets, this time on grounds of contempt following from the magazine's report (dated August 20th) of the proceedings before Mr Justice Donaldson. The court also refused Goldsmith leave to appeal to the House of Lords. Goldsmith applied to the Appeals Committee of the House of Lords for such leave.

On November 19, I was committed for trial at the Old Bailey on a charge of criminal libel, as the writer of the Elwes article.

On November 22, Goldsmith was refused leave by the Court of Appeal to postpone his appeal against Mr Justice Donaldson's refusal (in July) to grant him an injunction.

On December 8, the Court of Appeal, Lord Denning presiding, began hearing *Private Eye*'s appeal against Mr Justice Stocker's decision to allow Goldsmith to proceed against the seventeen newsagents. Goldsmith dropped his appeal against the Donaldson decision.

On December 9, the House of Lords Appeals Committee refused Goldsmith's application for leave to appeal against the Lord Chief Justice's decision of October 29.

On February 23, 1977, the Court of Appeal (Lord Denning dissenting) refused the appeal of the seventeen newsagents.

On April 29, the House of Lords refused *Private Eye* leave to appeal against the above.

On May 10, the settlement of the criminal libel case was announced. All outstanding civil actions were also settled.

On May 16, the two accused in the criminal libel case were formally acquitted at the Old Bailey.

While the maelstrom lasted *Private Eye* published very little about Goldsmith, apart from the details of the battle, and everyone was far too busy to discover what exactly he was up to. But Michael Gillard considers that enough has now emerged for a sensible theory to be developed.

In October 1975, when Goldsmith was appointed chairman of Slater Walker by the Bank of England, he also faced financial loss as a result of his deals with Slater. Jim Slater at that time wanted to leave the country. He changed his mind when he was told that he must stay. But if Slater was going to stay he needed a reliable and sympathetic successor. Goldsmith's companies were major shareholders in Slater Walker and major customers of the SW bank.

The Department of Trade was pressing for a full, open inquiry under section 165 of the Companies Act. This was opposed by the Bank of England on the grounds that it would damage confidence in the City, as Slater Walker Ltd had been a fully authorised bank. The DoT did carry out a private inquiry under section 109 but Wilson was persuaded by the Bank to overrule the DoT request to go further.

This suited Slater and Goldsmith as it meant that little about the interlocking share dealings and bank loans would be revealed. If they had been revealed, as they later were – to some extent – when Jim Slater was prosecuted, there could well have been City opposition to Goldsmith staying on as chairman of Slater Walker.

It was this position that was also threatened by the *Eye*'s disclosures and its questioning of his suitability and impartiality. If Goldsmith had been forced out as chairman he would not have been able to influence what was revealed about the details of his own dealings with Slater and Slater Walker, or those of his friends like Frost. But the more the *Eye* raised questions and eyebrows in the City the more 'this sweetheart deal' was threatened.

The Elwes article attacked Goldsmith as a public figure,

and the two 'In the City' pieces attacked him on financial grounds. The only real threat to the cosiness of the Slater–Goldsmith deal seemed to be *Private Eye*, in particular its City column. So it was that the last of the three stories, the Levine story, launched a thousand writs. So, in Gillard's view, Goldsmith's avalanche of litigation against *Private Eye* was partly a colossal bluff, intended to distract attention from the crucial arrangements he was making to rescue the millions he had locked up in Slater Walker. (At the time none of this was known. In fact it was not to be until September 1976 that the public heard that the Bank of England had spent £110 million of public money to bail out Slater Walker.)

An alternative theory is that Goldsmith was hoping to please Harold Wilson and Marcia Williams. The latter had assisted him to get the section 109 inquiry, and her pleasure in his actions against the *Eye* was confirmed by his knighthood. Before going over the top Goldsmith attended a dinner given by Paul Johnson where he was urged 'to throw the book at *Private Eye*'. He felt, wrongly as it turned out, that in doing so he would become a popular hero.

Both Ingrams and Goldsmith saw the struggle in personal terms and all early attempts to arrange a settlement failed. Anthony Blond remembers one meeting with Goldsmith, who was an old friend of his. 'Jimmy became wilder and madder whenever I suggested he stop persecuting *Private Eye*. "They have attacked my son," he said. "I will throw them into prison. I will hound their wives, even in their widows' weeds." Then he gripped my arm. It was quite anxious-making.'

By far the greater part of the burden throughout the battle against Goldsmith was borne by Richard Ingrams. This was partly of necessity but partly from choice as well. He gave his usual impression, for the most part, of being generally unworried, but Gillard considers that this was misleading. Sometimes in the early days Gillard wondered whether Ingrams realised the seriousness of Goldsmith's determination. At that time he christened Ingrams 'Colonel Bumble' and suggested that the *Eye* operation resembled a rifle section of Dad's Army taking the field against a Panzer division.

He misjudged it at the beginning, partly because of the advice we received before we consulted James Comyn. Then after the amazing Wien judgement, when Goldsmith got permission to go ahead with the criminal libel, Ingrams was shattered for a bit – we all were – but he woke up to reality and began to play it very well. I think he continued

to play it very well until right at the end when he lost his
nerve. My impression was that after Simon Jenkins (editor
of the *Evening Standard*) came round with the last-minute
offer of settlement, just before the Old Bailey hearing was
due to start, Goldsmith had really got to him. It had been a
war of attrition and it had worked. So he grabbed the peace
offer like a drowning man thrown a line. He had started to
see the prison gates.

Gillard always resented the terms of the settlement (not a
resentment incidentally which I shared. The prison gates were
clearly visible from my house in Abergavenny as well. When
news of the settlement eventually reached South Wales it
came as a welcome relief.) For in Gillard's view *Private Eye*
had also got to Goldsmith, and he too wanted out. The case
had already cost him his attempt to buy *The Observer*, and it
was about to cost him his attempt to buy the *Evening
Standard*.

So at last we had a strong card. But Richard wouldn't even
speak to me or Geoffrey Bindman, our solicitor. He
arranged the settlement without telling anyone. He just
grabbed it. I *really* objected to us agreeing to take ten years
to pay and then continuing to attack him. That was not on.
That was like asking him a favour and then kicking him. He
tried to make a similar offer in my slander case, and I gave
him the money immediately. I was not being put in that
position.

   Also, because of the settlement a lot was left on the table
unresolved. The distributors' case and the criminal libel
were the two standards to which people had rallied. We
had gone as far as we could with the distributors, but we
had spent fifteen months banging the drum about the
criminal libel case, saying 'Onwards, into the Valley of
Death', and then suddenly it was all off. I felt we had
perpetrated a fraud. 'The game's over,' we said, taking
away the ball and the stumps. Then within a month
Richard was back in there hitting out again. It looked like
we hadn't had the bottle. Would people rally again after
that?'

Ingrams does not agree with this analysis and points out
that previous settlement attempts had included a proviso that
Goldsmith should be able to vet future articles about his
affairs. In this case there was no such restriction. He also
thinks that Gillard fails to appreciate the difficulties of

Gnome

A variety of highly spiced accounts appeared in various papers last week regarding my state of health and, more importantly, my relationship with Ms Rita Chevrolet described by one paper as "confidante & masseuse".

It was widely alleged that Ms Chevrolet had taken advantage of what was described as my "senile condition" — one report stated that I have been reduced to a pathetic shadow of my former self and spend my days in a state of sedated euphoria propped up on a variety of highly-coloured Oriental cushions.

Furthermore it was alleged that Ms Chevrolet — "the only person who can make him smile" -- is in the habit of bringing me cheques made out for huge sums of money, thrusting a pen into my hand and forcing me to trace a barely legible signature.

"Meanwhile," continues one of these fanciful fairytales, "the legendary Lord Gnome whose forceful character once dominated millions of employees, lies in a state of drugged stupor, an imbecilic smile playing about his ravaged features."

Messrs Sue Grabbit & Runne in collaboration with John Addey Associates have already issued a categorical denial of all these so-called allegations. Contrary to what has been stated, I am in robust health and full possession of my faculties.

Rita Chevrolet,
pp Lord Gnome,
c/o Banque Maritime,
10,000 Rappoport
Avenue,
Geneva,
Switzerland.

A Gnome column printed during the Goldsmith affair.

bringing out the magazine and conducting non-stop litigation at the same time.

Gillard's views about the Goldsmith case may to some extent be coloured by the aftermath in which he sued Goldsmith for slander, and lost. Goldsmith had alleged to several Fleet Street editors that Gillard had blackmailed John Addey, a public relations executive, into supplying false information. By his own admission, Goldsmith's only authority for this was Addey himself. Gillard then sued Addey and received a complete retraction, £5000 damages and all his costs. Addey admitted that there had not been a word of truth in the story. Instead of backing down at this point, Goldsmith refused to accept it and continued to oppose the Gillard action. When it came to court Goldsmith said that Addey had only apologised because he could not afford to fight the case. He did not, however, call Addey to confirm this idea, although Addey was in London at the time, and had even been subpoenaed as a precaution. Goldsmith called no one. He just went into the witness box and thundered away for a day and a half, using histrionic powers to mesmerise the jury.

Following the case a member of the jury wrote to *Private Eye*, 'Our decision has troubled me ever since. . . . I hope that Mr Gillard's appeal will be successful,' and enclosed a donation to his defence fund. Two other members of the jury also expressed serious doubts, one of them saying that they had only found in the way they did because they wanted to get home and that a young girl on the jury had finally been bullied into agreeing with the rest of them.

Gillard appealed as far as the House of Lords* but to no avail.

Gillard says that even though he lost the case he does not regret bringing it. 'If I had not done what I did he would have repeated his allegations for ever, and he might have stopped me working anywhere else.' To Gillard's professional colleagues the allegations have always been patently absurd, and are regarded as evidence merely of how desperate Addey was when faced with Goldsmith and Levine.

---

* The judges of the Court of Appeal said that Addey was 'a liar' who 'was not to be believed in any particular'.

A little pot of money   10

All I wanted was a little pot of money for my old age.
Reginald Maudling

When we started *Private Eye* none of us expected it to be anything more than just an enjoyable way of continuing our old school magazine, but we found ourselves caught up in the rage for satire,' says Christopher Booker. But it was to be some time before the rage for satire was to make *Private Eye* into a prosperous business capable of withstanding the onslaughts of an enraged multi-millionaire.

The company balance sheet to 4 May 1962 showed an overdraft of £216, a loan from Andrew Osmond of £294, and legal expenses – already – of ten guineas. This was a shoestring business, and the importance of the Cook–Luard takeover is shown by the next balance sheet, to 6 October. The loan from Cook–Luard was £763, money banked for subscriptions had risen from £364 to £1960, and payments in contributors' fees and salaries had risen from £150 to £2361. There was an overall loss of £2191, most of which had been met by a subvention payment from Cook-Luard Productions Ltd.

Plans for the future of the new enterprise varied. Booker thought it was a temporary phenomenon. Rushton thought it was 'bound to work'. Usborne had plans for a European edition, and at one point started to ship copies out to be sold at Munich University. Ingrams, according to Usborne, was 'the only person mature enough to see that it might last for life'. But he was adamant that it should not be allowed to grow into a big organisation. 'He had a dread of it getting big and glossy and heavily involved with money. There was a terrific anti-profit spirit in those days among every one involved.' This rather depressed Usborne who had always had tycoon fantasies.* He found that many of his brainwaves,

* These have since been realised with Usborne Publishing; last annual turnover £2 million.

thought up to relieve boredom, were deposited in a file marked 'Usborne's Mad Ideas.'

For a short time when the Luard empire started to go under it looked as though *Private Eye* might even become an offshoot of the porn industry. The Establishment fell into the hands of a Lebanese 'businessman' called Raymond Nash who owned strip clubs and whose arrival coincided with a change in the gaming laws. He had a partner called Anthony Coutt-Sykes, the 'Coutt' having been added to instil confidence. Nash was last heard of in a Philippines jail. Before that there had been visits from a few of the protection racketeers but they had always found the place a bit too bizarre to start on; they were never quite sure who they were dealing with. Once a very large man interviewed Peter Cook during the evening show and mused over how terrible it would be if a mob of yobboes got in one night and got drunk and just smashed The Establishment up. Cook agreed with him, but never heard any more about it. Then a burly detective sergeant called Challenor called round, 'a man possessed' it seemed to Cook, who said that if there was ever the slightest sign of trouble he was to be told at once. Detective-Sergeant Challenor was later imprisoned for planting a brick on a student demonstrator, but Cook considered that he was the proverbial honest copper – most unusual in Soho – who was simply driven by overwork into lunacy.

For a short time, before the memo to Cook from Luard was dug out, the *Eye* teetered on the brink. Elizabeth Luard, the days at the Paris Ritz seeming rather far away, had to make the traditional journey to the pawnbroker with her jewel case in order to meet the wage bill. Then Cook took over, just in time to face the sales slump.

At this time, 1964, even Ingrams began to wonder if the show could stay on the road. He recalls it as 'a very dodgy period', when everything hung on Cook and Claud Cockburn being able to raise some money. The crisis lasted for about five months from March to July. Usborne then wrote to Cook, who owned about 80% of the paper, but who was still in New York. Usborne's letter said that: 'David [sic] Deutsch, Malcolm Muggeridge, Anthony Blond, John Calder and Claud Cockburn' were 'helping us look for money', and that among those who had been approached were Harold Lever, George Strauss, MP, Woodrow Wyatt, Cecil King, Jeremy Fry, Tony Richardson, Peter O'Toole and 'any others we can dream up'. The letter continued: 'As you can see from the enclosed appeal we have emphasised our expansion plans more than our financial crisis to make the thing look more attractive. God only knows whether it will succeed. I estimate that without further finance we could run two more issues before Thorpe's temper breaks.' The *Eye* had done what all small magazines try to do when the going gets rough – they had increased their credit with the printers. They had also offered John Thorpe a part share in Pressdram, but he took a sober view of its prospects and declined.

In April, Cook responded to this cry for help and returned to London with the news that he had been talking to the *Playboy* organisation about the possibility of an editorial link and financial assistance. He told the *Daily Mail* that in view of *Private Eye*'s falling circulation he was suggesting that it should carry more news in future. The *Evening Standard* reported that *Private Eye* was in such straits that it had approached the dishwasher king, John Bloom, for a loan. This was denied by *Private Eye* immediately.

In June, Peter Cook wrote to 'Mr Spectorsky' at the *Playboy* organisation, following up his earlier suggestion. The letter was an unashamed grovel:

I would like to thank you very much for all your hospitality and the time you spent discussing the *Private Eye* situation with me. I much appreciate your kindness. I find on my return that we are being fairly forcefully pressed by our printer. I am sure he can be held off for some time but it would of course be advantageous to settle with him as soon as possible so that we could move to our new vastly cheaper firm. I do think that the idea that our *Private Eye* team could do special features for *Playboy* on a regular basis is a good one. I know we have a unique and hitherto unexploited group of writers and artists whose talents would fit well into your format. For example, were I and Willy Rushton our fat cartoonist to go to Cuba or South Africa I think we would come up with a very different kind of humorous photo-cartoon documentary. ... I fully realise the strength of your argument that $40,000 is either too little or too much. I genuinely believe that as an investment it is very sound but obviously the sums involved are ridiculously small. I hope that it will be found that our loss may be of some use to you, but once again the amount is piddling. ... I would think that the history of the magazine with all the powerful opposition it had encountered would appeal to Hefner.... Once again many thanks for all your kindness, with best wishes,
Yours sincerely,

Peter Cook

P.S. I see today that Chrysler have bought 30% of Rootes Motors.

The point about changing the printers seems to have been a false lead to disguise the falling sales, for the document which *Private Eye* were at this time circulating hopefully around London's millionaires made no mention of a change of printers. Instead it spoke of Thorpe's as 'small and unique in its readiness to handle' the magazine. 'In the last few months,' it continued, 'the editorial content of the magazine has begun to change very considerably, swinging deliberately from the fashionable and partly extremely young readership of the past towards more news and an adult approach. In January Claud Cockburn joined the editorial board full-time, immensely increasing the average age of the board and at the same time its range of contacts and coverage.'

There is something rather touching about this attempt to present Claud Cockburn, in his own description 'one of the real hard men from the thirties', as an elder statesman who might be counted on to quell the young hot heads, and reassure millionaires who were being asked to cough up £15,000, for that was the sum being sought. 'We hope that there are enough people who consider *Private Eye* to be worth a good deal more than £15,000 by the unique function it performs, to provide that money each in lots of £5000 or £1000 virtually as gifts.'

As a further incentive there were plans for several new features, including book reviews. The document burbled on:

> There has been no time in the past six months during which there has not been published a book which could have been, space permitting, the theme or 'newspeg' for a *Private Eye* story, a review of the book but at the same time a satirical and revealing story. Within a very short time as *Private Eye* reviews become known and talked about as unique and distinctive features of literary journalism, publishers' advertising could become a major and solid source of income.

Nothing came of Cook's approach to *Playboy* and the English total of £15,000 proved over-optimistic. But the appeal was not a complete failure. Nine people were found who were prepared to give at least £100 each. They were the sort of people who might have agreed to become theatrical angels; the difference was that angels stood to make a handsome profit, whereas it was agreed in this case that, though the benefactors would receive shares, the money would be provided as a gift. In the event, their money was just enough to ensure survival.*

The transformation of this struggling little firm into the multi-billion dollar corporation that it is today can be traced very simply through the sales figures. Right up until 1971

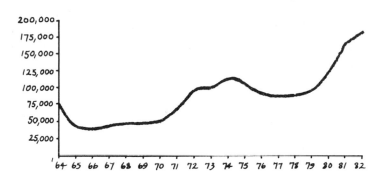

when the sixty thousand barrier was broken, *Private Eye* remained healthy but poor. The top salaries being paid in 1971 were £90 a fortnight. By 1976 this had only risen to £230 a fortnight. In 1980 it was £550 a fortnight. There were two elements in this success. One was simplicity. The other was the ban by W.H. Smith.

The refusal of Smith's, who had a virtual monopoly outside London of wholesale and retail distribution, to handle the magazine at all could easily have sunk *Private Eye*. Smith's attitude was the same from the start. Nicholas Luard recalls that even in 1962 the managing director of Smith's refused to take the paper for reasons that could be summarised as 'it probably isn't very nice'. After their conversation Luard discovered that he had not actually seen a copy.

In 1969, *Private Eye* revealed that Smith's were operating a black list of forty to fifty books that were generally available from reputable publishers. They included *Tropic of Cancer*. At that time they had also banned *Penthouse*, *Oz* and *Black*

---

*The generous enthusiasts were Jane Asher, Anthony Blond, Dirk Bogarde, Bernard Braden, Lord Faringdon, David Kunzle, Oscar Lewenstein, Martin Page and Peter Sellers. David Kunzle gave £1000 and was eventually repaid with interest. Martin Page and Peter Sellers also eventually accepted repayment. The others, like all current shareholders, are paid an annual dividend in the form of wine at Christmas. Lord Faringdon strolled in off the street with his cheque. He was notable as the only homosexual Communist peer, and once started a speech in the House of Lords with the words 'My Dears' (instead of 'My Lords').

The man who asked for Private Eye *at W. H. Smiths.*

Dwarf. Subsequently of course, Smith's have become pace-setters in the display and selling of soft porn, so that it is impossible in some branches to get to the magazine racks for the preoccupied male customers standing in front of them leafing through girlie magazines.

In 1971 Smith's told *Campaign* that their main objection to *Private Eye* was legal and that they would be prepared to take it if the libel laws affecting distributors were changed. Ingrams pointed out in reply that *Private Eye* had paid out £30,000 in cash on the nail in libel damages over the previous five years and that their distributors Moore-Harness had never had to pay anything and were in any case indemnified. In 1972 Smith's said that if they did sell it there would be more writs. That was quite possibly true, though it had taken them ten years to think of it.

Faced with this potentially disastrous situation, *Private Eye* has reacted by building up its own distribution network. In Evelyn Waugh's words, 'the muscles which encounter the most resistance in daily routine are those which become most highly developed and adapted'. By the time that Smith's, seeing the soaring sales, were beginning to make occasional conciliatory noises, *Private Eye* had decided that they no longer wanted them anyway. David Cash set up a trip to the boardroom of John Menzies (the W.H. Smith of the North) in Edinburgh in 1972 but nothing came of this either. Some of the senior people at Menzies really wanted to take *Private Eye* but they were far too timid. At that time – pre-Goldsmith – there was no record of a plaintiff in libel recovering damages against the distributor more recent than the *Shirley Temple v. Graham Greene* case; indeed that seemed to be the only example in the twentieth century. Nonetheless, Menzies wanted an indemnity of £50,000 per annum which in those days seemed wildly unreasonable. Cash went as far as looking for insurance, but the premiums quoted by Lloyds were absurdly high.

By this time, 1973, with sales moving over the one hundred thousand mark for the first time, *Private Eye* decided that it would manage very well without both Smith's and Menzies. Sir Charles Harness became a director of Pressdram and devoted more time to selling *Private Eye* alone, and Osmond realised that if Smith's and Menzies did take the paper it might not result in any immediate increase since a lot of buyers would merely switch to the more convenient shop, thereby hitting all the loyal small firms which had provided the paper to date. Furthermore, Smith's would probably be more trouble than they were worth, insisting on sending their own lawyers to see the occasional issue for instance. The grievance-value and the scarcity-value far outweighed the convenience.

Smith's were not the only potentates to take exception. The eight issues produced in 1966 up to March were banned by Australian customs for 'undue emphasis on sex, violence, crime and horror', which seemed a very fair description. And in October of the same year, Issue 124 was banned in South Africa. The *Cape Town Post* said that the main reason for the ban was the cover, which it described as 'four African men in tribal garb, leaping into the air.... All four are smiling broadly and appear to be extremely jubilant.... There is a sarcastic caption. The Publications Control Board has described it as vicious and repulsive filth.' This was praise indeed.

At home all efforts were made to build up a reliable network of independent suppliers. Moore-Harness were

PRIVATE EYE

No. 124
Friday
17 Sept. 66

1/6

VERWOERD

A NATION MOURNS

strong in London, but outside the capital there were several sales drives. In October 1966, during a Northern sales drive by Peter Cook and Richard Ingrams, it was revealed that one-third of the forty-one thousand sale was in London and that only one thousand copies were sold throughout the whole North-East. Asked by local journalists which North-Eastern personalities might have appeared in *Private Eye*, Cook replied that the only one 'was T. Dan Smith, but we suppressed the article'. This was some years before questions began to be raised about T. Dan, but he paid no heed to this early warning. A further publicity tour was made in the West Country in 1967 and both contributed by the end of that year to a five-thousand increase in sales. From then sales were to rise fairly steadily until 1974, when they reached an early peak of 117,000.

The other characteristic of the paper's business success has always been simplicity. The staff today, apart from the editor, are the managing director David Cash, Tony Rushton who is in charge of advertising and layout, one editorial secretary, Liz Elliott, and one accountant, Sheila Molnar, who also does the bookkeeping for the other companies. In a separate office there are a circulation manager, George Rankin, with a staff of two, and a subscription manager, Ena McEwan, with a staff of four. There are two reporters, Paul Halloran and Jane Ellison, and one part-time sub-editor, Mary Brooke. There is also Cyril Bottomley, who was formerly a paper salesman and now works two days a fortnight for *Private Eye*. David Cash says: 'On any other publication everyone would have a secretary, but we've never gone in for that.'

The business reorganisation was started by Andrew Osmond when he rejoined the paper as managing director in 1969. At that time the mail-order business which had been one of Usborne's pet schemes was in a state of collapse. It never revived. (This disappointed Ingrams who liked to turn a joke into solid form, as with the Quintin Hogg cushion.) But there were two other successes. A classified page was created by making up bogus but interesting ads. This just seemed the best way to start one. There was one rate for normal ads and twice that for 'filth'. Slowly over the years most of the filth (i.e., contraceptives) has been weeded out.

Then the subscriptions were re-organised. Subscriptions are gold-dust to any magazine. There is no distributors' discount and it is money in advance. In 1969 there were about

175

Andrew Osmond returns as managing director. Bubble by Ingrams.

five thousand subs, which was 10% of the total sale. By the time Osmond left in 1974 there were twenty thousand subs in a total of 117,000 – 17%. Osmond says:

> We figured we had many occasional buyers. So we tried to turn them into subscribers, by catching them with a tear-out insert. We never advertised for subs outside the magazine. We made offers that ran for months. We gave away books and big reductions. We had a lower fall-off rate than most. Two out of three new subscribers signed on for a second year, and one in three signed up indefinitely.
>
> All through that period, when the business doubled in both subs and other sales, we never took on another person. I was always amazed when dealing with rival periodicals at the number of people in their offices. What other paper has an advertising manager who also does the layout? At one point we even considered dropping all the ads. Instead we just kept putting the rate up until the ads thinned out to fill the available space. Other magazines always operated by the rules of the game. We just had the amateur touch and utter self-confidence; it was the same right at the start. I don't know where we got it from. There was one other important factor in our success and that was Richard's emergence as a national figure. His continual appearances on the radio and television were wonderful free publicity.

The other main activity of *Private Eye* is book publishing.

Again this was started by Osmond and Cash, and again no one extra was hired. It was all done by the existing staff of the magazine. In that way *Private Eye* had the great advantage that it had no wheels to keep turning. It did not have to publish a certain number of books a year. The company could be virtually dormant for nine months and then take advantage of the Christmas boom. They started with six titles a year and so far only one has lost money. The real snag with all publishing, according to Osmond, is distribution. There was a link with Michael Joseph for a time, and then, through Nicolas Bentley, the list was moved to André Deutsch in 1972.

Recently the number of titles has averaged three books a year. Successes have included *The Country Diary of an Edwardian Gnome*, which sold twenty-two thousand in hardback, and the book of *Dear Bill*, which has sold 125,000 in paperback and was in the charts for six months. Book publishing (at £250,000) now accounts for one-quarter of total turnover.

Osmond was succeeded in 1972 by David Cash, who had left Ridgeway School, Wimbledon, with ambitions to be an architect. It was due to Cash that *Private Eye*'s distribution became independent even of Moore-Harness, who had been their distributors since 1962. Dissatisfaction arose as Moore-Harness became more and more involved in the pornography trade. Cash knew that Moore-Harness had been able to persuade many of the small newsagents, who were prepared to take *Private Eye*, to take porn as well. Then, as sales of the *Eye* soared, Cash discovered that in many cases Moore-Harness were refusing to supply the *Eye* unless the newsagent also took a certain amount of porn. On more than one occasion Moore's warehouse was raided by the police and 'a quantity of material removed'. Cash was able to obtain Moore's list of newsagents who were taking the *Eye* and in 1977 *Private Eye* started doing its own distribution. They started with sales at ninety-one thousand, and since then, with the aid of their own circulation staff, had built this up to 190,000 by December 1981, including forty thousand subscriptions – 21%. It has been one of the most spectacular aspects of the paper's success. Shortly after *Private Eye*'s departure, Moore-Harness went bust.

The present position is that *Private Eye*'s income comes 'mostly' (90%) from trade sales and subscriptions, and only about 10% from advertising. 'This is a great strength. Most magazines get about 60% of their income from advertising,' says Cash, 'and it is particularly useful because in a recession ads get scarce, and other papers have to increase their price to their readers. For *Private Eye* the advertising revenue is merely the cream on the top. It also has obvious editorial advantages.'

The experience with FebEdge the printers has been excellent. There was a suggestion at one time that because it was such a militant left-wing shop there would be union problems. But FebEdge have no more union problems than Thorpe had. Nor have they objected to the contents of *Private Eye*. Once a junior manager complained about an Idi Amin cover. He was dismissed.

The change from the fringe publication that 'might not last three months' to today's thriving business (1981 turnover: £1 million) has been gradual, but it is now a fact.* Barry Fantoni says, 'I'm afraid *Private Eye* is here to stay. I don't see any of us escaping it now.' And Tony Rushton considers that, 'It'll give me a living for as long as I want. Even if you took Richard away it wouldn't matter now. We have reached the *Punch* stage, the editor is no longer vital. You couldn't have said that ten years ago, but the Goldsmith case brought us onto a new plateau of respectability. Commercially the magazine will undoubtedly continue. Richard has now created something with its own momentum.'

There speaks the member of a company pension scheme. One was started in the mid-seventies, in Cash's words, 'as people began to approach the age of forty'.

There are now three companies, apart from the original Pressdram. The villa in the Dordogne is owned by Springvale Finance Co Ltd. Private Eye Distribution is also separate, and the books are published by a third independent company, Private Eye Productions. Pressdram, which is always the company sued, does nothing but publish *Private Eye* and owns nothing but the title, which is copyright. Peter Cook retains 70% of the shares in Pressdram and so still remains 'the proprietor', but if he wishes to sell his shares he has to

---

* My inquiries about profits met with no response. Anthony Blond estimates that there was a profit of £90,000 in 1980. In the past the practice has been to distribute profits among the staff in bonus payments, rather than to pay dividends to shareholders. The libel provision (£100,000 in 1981) has also eaten into profits.

However in 1981, a highly successful year, a surplus of £106,000 remained to be distributed among staff and contributors. This brought the editor's earnings up to £25,587 and the managing director's up to £27,028.

offer them first to the other shareholders* *at cost*. This is a recent provision in altered articles of association. In fact, during the Goldsmith case Cook was approached by some prospective buyers who he agreed to meet out of curiosity.

'Two people turned up, both called Simon Fraser,' Cook recalls.

> One of them owned half Scotland, and the other did not. They said they wanted to buy *Private Eye*. I was quite suspicious of them because I thought that they might be put up to it by Goldsmith, but anyway they rambled on for a couple of hours about their plans for the paper. Then Oscar Beuselinck, my lawyer, got a bit bored and suddenly said, 'What about the fucking ackers then?' It turned out they were thinking of between £25,000 and £50,000. Oscar couldn't believe it. 'But you're talking about the price of fun,' he said. 'How do you put a price on that?' Finally I told them that I would sell it to them for £5 million. So we heard no more about it.

Cook is not entirely clear about his present position *vis-à-vis* Pressdram. 'I think I'm still the proprietor,' he said. 'I own the same number of shares, so I must be, mustn't I?' The answer seems to be yes, but if he wants to sell it, he will receive £1500, although the market value of his holding is probably closer to £250,000. He has by choice never been paid for any of his contributions to the paper over the years.

* The current shareholdings are as follows:

Peter Cook 16,080	Mary Ingrams 400
Peter Cook Ltd 1200	Barry Fantoni 160
Anthony Blond 2400	Tessa Fantoni 160
Peter Usborne 2160	Dirk Bogarde 103
Private Eye Productions 1530	Bernard Braden 103
Andrew Osmond 720	Oscar Lewenstein 103
Tony Rushton 420	Jane Asher 102
David Cash 400	The Estate of Lord Faringdon 102

11 The prisoners of the Fleet

Fleet Street is as prudish now about power as it once was about sex.
Richard West

I find that if I write about the world of journalism, literature, art or culture with the same irreverence as people in that world write – the right and proper irreverence – they scream like meanies over a wood fire.
Tom Wolfe

One could trace the relationship between *Private Eye* and 'the media of communications' – mainly the national press – as a sort of Rake's Progress.

In the early days, Fleet Street loved *Private Eye*. It was part of the satire boom, it was the Latest Thing. Then Fleet Street declared 'the satire boom' to be over and *Private Eye*'s imminent demise was announced. The paper became almost invisible overnight, Fleet Street ignored it. The third phase was a reaction to *Private Eye*'s early libel battles. Since these frequently involved well-known names they could not be ignored, but they could be made the occasion for taunting. The *Evening News* could report the award of 'substantial damages to Sir Cyril Black' under the headline 'The Price of Trying to be Funny'. *Private Eye* was becoming a steady financial contributor to the members of 'the establishment', it said. Then, as *Private Eye* started to print interesting stories regularly, Fleet Street started to steal them. The phase of unattributed 'lifts' lasted from about 1966 to the early 1970s.

Private Eye also carried stories which Fleet Street frequently did not care to lift, with or without attribution. When they eventually became national news it was not because of an unattributed lift but because there had been some new development which Fleet Street could no longer ignore. By the time the Poulson bankruptcy had made *Private Eye* into a national magazine, a grudging respect had turned into admiration. Many long-standing *Private Eye* readers were by now established Fleet Street journalists, and they were prepared to say that they liked the magazine despite which-

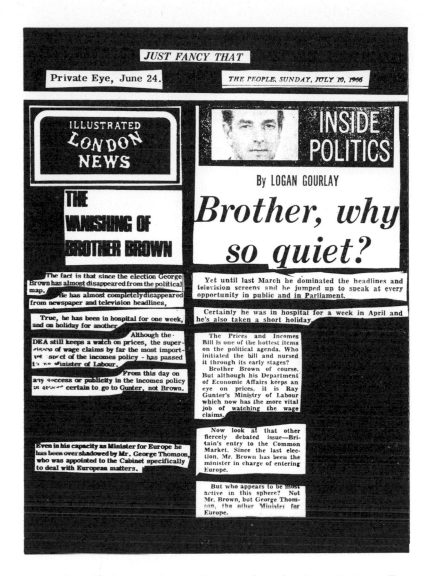

JUST FANCY THAT

Private Eye, June 24.

THE PEOPLE, SUNDAY, JULY 10, 1966

ILLUSTRATED LONDON NEWS

INSIDE POLITICS

By LOGAN GOURLAY

THE VANISHING OF BROTHER BROWN

Brother, why so quiet?

The fact is that since the election George Brown has almost disappeared from the political map. He has almost completely disappeared from newspaper and television headlines,

Yet until last March he dominated the headlines and television screens and he jumped up to speak at every opportunity in public and in Parliament.

True, he has been in hospital for one week, and on holiday for another.

Certainly he was in hospital for a week in April and he's also taken a short holiday.

Although the DEA still keeps a watch on prices, the supervision of wage claims by far the most important aspect of the incomes policy - has passed to the Minister of Labour.

From this day on any success or publicity in the incomes policy is almost certain to go to Gunter, not Brown.

The Prices and Incomes Bill is one of the hottest items on the political agenda. Who initiated the bill and nursed it through its early stages?

Brother Brown of course. But although his Department of Economic Affairs keeps an eye on prices, it is Ray Gunter's Ministry of Labour which now has the more vital job of watching the wage claims.

Even in his capacity as Minister for Europe he has been overshadowed by Mr. George Thomson, who was appointed to the Cabinet specifically to deal with European matters.

Now look at that other fiercely debated issue—Britain's entry to the Common Market. Since the last election, Mr. Brown has been the minister in charge of entering Europe.

But who appears to be most active in this sphere? Not Mr. Brown, but George Thomson, the other Minister for Europe.

ever of its faults was being discussed at the time. *Private Eye* had lost its *samizdat* status and become desk-top reading. It was praised in the courts, in Parliament and in the letters column and leaders of *The Times*.

During the next phase *Private Eye* began to influence Fleet Street. When the magazine was founded, the stereotype of the investigative journalist was a cheerful rogue with his foot in your door who was prepared to do anything legal and quite a lot that was illegal in order to get a story for his news editor, a man who was usually a bigger rogue than he was. Then these toothless, grinning men with bulging wallets were gradually replaced by earnest young graduates with a mission in life. Even the Glasgow papers acquired mini-'Insight' teams. *Private Eye* played some part in bringing that change about.

The Private Eye Story

In the penultimate phase reporters who could find full-time work in Fleet Street also began to work on every issue of *Private Eye*. Slowly but surely this process was reversed and the values of Fleet Street began to influence those of the *Eye*. The final stage was reached when *Private Eye* became susceptible to the same pressures. It too had friends to protect. It too was capable of misusing its considerable influence. The editor of 'William Hickey' (not an *Eye* contributor) professed himself too frightened of the editor of *Private Eye* to write a story about him, even though it was the proprietor of the *Daily Express* who was instructing him to write it. 'Why should I make a stick to beat my own back with?' 'William Hickey' replied. *Private Eye*'s influence was capable of suppressing news as well as circulating it.

The secondary success of *Private Eye*, after the 'satire boom', was very largely due to Fleet Street's failings. The national press has great power but this is shackled by great constraints. Some are imposed by law, others are self-imposed in response to vested interests or commercial pressure. It was in avoiding these constraints that *Private Eye* discovered a unique role.

Anthony Sampson, in *The New Anatomy of Britain* (1971), wrote of the frustration which can arise on a national newspaper.

CHARLES KRAY, elder brother of the Kray twins yesterday demanded a public apology from Independent Television for comments made by a Tory MP on a TV show.

Kray, 49, alleged that Mr Michael Brotherton, MP for Louth, made a "vicious attack" on him and his mother Mrs Violent Kray during Thames TV's Today programme.

The unintentionally humorous press cuttings were first suggested and supplied by Fritz Spiegl, the Liverpool composer and musicologist.

Journalists have remained in a weak position, and their weakness is shown by the fact that, while most of them are on the left, the majority of their newspapers, like their proprietors, are predominantly on the right. Licensed rebels can hold forth in Conservative newspapers like the *Daily Mail* or the *Evening Standard* but they are like eccentric radicals invited to amuse or provoke a Tory dinner-party. The 25,000 journalists are caught unhappily in the commercial cogs of Fleet Street. British journalists are aware of being less respected than Americans; there is no British equivalent to the American journalist-pundit. ... American newspapers helped to create their democracy, spreading news from coast to coast – in a country without traditional social networks, journalism was crucial. But in Britain the secretive ruling classes in the eighteeth century had no love of journalism, and it began as an eavesdropping profession, where even parliamentary reports had to be smuggled out. In spite of such eminent journalists as Churchill, Milner or Dickens, journalism has never quite recovered from this backdoor complex.

Private Eye was in direct line of descent from the original eavesdroppers. There was no sense of a dead proprietorial hand, and it was this that explained much of its early appeal to readers and to 'mainline' journalists alike.

Another reason for *Private Eye*'s success as a newspaper was Fleet Street's fondness for the lobby system. In other countries people had long since discovered the need for a journal that would print what only journalists knew, because the journalists were prevented from printing it in the usual way by the power of the national press which employed them. The extraordinary thing was that such a paper had not existed in Britain for many years. Under the lobby system journalists could become insiders, but only on condition that their readers did not. *Private Eye*'s readers were made to feel that they, too, were insiders. The lobby system, which is obviously in the interests of the government, or the great industries and trade unions which operate it, and which gives those journalists who cooperate with it a privileged and relatively easy life, is completely against the interests of newspaper readers. The implicit contract between *Private Eye* and its readers was different; it was that, provided the paper could find out what was going on, it would print it. No other newspaper could promise that – they all knew far too much.

Jim Perry, formerly a City reporter with the *Daily Express* and the *Daily Mail* and one of the early contributors to 'In the City', can remember vividly how difficult it was in those days to smuggle information into the national press.

The lawyers were the real impediment. We had the same problem again and again. I would come in late afternoon and say something like 'IOS are goin' up the wall' but the lawyers would never let us write the story. If you got a good story *your own side* immediately tried to prove you wrong. In fact the *Daily Express*, despite what I'd told them, printed a 'Boom Boom IOS' story one month before the company crashed.

The City pages were in the 'good news' business. The idea was that readers just wanted to know how to make money. City public relations were created between 1968 and 1973. They had not really existed before. The PR man's line was 'His company's shares are on a p/e of 10 because people write about him. I can get you written about.' And the top PR men were formerly good journalists. An industry suddenly appeared and they had to recruit for it. That was one of the good things about the early 'City

Slicker'. We could use it to attack the City PR men.

Nowadays the City columns are staffed by *serious* financial analysts, even economists. They have little if any idea about scoop stories. But before PR, the journalist had to know the guy he wanted to speak to. If you didn't know the guy he didn't say 'No comment'. He said 'Fuck off'. And it was sometimes hard to get to know the right people. My job was really to spend most of the day in bars and clubs talking to people who knew what was goin' on. I remember I had enormous expenses. £50 a week, which was bigger than many people's salaries in those days.

The policy of sending Perry out into the bars of the City sometimes backfired. On one occasion he returned to the office at about 7 pm and stood in the doorway gently swaying. Then he said: 'I've got the most amazin' story. If only I could remember what it is.' Then he passed out. On other occasions things went better.

Once I was tryin' to talk to a guy called Harold Lotery. No matter what I did I couldn't get hold of him but I discovered that he was spendin' most of the day in the RAC, playin' bridge. The point was that Jim Slater was quietly tryin' to take over his company and the shares kept goin' higher and higher. Finally I got through to his secretary and told her the position. 'Who is Slater?' was all she would say, and 'Mr Lotery does not know why the shares are goin' up.' 'Look,' I said. 'Unless he talks to me I will write that he has spent the last six months in the RAC, playin' bridge. Even though his shares have been goin' up steadily and he doesn't know why.' He phoned back at once. 'Come and have lunch, dear boy. You've got it all wrong.' That was it. Once you knew people they spoke to you.

Perry was also known for interviewing Sir Julian Hodge in his bath. The rumour was that the Hodge Group was collapsing so he called round at Hodge's home in Cardiff one evening in an attempt to get some answers. Lady Hodge came to the door and said it was quite impossible to talk to Sir Julian as he was in the bath. Perry persuaded her to ask him one question through the bathroom door. In this way he obtained one answer. Next day he was able to start his story in the *Daily Mail* 'From his bath last night, Sir Julian Hodge said...'

But such triumphs were infrequent. Apart from the

lawyers there was increasing trouble with the PR men. For most newspapers, the greatest single generator of advertising revenue was the City page. The PR men decided to control this. There were constant complaints that 'not enough advertisers were being written about' and this put a lot more pressure on the journalists. The solution for Perry and his *Express* colleague Michael Gillard was 'In the City', a column which was first suggested to Perry by Paul Foot.

Private Eye, on the contrary, had, for many years, adopted a policy of keeping advertisements out of its pages and using its cover price as its financial base. This was out of line with virtually every other magazine and paper in the country and was only possible because *Private Eye*'s overheads were so low. The great advantage of the arrangement was that *Private Eye* gave no hostages to fortune.

By 1971 *Private Eye* had established such a reputation that Tom Hopkinson wrote: '*Private Eye* is by far the most original and effective magazine launched in Britain since the war.' And Jo Grimond, then recently retired as leader of the Liberal party, said in his Beveridge Memorial lecture: 'One of the most curious features of the press today is that you have to see *Private Eye*. There you will find stories, sometimes of importance, mentioned nowhere else, and on the whole more accurately reported than in at least the so-called "popular" press.'

The *City Press* agreed. '*Private Eye*,' it said, 'was indispensable reading for political journalists and nowadays [April 1971] for City editors as well.' This was a tribute paid only two years after 'In the City' began in Issue 201.

By contrast, the popular press had taken advantage of the easing of the wartime constraints to print pictures and sex stories rather than more news. Tom Hopkinson noted that *Private Eye* had used bawdiness to rather more point. 'Blowing apart the established barrier of "good taste" which is one of the subtlest protections for people in positions of power and prestige, it made its mark by a mixture of satirical extravagance and comment so savage that few readers of the early numbers can have predicted more than an exceedingly short life.'

Much of 'In the City' was an implicit criticism of Fleet Street's own standards of reporting, but there were also many stories about the national press. Two of the best examples were the stories about the Harmsworth's groups plan to close the *Daily Mail* and develop its immensely valuable property, and the coverage given to the position of the powerful Fleet Street union leader, Richard Briginshaw of NATSOPA.

185

Throughout the seventies Fleet Street continued to oppose *Private Eye* and to steal from it on occasion. As late as 1972, by which time the *Eye*'s investigations were widely known, *The Guardian* lifted without attribution a piece on the Rio Tinto Zinc Co., the plagiarism being proved by the inclusion of mistakes.

And there was a still more recent example when Adam Raphael of *The Observer* copied out a long article on the Thorpe affair.

In December 1970 the house journal of *Times Newspapers* noted that *Private Eye* had recently carried an accurate report of a private *Times* editorial committee meeting. The story read:

> Somewhere in Printing House Square (on one or more of its seven floors) there are those who are selling out *The Times*. They are probably hard-working individuals, each doing a good job for the paper, but possessed of a misguided sense of humour, or a feeling of dissatisfaction: 'loyalty' to them appears to be a dirty word. All we can suggest to the self-detractors is that when they are cornered in the club or pub with a request for the inside dirt ... the appropriate brush-off for that scavenger [*Private Eye*] is 'Bugger off'.

Needless to say, this article was immediately sent on to Greek Street by several of the hard-working individuals in question. The headline to the piece in the house journal had been 'You don't foul your own nest'.

While happy to use the *Eye*'s information when it came in handy, Fleet Street also took steps to restrict the amount of information *Private Eye* could obtain. An application by Auberon Waugh to join the parliamentary lobby was consistently sabotaged by the existing lobby correspondents on the premise, perhaps, that the only reporters who should be allowed unrestricted access to members of parliament were those who most resembled the politicians in instinct, behaviour and sympathies. The members of the lobby were of course rightly suspicious that if *Private Eye*'s parliamentary correspondent had been allowed into the lobby he would have used his position to publish much more information than would have been generally convenient.

The reactions of the editors of Fleet Street to the attentions of *Private Eye* varied. The editor of *The Times*, Mr (now Sir) William Rees-Mogg, remained steady under fire. He was on one occasion reported to be marooned at Bordeaux airport

Le Président M. Anouar El Sadate a reçu, hier, M Wright Fogg. Rédacteur en Chef du «Times».

surrounded by drunken British rugby supporters in circumstances that exposed him to some ridicule. Then it was noted that an Egyptian newspaper had referred to him as 'Mr. Wright-Fogg'. Later, the fact that he had suppressed reports from Washington which were critical of the appointment of Peter Jay as Washington ambassador was documented. In the face of all this Mr Rees-Mogg maintained a serene front. Once, as an additional tease and out of curiosity as to his reaction, he was placed on the contributors' list after some trifling item of information had been checked with him. (It was one of his more amiable characteristics that he was always prepared to talk to *Private Eye* on the telephone.) On receiving the money the editor of *The Times* sent the following letter:

March 24, 1976

Dear Mr Ingrams,

Thank you very much for your cheque for £1.00 which I am returning herewith. I never charge for acting as a news source and am always happy to speak to any member of your staff in order to check facts.
Yours sincerely,

William Rees-Mogg

The only time when he took exception to a story and actually sued was when *Private Eye*, in relative innocence, wrongly suggested that in directing *The Times*'s editorial coverage of the October 1974 General Election he was intending to influence the result. Mr Rees-Mogg considered this an outrageous statement and was eventually awarded a sum of money in damages after an out-of-court settlement. Those who had always considered that it was one of the first functions of the editor of a national newspaper to influence public opinion were left with glazed eyes.

Other editors took a very different view of an adverse press.

The apology to Paul Johnson, in March 1968, when he was editor of the *New Statesman*, was a classic. The plaintiff claimed that the libel lay in suggesting that under him the paper had tempered its socialist principles. Since then Mr Johnson's politics have continued along a predictable course towards extreme right-wing Toryism. It must be rather unusual for a plaintiff to win damages for the suggestion that his political principles are what he himself proudly proclaims them to be shortly afterwards.

The position of Night News Editor on *The Times* might be thought an absorbing and responsible one. Here is how that person spent his time one evening last month.

At 7.30 he was telephoned by the editor of *The Times*, Mr William Rees-Mogg. Where was Mogg? He was in Bordeaux. Why? Because he had been invited to taste claret. And was it fun? No; he was stuck at Bordeaux Airport. He had been stuck there for five hours because the British Airways plane had broken down. Nobody seemed to realise how important Mogg was. They had only given him two cups of tea and some old cake.

Anyway, Mogg wanted action. He wanted the Night News Editor to phone the Chairman of British Airways and the Managing Director of British Airways, and he wanted to come home.

As Mogg spoke, the Night News Editor could hear the sound of breaking glass and obscene songs. There seemed to be a crowd around Mogg, and they seemed to be having a jolly time.

Immediately the *Times* machine was started. Telephone calls were made. Messengers were sent. The capital and the Home Counties were combed for Sir David Nicholson (chairman, B.A.) and for Henry Marking (man. dir., B.A.). Neither could be found. At 10 p.m. Mogg rang again. He was still at the airport. He still wanted to come home. The noise around him had grown and he explained, at the top of his voice, that his new friends were members of the British Rugby League team who had just won a football game and were very drunk. Everyone else, he said, seemed to have left the building.

Eventually, at 12.30 p.m., the Night News Editor and the press officer of British Airways came to an arrangement. A relief plane could not be sent to Bordeaux as this would cost many thousands of pounds. But a two-engined plane would be sent carrying spares for the broken-down airliner and hot food for Mogg.

So back at Bordeaux as the night closed in, surrounded by the berserk crowd of happy footballers who were by this time calling him "Willy", the bespectacled Mogg clung to the thought of the rescue which was approaching. British Airways had promised.

Unfortunately Bordeaux Airport closes at night. And just as the BA plane approached, a French military aircraft arrived on the scene. This too wanted to land at Bordeaux, and it got priority. The French military aircraft approached the runway, touched down, and then crashed. The airport was closed again, and the BA plane was diverted to Biarritz. There, in the early hours of the morning, the engineers, the spare parts, and Mogg's food (no longer very hot) boarded a taxi and set out on the long road journey to Bordeaux. They did not get there before dawn. And it was many hours later before the wrecked plane could be moved and Mogg could return to England.

Paul Johnson, then editor of the New Statesman, *by Scarfe.*

The dispute with Fleet Street continued in 1969 with *The People* case. On April 26th that year Richard Ingrams wrote to *The Times* to draw attention to a new tactic employed by lawyers representing newspapers which had sued for libel. In the case of the *Daily Express*, the *New Statesman* and the *Spectator* an unpublicised clause had been included in the settlements preventing *Private Eye* from mentioning these papers again. In the case of the *Daily Express* and its editor Derek Marks this had read: 'None of us [at *Private Eye*] will publish anything in future that is defamatory of Mr Marks or the *Daily Express*, or anything which reflects directly or indirectly on his editorial competence or integrity.'* This wording gave the plaintiffs an immunity from criticism far beyond the bounds of libel. The point was taken up by Michael Foot in the House of Commons. It was also noted that even when the *Spectator* was attempting to stifle comment from *Private Eye* it was itself engaging in unusually violent attacks on Harold Wilson, then Prime Minister, through its parliamentary correspondent, Auberon Waugh.

Mr Harold Evans, when editor of *The Sunday Times*, also proved to be highly sensitive to any form of ridicule. This first became apparent when a columnist in the *Evening News*, Lord Arran, dubbed him 'Dame' Harold Evans, apparently finding him rather self-important and not unreminiscent of the great theatrical Dame, Edith Evans, in manner. *Private Eye* took up this harmless nickname and Mr Evans became extremely hostile. On one occasion, when approached by a reporter (myself) about a story,† his reaction was to say that he did not wish to speak to anyone from *Private Eye* in order to check such stories. After a while Mr Evans began to respond to a long series of teases with threats of legal action. He received various apologies which culminated in October 1977, with the comprehensive settlement of a multi-thousand pound action brought by Mr Evans in response to numerous references to him in Auberon Waugh's 'Diary'. The settlement included a memorandum to the staff of *Private Eye* signed by Richard Ingrams but written by Harold Evans. It read as follows:

---

*On the day that this agreement was reached the *Daily Express* named the head of MI6 (justifying this because the *Saturday Evening Post* had just done it in America). *Private Eye* had of course first published the name in Britain four years earlier. The *Express* nonetheless claimed a scoop.

†The story was that he had asked Anthony Howard to write a critical article about *Private Eye*.

In view of Mr Evans' complaints and the litigation, past and present, which he has commenced against *Private Eye*, and in view of the binding undertaking I have given (both personally and on behalf of Pressdram Ltd) that we will *neither initiate nor pursue any campaign of malice misrepresentation or denigration of him whether in his personal or professional capacity, nor publish refer to or repeat directly or indirectly the libels in the action he brought in 1974 nor any other libels*, I am now issuing the following instructions, which are to remain in effect permanently.

No reference, *direct or indirect*, to Mr Evans is to be made in anything printed by *Private Eye* unless it is

1. True
2. Unambiguous
3. Not malicious
4. Approved by me personally or by any acting editor.

Harold Evans, by Rushton.

To ensure that these instructions are properly carried out I have asked our libel reader to draw to my attention *any* reference to Mr Harold Evans other than references he already knows to have been approved by myself or any acting editor.

References to Mr Evans which disregard the spirit or the letter of these instructions will be excised without reference to the contributor in question.

Contributors should realise that if *Private Eye* publishes references to Mr Evans in disregard of the undertaking both I myself and Pressdram Ltd will be liable to proceedings for breach of the undertaking, and there will be the possibility of actions for libel. This will place *Private Eye* in serious trouble which could endanger its future.

Mr Evans has been provided with a copy of this memorandum.

Copies to: Auberon Waugh
           Nigel Dempster
           Your [sic] libel reader

This absurdly carefully worded document did perhaps place rather too much confidence in the formality of normal bureaucratic arrangements at *Private Eye*. It was effective in restricting news or gossip items about Evans but in the following month there was a reference to 'The Sunday Dames', and spirited attacks on *The Sunday Times* for its attitude to the Thorpe affair continued throughout the negotiations. An important aspect of the above memorandum was that no reference was made to it in either paper, and it was not until January 1979 that Mr Evans was once again driven to bring his objections into the open. He was awarded a further £1000 and an apology for the 'unfair and untrue' references to him.

In reacting to hostility *Private Eye* could be relied on to be true to its principles. It was less sure of itself in reacting to praise. For years the magazine has attacked the Fleet Street habit of giving itself awards. This criticism might have been more convincing had the magazine and its staff not been quite happy to accept such awards whenever they were offered. In January 1969 *Private Eye* became the 'Irritant of the Year'. In January 1973 it employed the 'Journalist of the Year'. And in February 1982 it received a special award. The 'Irritant' award was collected by Ingrams from Edward Heath. At the prize-giving Heath made a fairly irritating speech calling for a review of the Official Secrets Act and the laws of libel and contempt. Needless to say, at the end of his term of office as Prime Minister nothing had been done about any of these laws. The speech's only purpose had been self-serving. Such awards are of rather dubious value to the *Eye*, whose readers would probably sooner see it attacking the Grocer than receiving awards from him.

None of this distracted the paper for long from its proper function throughout the seventies, which was to be a pacemaker for the national press and to print stories which established papers could not touch. In particular, there were the numerous stories about the cronies and crooks surrounding Harold Wilson when he was Prime Minister. There were also the Jeremy Thorpe story and the Ladbroke's story.

The Ladbroke's story was an interesting example because there was, on the face of it, nothing to prevent one of the national papers from running it in the normal way. It was originally prepared for the *Evening News* by a reporter, Jack Lundin, who was able to check every allegation made, entirely to the satisfaction of his colleagues. On this occasion there could be no legal cop-out, but when the story was ready it was spiked at the last moment by the editor. Lundin never received a satisfactory explanation for this craven behaviour, but Ladbroke's were a major advertiser with the *Evening News*.

In the case of the Thorpe story, it was his homosexuality

PRIVATE EYE

No. 458
Friday
6 July '79

25p

GRAND ACQUITTAL SOUVENIR

which caused Fleet Street's hesitation. Unable to see that the allegations were of serious criminal misbehaviour, Fleet Street fluttered around not daring to mention that the whole story only made sense if it was accepted that there was a suggestion that the leader of the Liberal party might have been, at some time in his life, of homosexual inclination. Long before Thorpe was charged, the *Daily Mirror*, for example, had an enormous file on the case which never looked remotely like getting past the libel lawyers. Nevertheless, two *Mirror* reporters continued day by day to collect the most detailed information purely for purposes of 'background' if Thorpe ever came to trial and was found guilty. They considered this to be standard Fleet Street practice.

In the case of the Wilson/Marcia Williams story, Fleet Street only felt bold enough to follow up some of the *Eye*'s original allegations after John Peyton, MP, had asked a question in the House about them. To take the *Daily Mail* as an example:

> Mr Wilson yesterday denied allegations that red boxes used for carrying State papers – received 'somewhat odd circulation' in his previous administration. . . . The Prime Minister retorted: 'You must be hard up for information if you rely on *Private Eye*. The story is entirely untrue. No red boxes, blue boxes, black boxes or green boxes moved as you seem to think. Perhaps you will check the facts. I wish you would get in touch with me instead of lowering what was a moderately distinguished Ministerial career with allegations of that kind.'

Presumably parliamentary insiders would have seen at once that the question had rattled Wilson. The report continued:

> The story which Mr Wilson denied appeared in the magazine *Private Eye* a fortnight ago but until yesterday there had been no reference to it in Parliament or in the newspapers. Mr Peyton did not mention the magazine in his question to Mr Wilson. The Prime Minister's bald reference to *Private Eye* caused astonishment among MPs and probably some embarrassment to his close associates. For when he surprisingly dragged in the name it drew attention to what has so far been a story which had only had a limited readership.

At this point the amazed *Daily Mail* reader might well have been forgiven for saying. 'Yes, and why?' Nothing daunted, the paper's lobby correspondent, that intrepid *ex officio* insider, continued his explanation:

> The *Private Eye* story alleged that official papers from 10 Downing Street were regularly delivered to the home of a member of Mr Wilson's staff . . . but that delivery of them was sometimes taken by another person who had nothing to do with the Government.

As a matter of fact, the magazine had said a great deal more than that. The report in question had been about the extraordinary influence which Marcia Williams exercised over Wilson. It had alleged:

1. That the Prime Minister's former Principal Private Secretary had (according to his widow) been driven to an early grave by Mrs Williams's tantrums.
2. That Mrs Williams had had two children with the *Daily Mail*'s then political correspondent, Walter Terry.
3. That it was Walter Terry who had taken in the red boxes at Mrs Williams's flat (the lease of which had been financed by Joseph Kagan, a man with KGB connections).

There was a certain amount here that might have been of mild interest to a keen-eyed journalist, but only two papers in the country even acknowledged the existence of the *Private Eye* story before John Peyton's question. The *Cornish Times* (on sale in the Isles of Scilly) said (26 April) that *Private Eye* had a sensational story about Marcia Williams, and that the magazine was on sale in Liskeard, 'one of the few places in Cornwall where you can buy it'. The only comment the paper made was to say, 'Women are allowed to fall in love surely, and fall in love the same as men.' The other paper was the *New Statesman*, an old adversary of *Private Eye*, although by this time it had a new editor, Anthony Howard. Ignoring all the more serious possibilities raised by the *Eye* story, the *New Statesman* chose to devote its front-page leader simply to attacking *Private Eye* for breach of privacy while repeating the details about Mrs Williams's family. The following week a *New Statesman* reader objected to Howard's own hypocrisy in both repeating the story and saying it should not have been published. Another letter, from Edward Mortimer, strongly supporting the *Eye*'s decision to publish, was not deemed worthy of inclusion.

In the case of Thorpe, police officers were determined to ensure that prosecutions were brought, despite the wishes of the Director of Public Prosecutions. So they leaked information not to Fleet Street, which was considered too tame, but to *Private Eye*, as the only way of forcing the issue. The *Private Eye* story 'The Ditto Man', which contained details about police interviews with Thorpe, was the final factor in persuading the DPP, Sir Tony Hetherington, that a prosecution was unavoidable. In another story, the Heyman case, where the identity of a former diplomat involved in 'child pornography' was protected, although the issues raised were thoroughly aired in all the papers after a story appeared in the *Eye*.

The *Sunday Telegraph*'s coverage of the Heyman story included one of the most unexpected compliments Fleet Street had ever paid *Private Eye*. Much of the story (of 22 March 1981) was devoted to the question of how *Private Eye* had obtained its facts.

> Within weeks of the committal hearing, the satirical magazine *Private Eye* published a detailed account of Sir Peter's activities. ... It is now clear that this came from a police officer. ... [Some officers believed there was] the beginning of a cover-up to protect the one distinguished man in the case. It led them to criticise the DPP Sir Tony Hetherington, and a private decision by an unidentified officer to organise a leak to *Private Eye*.

Considering what had previously happened in the Thorpe case, the police suspicions of a 'DPP cover-up' may not be thought entirely surprising. What clearly did not seem to occur to the writer of the *Sunday Telegraph* article was whether it was entirely dignified or satisfactory for a national newspaper to be trying to work out how 'a satirical magazine' was doing the national press's job for it. The only implication the piece seemed capable of sustaining was the old one – that if something had appeared first in *Private Eye* then it must be in some way illicit. In normal circumstances Fleet Street relies heavily on police sources. But it is an interesting sidelight thrown by the Thorpe and Heyman stories that in order for one faction of the state's prosecutors to get around another it had to circumvent the national press, which was itself considered too establishment-minded to work the trick.

One editor in Fleet Street appears to have noticed this possibility. Writing in *Punch* on 25 March 1981, William Deedes, editor of *The Daily Telegraph*, said:

> To found, to innovate in journalism is one of the peaks,

and a high one because the slopes have got steeper and slipperier and the air more rarified.... None of the legendary successes in journalism were achieved without risk – risk of offending, displeasing, or incurring wrath of transgressing the law or even getting the sack. You can't have success and security in journalism ... which is why the whining of some contemporaries about the unfairness of our laws on libel, contempt and official secrets strikes me as misconceived. ... If established newspapers seek too much security from law commissions, then the fieriest part (sic) of the torch may well pass to the *Canards* and *Eyes* of this world.

What Mr Deedes does not say is that as long as people like himself, who control part of Fleet Street, are happy to accept the present restrictions on press freedom represented by the laws of libel, contempt and official secrets, *Private Eye* will continue to be presented with a three-lap start every time a 'difficult' story breaks.

The last phase in *Private Eye*'s relations with Fleet Street has been more ambivalent than before. Richard Ingrams is now a highly acceptable figure in Fleet Street, and is a personal friend, for example, of Sir John Junor, the editor of the *Sunday Express*. The *Eye*'s use of classic Fleet Street figures such as Nigel Dempster and Peter McKay has caused the values of Fleet Street and Greek Street to resemble each other. This has not been universally welcomed by Greek Street veterans. John Wells is not enthusiastic. He compares McKay and Dempster to 'Ingrams's Dobermann pinschers'. 'From a position of unassailable morality Ingrams uses utterly immoral people to attack other people's morals. But if his Dobermanns ever bite him they get whipped. For instance, when Ingrams found that McKay was using *Eye* material in his *Mirror* column he inserted a reference to McKay in the "Grovel" column.' Wells sees the 'Grovel' cast-list as 'just the same as "Jennifer's Diary" but with abusive names'. He recalls a chant written by Belloc which was sometimes recited in Greek Street.

These are the things that people do not know.
They do not know because they are not told.

'The point should be,' says Wells, '*what* to tell them. Do you tell them about Rio Tinto Zinc or about some peer shagging a starlet?' In his view you cannot expect the Dobermanns to ask themselves this question, but it is time their master did so.

There are signs today that the brief fashion for serious investigative journalism is already over and that the press is once more trying to take itself even less seriously. If so, *Private Eye* is for once in step.

Private Eye now knows a lot about people in Fleet Street. As Peter Hillmore put it, 'People have a tendency, media people, before embarking on some course of action to ask themselves, "How would it look in the *Eye*?"' But the suggestion has also been made that some people in Fleet Street are now in a position to control whether or not a story appears in *Private Eye*. Reports in *Event*, compiled by various people, including Martin Tomkinson who had just left *Private Eye*, stated that McKay and Dempster had prevented a story appearing in *Private Eye* because it placed senior executives of the *Daily Mirror* in a bad light. Although the story which had allegedly been suppressed was hardly of sufficient interest to be printed in the first place, and although *Private Eye* denied that there had been any question of suppressing it, the relationship between Fleet Street and *Private Eye* on this occasion did look sufficiently close to have made suppression a possibility.

Pulling wings off flies 12

Forster's contribution to our present collective society is the reminder that it will become an arid and destroying desert if we remove the oasis of private life ... [but]. ... Does he feel that, in England at any rate, a younger generation is carrying the cult of privacy and personal relationships to the lengths of whimsicality and eccentricity? It often strikes one that far too large a portion of educated energy is going into running England as a kind of private joke, an ingenious personal crossword. We are more gentle with one another ... indeed ... we are bathed to the point of sleep in tolerance and understanding. Forsterian teaching has been taken on without our recognising that it had the virility of a reaction.

V. S. Pritchett, *Mr. Forster's Birthday*

Three criticisms of *Private Eye* are that it is heartless and cruel in its intrusions into private lives; that it is philistine; and that it is anti-semitic. The first of these was put most eloquently by Clive James, who said that it was extraordinary that Ingrams, who could write a book as sensitive as *God's Apology*,* could also edit a paper which 'sent people's children crying home from school'. Auberon Waugh responded in his 'Diary' of 12 May 1978.

Brooding over children, I fall into a gloom, Nobody ever stops to consider what effect all this publicity about Princess Margaret Rose's malarkey with 'Roddy' Llewellyn might have on her young children, the Viscount Linley aged 16, and the Lady Sarah Armstrong-Jones, who was 14 on May Day. ... It is probably time we had a law forbidding publication of any news or comment which might embarrass the young children of those concerned. I remember how a callous remark I once made at school about Attila the Hun caused Sir Ian Moncrieffe of that Ilk

---

*The story of a friendship shared by Malcolm Muggeridge, Hesketh Pearson and Hugh Kingsmill.

(a direct descendant of Attila's) to burst into uncontrollable sobs. In fact it would probably be better to suppress all news of any description rather than make a young child, anywhere, cry on the way home from school.

My only direct experience of the reaction of children to an attack on their parents was in the case of the late George Hutchinson, who once complained bitterly that whenever *Private Eye* referred to him as 'characteristically inspired' his son came *running* home from school, waving a copy of the paper, in order to laugh at him.

Be that as it may, it is true that many other of *Private Eye*'s attacks have drawn innocent blood. Michael Frayn noted this as long ago as 1963 when he made his satirical commissar 'Ron Knocker' say in *The Observer*:

> Far too much of *Private Eye*, for instance, is still devoted to ends other than wounding. The proportion is decreasing all the time, but the editors should bear in mind that what the public wants is not to be made to laugh or done good to in some nebulous way, but to see people hurt, hurt and hurt again.
>
> I am delighted to see that in the current issue there is an extended parody of *The Guardian* in which the criticisms of *The Guardian* itself are deliberately stale and second-hand, whereas the innuendoes against individual members of the staff are superbly personal, wounding, and irrelevant to their public functions. That, I think, shows the sense of values we should aim at.
>
> We certainly seem to have got the public beaten. A year or two ago, if we had ridiculed a man for being a drunk, or writing a flop, or having a detached retina, all the namby-pamby do-gooders would have whined. But nowadays everybody joins in the fun. Or at least looks the other way. Perhaps they are afraid of being hauled off and satirised themselves as the namby-pamby do-gooders that they are.
>
> It is strange now to think that our movement started by appealing to men's intelligence and sense of justice to laugh at injustice and stupidity. How limited that appeal was! How much more universal and powerful is our appeal to men's malice, resentment, destructiveness, and envy! And how much more successful we have become since we grasped that truth!

As time has passed *Private Eye* has tended to attack even more personally. Most journalists, as they get older and more

"... no I think there should be a law against it myself the way these newspapers pry into people's private lives I mean to say did you see that story the other day about that MP who's living with his secretary I mean who wants to read that sort of thing? surely what a chap does with his private life is his own affair don't you agree? take that story in yesterday's paper about that Lady Whatsername running off with that pop star what earthly interest is that to anybody I mean the fact that she's been spending weekends down at his houseboat in Marbella while her husband's been left on their Scottish farm with the three children apparently so I read somewhere else one of those boys was chucked out of Eton the eldest I think it was Alan I mean I can't understand people reading that stuff let alone the minds of people who WRITE it..."

influential, become like everyone else in that position; they are absorbed into the corrupt magic circle of 'insiders', friends and contacts who become used to working together and to fixing what does and does not get into print. They subscribe to E. M. Forster's code of 'personal relations'. Anthony Blunt, among others, has good reason to be grateful for that tendency. Ingrams has replied to the 'breach of privacy' criticism before, in the words of Cobbett:

> Amongst the persons whom I have heard express a wish to see the press what they call free, and at the same time to extend their restraints on it with regard to persons in their private lives ... I have never, that I know of, met with one who had not some powerful motive of his own for the wish, and who did not feel that he had some vulnerable part about himself.

Against Cobbett it might be said that after a number of years of conscious life all complete people must acquire a sense of vulnerability about *some* part of themselves. Nonetheless *Private Eye* has generally resisted the code of personal relations, though the editor strongly objects to disclosures about his own private life.

One example of the triumph of personal relations over critical judgement is provided by Bernard Levin. On the whole, over the years, Levin has approved of *Private Eye*. In 1966 he used to contribute occasionally, and say, 'Gentlemen, more power to your elbows'. In 1971, reviewing the history of the first ten years of *Private Eye*, he wrote in *The Observer*, 'the magazine was founded as an enemy of cant and humbug in every area of our public and semi-public life. By and large, they have waged single-minded and unafraid war on those enemies ever since. . . . Again and again, reading this compendium, I found myself shouting with laughter as a shot went home.' Even in 1979 Levin was quoted by James Cameron as follows: 'Amid the din of special pleading for special interests, the thunderous rustle of wool being pulled over eyes and the rattle of skeletons being hastily thrust back in closets, *Private Eye*'s savage sanity provides a just counterpart to the swineries in public life.' Yet a year later, at the time of Tynan's death, the paper, for Levin, ranked with the '*marchands d'ordure*'. What had happened?

Ingrams suggests that the change of attitude was for personal reasons. Levin had fallen in love with Arianna Stassinopoulos, who had been libelled in the *Eye* and had successfully sued for an apology and damages. He had also become a devotee of an Indian religious cult run by the Bhagwhan Shree Rajneesh, a religion which had been mercilessly mocked in *Private Eye* after the Bhagwhan ('Bagwash') had appeared on television.

Levin was so angered by this that he wrote to the *Spectator* to defend the guru and to say, 'I am sick of being lied about by Richard Ingrams who, himself corrupt, is unable to recognise honesty in [others] . . . dealing in dirty little bits of gossip now constitutes practically the whole of Ingrams's life.'

Finally Levin himself had obtained an apology from *Private Eye* for the false suggestion that he had arranged for the *Radio Times* to scrap a cover which showed an unflattering caricature of his face. In Ingrams's view people like Levin are all in favour of the *Eye* being 'savagely sane about special pleading and public swineries' until they themselves are interested or among the swine. They either want to be associated with the gang, and therefore to some extent protected by it, or they are against it.

Certainly there are some people who are protected by the *Eye*, but they do not include its founders, or even its present contributors. Of the founders, Booker, Rushton, Foot, Cook and Wells have all received unflattering mention at one time or another; only Osmond and Ingrams himself have remained virtually sacrosanct. Waugh has been mocked and has not been able to prevent the paper from attacking his friends; nor have Booker, Foot, Cook or Wells (despite attempting to do so). Even close friends of Ingrams such as Dr Peter Jay have been steadily attacked (by Ingrams) once they ventured too far into the public arena, in Jay's case into the Washington embassy.

In taking this line *Private Eye* is at least opposing the suffocating tendency, described by V. S. Pritchett in the passage quoted at the head of this chapter, to run the country as a cosy, private club. One factor here is the relative isolation of Ingrams and Waugh from metropolitan circles. George Orwell was once asked by Stephen Spender why he no longer attacked him, and Orwell replied:

Even if when I met you I had not happened to like you, I should still have been bound to change my attitude, because when you meet anyone in the flesh you realise immediately that he is a human being and not a sort of caricature embodying certain ideas. It is partly for this reason that I don't mix much in literary circles, because I know from experience that once I have met and spoken to anyone I shall never again be able to show any intellectual brutality towards him, even when I feel I ought to.

This is the assumption of the importance of personal contacts over mere ideas or principles which runs so deeply through English life. It could therefore be said in defence of *Private Eye*, when it is accused of intrusion, that one small institution is still kicking over the tables so invitingly laid by the mutual admiration societies of the world. Osmond remembers how Foot once returned from interviewing Enoch Powell, utterly shattered. 'He buried his head in his hands and kept moaning, "I liked him. Oh God, I *liked* him."' This did not however prevent Foot from savaging Powell in the subsequent book.

A further defence against the charge of intrusion is that several of the most important news stories covered by *Private Eye* during the seventies started life as gossip. They included the arrangements made by Harold Wilson to run his private office when he was Leader of the Opposition, the charges against Jeremy Thorpe, and the public position of Sir James Goldsmith.

The second criticism is that *Private Eye* is philistine. It has 'attacked' the music of Mahler. It is hostile to the taste of the fine arts commissars of television and the public galleries. Certainly the magazine is unlikely to be offered an Arts Council grant.* But its only regular coverage of the arts is in 'Pseud's Corner'.

The first pseud of 'Pseud's Corner' had been K. Tynan in November 1968, writing in glowing terms of a poem by Christopher Logue. Two of the other entries that week were from the work of Tony Palmer. The Corner has appeared in every issue since. Its occupants have included Germaine Greer, Paul Scott, Michael X, John Wells, V. S. Naipaul, Candida Lycett-Green, Rebecca West, Anthony Burgess, Christopher Booker, Auberon Waugh, Barry Fantoni, Bernard Levin, Laurie Lee, John Le Carré and most British art critics. Its monitors have included Osbert Lancaster, Roy Fuller, Graham Greene, Germaine Greer, Diana Quick, John Osborne, Anthony Blunt and Christopher Logue.

'Pseud's Corner' is the modern equivalent of the little boxes which were nailed up in the streets of Revolutionary France into which righteous citizens could drop their denunciations; except that now the denunciations are signed – usually by the man in the street, that is by the humble consumers of the culture which the experts are so anxious to monopolise or capture. The denunciation does not, then, rely for its effect on the status of the denouncer (unlike so many other pronouncements on literature and the arts), but on the evident absurdity of the material denounced once it is

---

* Wells and Ingrams did once apply for such a grant. As Wells recalls, 'This was shortly after Jennie Lee announced her intention, as a member of the Socialist Cabinet, of subsidising the arts in a new and imaginative way. Gnome announced his intention of applying for a grant in the 'Gnome' column and we got a letter from the Arts Council inviting Lord Gnome to present himself in person and make an application. Emanuel Strobes wrote back explaining his Lordship was out of the country and in the end Ingrams and I went along explaining that Emanuel Strobes was temporarily indisposed. The meeting was conducted with unblinking seriousness on both sides, the only smile crossing anyone's face when the Arts Council's representative who was called Eric White showed us out, noting in passing some modern sculptures hanging on the wall which he told us, equally po-faced, were made by filling contraceptives with plaster of Paris. The grant never materialised.'

removed from the protective self-importance of its original context.

The most irritating failure of 'Pseud's Corner' is the tendency to confuse the reporter of a pseud and the perpetrator of it. So, if someone interviews a pseud and signs the article, he is quite likely to find the quote he extracted from the pseud – probably knowingly – displayed above his own name in the Corner. This happened to Raymond Williams, although he did not consider the relevant quotation pseudish. Another occasional fault has been a failure to spot irony.

The knee-jerk reaction of those who are denounced in 'Pseud's Corner'* is to denounce the paper as 'philistine'. Clive James wrote as follows in *The Times Literary Supplement* in November 1972.

Since attacking *Private Eye* on a late night television show early in the year† I have found myself making regular trips to 'Pseud's Corner' – without passing 'Go' and without collecting £200. Before I called it an institution no less comfortably placed than the College of Heralds, *Private Eye* had never heard of me.... After I called it that, suddenly I was as dear to the magazine as Sir Basil Spence.... *Private Eye*'s crusade against barbarism is decisively hobbled by its own philistinism, and even though its editor undeniably knows how to put one of his own sentences together, it doesn't necessarily follow that he's equipped to criticize one of mine. The general assumption that 'Pseud's Corner' is somehow the arbiter of what is semantically acceptable simply goes to show that we live in an age of poltroonery. I, for one, will be damned before allowing *Private Eye* to be the measure of anything.... The magazine is richer than it was and will probably continue until Doomsday – but let it continue, for heaven's sake, without our respect. For every fact it unearthed, it unleashed an untruth; for every guru it unmasked, it set up a shaman; for every injustice it condemned, it condoned a snobbery. *Private Eye*'s enviable flexibility of stance was always dependent on its having no brains. Now it has disappeared into success, where it belongs.

*The art critic Marina Vaizey once referred to *Private Eye*'s writers as 'art haters to a man', without mentioning that she has frequently been sent to the Corner.

†*Private Eye* subsequently noted that James had appeared in 'Pseud's Corner' *before* he attacked *Private Eye* on television.

Pulling wings off flies

And the characteristic mode of determinism is not investigation by criticism, but justification by description: an intellectual mode which might just as well be called anti-intellectual, since no matter how much information it aspires to deal with it can never arrive at a judgement. The rock culture grew up in a mental vacuum; and the fact that it grew at all - and grew so fast - was in itself sufficient proof of the aesthetic truism that creativity is a primal urge, antecedent to rational mentality.
CLIVE JAMES
CREAM

The merest moments in Tolstoy can take your breath away, as when you are suddenly shown a beautiful, self-possessed young lady at a soiree falling in love with her own arm. Pitiless is the wrong word for such a vision: it is simply, inescapably, pure.
CLIVE JAMES
SUNDAY TIMES

Her poems are tall drinks for grown-ups: the best ones are like swallowing a rainbow.
CLIVE JAMES
OBSERVER

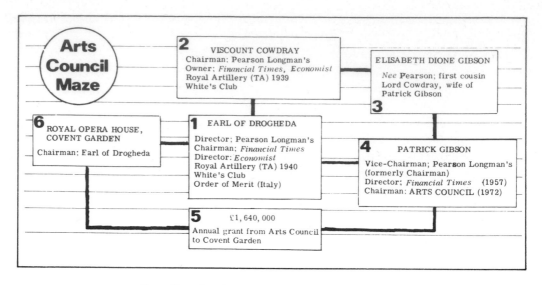

Arts Council Maze

2 VISCOUNT COWDRAY
Chairman: Pearson Longman's
Owner; *Financial Times, Economist*
Royal Artillery (TA) 1939
White's Club

ELISABETH DIONE GIBSON
Nee Pearson; first cousin
Lord Cowdray, wife of
Patrick Gibson
3

6 ROYAL OPERA HOUSE, COVENT GARDEN
Chairman: Earl of Drogheda

1 EARL OF DROGHEDA
Director; Pearson Longman's
Chairman; *Financial Times*
Director: *Economist*
Royal Artillery (TA) 1940
White's Club
Order of Merit (Italy)

4 PATRICK GIBSON
Vice-Chairman; Pearson Longman's
(formerly Chairman)
Director; *Financial Times* (1957)
Chairman: ARTS COUNCIL (1972)

5 £1,640,000
Annual grant from Arts Council
to Covent Garden

Standing in the Corner can be a painful experience, it seems. But apart from the slanging match between 'pseuds' and 'philistines', *Private Eye* also inaugurated another campaign against the arts. This was the exposure of the pretentious, wealthy and agile group of people who control contemporary patronage

In May 1975 James decided to defend his friend and patron Charles Osborne, the Arts Council's literature director who had been criticised for giving a £12,000 grant to *his* friend, Ian Hamilton, to run the *New Review* – a magazine to which Osborne himself contributed under a pseudonym. James's argument turned on the following point: 'As to the *New Review*'s contents, only people with a literary background are competent to judge and the only *Eye* staff member even partly in possession of such a background is Auberon Waugh.'

With that sentence James encapsulated 'the poltroonery' of academic literature and institutional patronage. The best reply to the James' position was made by Evelyn Waugh, writing in *Spectator* in February 1956.

In a civilised society everyone is a critic.... Even in the happiest days of the past it was only a small part of the population who fostered arts and graces. That world still exists and is the proper milieu of the writer. In that world the most acute and influential criticism is uttered in private conversation by people with no identifiable qualifications. ... Is Mr Wain [John Wain, his protagonist] totally unaware of the existence of these critics? Does he regard them as imposters because they have not taken classes in

204

English Literature? Does he really believe that one must hold a diploma from some kind of college before one can voice an opinion?

To the criticism that *Private Eye* is anti-semitic Ingrams replies that it is no more anti-semitic than it is anti-any other minority. He told Ann Leslie of the *Daily Mail* that he thought the Jews had 'become much too sensitive; they should be more tolerant of criticism, as they used to be.' Anne Leslie interpreted this to mean that he yearned for a Golden English Age, 'when Jews knew their place and laughed bravely when called "yids"'; not a word *Private Eye* has ever used, though quite a useful one for adding a little red racialist meat to Miss Leslie's article.

Others, apart from Zionists, who accuse *Private Eye* of anti-semitism are those who are attacked by it. Esther Rantzen once seriously claimed that *Private Eye* only wrote about her husband, Desmond Wilcox, because she herself was 'both a successful woman and a Jew'. Sir James Goldsmith also tried to explain the *Eye*'s hostility on the grounds that he was a Jew. The *Jewish Chronicle* was not very impressed. Its columnist Ben Azai wrote on 13 May 1977: 'Apart from an intermittent concern about Israel, Goldsmith was only vaguely aware of his Jewishness until *Private Eye* began what he regarded as a personal vendetta against him. Scratch a semi-Jew and one will discover a full one.'

There is a fourth criticism of *Private Eye*, which may by now be impossible to answer, since it springs from the magazine's success in its struggle to survive. It was delivered by Graham Greene in 1968, in the *New Statesman*, in the course of reviewing Patricia Cockburn's book *The Years of The Week*.

> . . . while *The Week* survived without libel actions because there were no printers to prosecute and nothing to seize against the costs of the action but a secondhand shoelace, *Private Eye*, by becoming a valuable property, has made libel actions worth while. Behind *The Week* was one enthusiastic truth-diviner at the service of increasingly communistic beliefs. When Cockburn wrote that the king had no clothes, his opinion had to be treated with respect: one felt sure that more often than not he had good evidence for the king's nudity. But the comic pages of *Private Eye* clash with the inside news – Lord Gnome is necessarily a figure we cannot trust, and the statement in his pages that

the king is naked may be only another Spike Milliganism. One doubts whether *Private Eye* could have so nearly played an important part in the Abdication Crisis or been able to hound Howeson, the Tin King, into the Old Bailey dock. . . . I have an uneasy feeling that under the same circumstances a small notice might have appeared in *Private Eye* regretting some minor inaccuracy in its report on the Tin King. I don't think *The Week* ever apologised to anyone. Success in journalism can be a form of failure. Freedom comes from lack of possessions. A truth-divulging paper must imitate the tramp and sleep under a hedge.

A faint holiness? 13

The struggle between Ingrams and Goldsmith revealed much about the characters of both men. Both came close to ruin as a result of it. Goldsmith was transformed into a national figure but it cannot be said that he emerged from the business in a stronger position than he entered it. Ingrams said that throughout the case he had an eerie feeling that Goldsmith rather wanted 'to be Ingrams'. This to some extent came true when Goldsmith, unable to buy a newspaper or a magazine, launched his own magazine, *Now!*, a disastrous venture which culminated in him leaving the country in a state of some humiliation. After the settlement Ingrams published an account of the campaign from his point of view, *Goldenballs*. Goldsmith commissioned a book on the same subject from the trials historian Montgomery Hyde. Mr Hyde was paid an embarrassingly large sum, but although Goldsmith said he was very pleased with the result the book never appeared.

On the other hand, just as Goldsmith began to resemble Ingrams, so the opposite happened. As the battle progressed it was widely said in Fleet Street that 'Ingrams and Goldsmith were made for each other in heaven.' Actually Fleet Street, though too circumspect for the most part to get involved, was on the side of *Private Eye*; it had to be. But though Ingrams and Goldsmith did not become identical people, there is no doubt that Ingrams was changed by his experience. The drastic side of his character became more evident. Goldsmith was a much rougher customer than *Private Eye* had previously dealt with.

The two men come from different backgrounds. Goldsmith traces his family back to the sixteenth century when the Goldschmidts were merchant bankers in Frankfurt connected with the Rothschilds. They then moved to Paris, and by 1870 had a London branch called Bischoffsheim and Goldschmidt. Goldsmith's father, Major Frank Goldsmith, was brought up in Suffolk. He went to Magdalen College, Oxford, was called to the Bar and was then elected to the LCC. In 1910 he became Conservative MP for Stowmarket. He served in the Suffolk Yeomanry in the First World War, was decorated with the Legion of Honour, but was then removed by the British to the Dardanelles because they were suspicious of his German connections. After the war Major Goldsmith took umbrage over this treatment and moved to France where he bought three hotels. There he met Goldsmith's mother, Marcelle Mouiller, the daughter of a French peasant farmer from the Auvergne. Goldsmith is therefore a French citizen (as well as a British subject) and is fluent in French. During the war Goldsmith was evacuated to the Bahamas, and then to Canada. In 1944 he was crammed at Millfield in order to get into Eton. He was no good at games so at Eton he took to gambling. At the age of sixteen he won £8000 on an accumulator and left school. After that he became a waiter in Paris, and then graduated to being deputy head of the *hors d'oeuvres* trolley at the Palace Hotel in Madrid. He ended up £2000 in debt and had to return to England where his father paid his debts provided he did his national service. His childhood ended in 1954 when, at the age of twenty, he eloped with Isabel Patino, the eighteen-year-old heiress to a £75 million tin-mining fortune. It was a story which made national headlines. His wife died four months later of a brain tumour. His father died in 1967, having spent most of the family fortune. By that time Goldsmith had founded Cavenham Foods and was on the way to making a fortune of his own.

The only resemblance between Ingrams and Goldsmith is that Ingrams also comes from a banking family, his maternal grandmother was a Baring. Ingrams's father, as a young man, had flown a private aeroplane between the towers of Munich Cathedral. He was a Germanophile and a merchant banker who ran the black propaganda department during the war. He died in 1953 before Ingrams really got to know him. (Rushton and Osmond also lost their fathers when they were young.) Two of Ingrams's three brothers have died, and his youngest son died aged six.

Over the years, Ingrams's nature has changed considerably. As a young man he was an unforgettable sight, once described by James Fenton in the *New Statesman*. 'His face ... [for the student of character] poses an absorbing problem of interpretation – what are those expressions that disturb its uneven surface? Was that a smile? Was that interest, annoyance, worry, fear?* The lines change, and the

---

* No, says Ingrams. It was the expression of a man attempting to simulate interest in the conversation of James Fenton.

troubled eyes do not reveal their secret. It's like catching a badger in the headlights: before you can slow down, the animal has escaped into the undergrowth.'

This facial dumb-show, a curious sequence of billowing expressions unrelated to conscious stimuli, tends to transfix other members of the company, who can be further disconcerted by the silences. Ingrams is a master of the strategic silence. One moment he is making a joke and the centre of a happy group; the next someone else is talking, the moment comes to react, everyone reacts and then a yawning gap opens up in a corner of the room. Ingrams is lying doggo. Then, just when they think that he may be about to lay an egg, Ingrams is off again, a fully *compos* member of the conversation. Simpler souls can be made to feel very uncomfortable by these methods.

Those habits have not changed, but in other ways the middle-aged Ingrams – he is now forty-five – could be a different man. In 1966 Ingrams used to drink, smoke, make a lot of noise, make ribald remarks which caused girls to giggle, and generally give the impression of being a highly irresponsible, not to say contented, member of the human race. The sheer high spirits of the office in those days were entirely to his taste and very largely his creation. Some afternoons he would skive off to watch *flamenco*. Others he would fall into a light sleep over an empty bottle of whisky. Where he gave the impression of a deep self-control it was only against the possibility that, if he ever let go, he would end up in the Trafalgar Square fountain, splashing policemen. He was a kind, thoughtful and cheerful employer. And he rarely opened his mouth except to make people laugh. Unlike many professional humourists, one had no sense of strain about listening to his jokes. He was not giving a non-stop performance, he was simply an extremely funny man.

Then, in 1967, Ingrams went off the booze. He was told that if he did not stop drinking he would shortly die. Other drinkers have been puzzled by this diagnosis, but Ingrams believed it. He went home to Berkshire, took some sickening pills, took to his bed for three weeks, and returned to London an abstentionist. The drama of this abrupt convers probably appealed to him.

He is now a lonely, public campaigner against the 'Gay Rights' movement. (Tony Rushton wonders whether 'something nasty' happened to him during his national service.) As for heterosexuality, Alan Watkins formed the impression that he has a horror of marital infidelity, a misdemeanour which he castigates regularly in *Private Eye*.

John Wells and Andrew Osmond both remember the family pressure Ingrams had from the start to 'go and get a proper job', pressure which continued far into the years when *Private Eye* was a success and which it must have required a considerable stubbornness to resist. For Ingrams *Private Eye* has been his escape route from 'the bank'. Wells says that he

... has considerable leadership qualities and would probably have made a good politician, although he tends to run the office more as a gang leader. He is not really open to discussion. He can't argue and he can't admit error. But it is a very lonely job and he is probably on the edge of his nerves a lot of the time. I would like to think that he was my best friend, but his shyness and his pride do make him extremely difficult. He is far *less* sure of himself than he appears. He does not give credit, he does not like his friends writing plays and he does not want them to succeed. It's all a question of what he sees as disloyalty to *Private Eye*. The fact that *l'Etat c'est moi* applies, I mean that disloyalty to the *Eye* means disloyalty to him personally, is something he is slow to recognise. He once told someone that he disapproved of me because I was no longer 'a pure hack'. There is a good deal of self-denigration in his denigration of others.

Wells is not impressed with the view that Ingrams is in some way 'outside society'. He remembers a party which Ann Fleming gave at Brooks's for Angus Wilson. It was crowded with figures from the Ingrams' demonology: Pamela Hartwell, Diana Cooper, Edward Heath. Ingrams walked in on an impulse and was immediately the centre of attention. People clustered around him in admiring groups. 'He ended up walking out of Brooks's wearing a laurel wreath that Ann Fleming had meant to present to Angus Wilson.'

Of the original founders, Andrew Osmond has drifted furthest from *Private Eye*.

Nowadays I tend to wince for the victims, who often seem small, inoffensive people. In that sort of case, especially when the story is wrong, the consequences are rather troubling. A paper going to press is like a military unit in battle. One man has to make instant, irrevocable decisions; no glimmer of doubt is permissible. The best papers are always the product of an autocrat's whims. Certainly that's how it is at *Private Eye*. Once Richard leaves, the magazine we know will wither away. It may survive in name, but it will be no more recognisable than Beaverbrook's *Express* today.

The price of this editorial style, of course, is a lack of independent voices. There is Logue, and there is Waugh, but the rest is tightly strapped into Richard's own world view, which can get a little predictable. It would be nice to see a few more breezes blow between pages 1 and 24.

His effect as editor is obvious. What is less often discussed is the effect on him of the job. The pressures are intense, and get no less so with time. He is often so tired he looks in need of a doctor. This makes him favour the old routines, and regular suppliers of dependable stuff will stand very high in his affections. He likes to keep people in their slot – the slot which is useful to him. His life is so demanding, so surrounded by enemies, that he draws heavily on the praise and support of his friends, and can sometimes forget to give the same back in equal measure. And of course he's been going so long he gets bored. He lashes out to keep himself interested.

Fame is the other thing the job has brought him, and he enjoys it, there's no doubt of that, perhaps rather more than a satirist should, certainly as much as some of those he attacks. In his own mind, I suspect, his status as a British Public Figure is one in the eye for all those who said he was wasting his talents in youth.

Most of *Private Eye*'s contributors have had experience of Ingrams's ruthlessness. Barry Fantoni was put out when, during a media campaign to make the poet E. J. Thribb into a national figure – on which Fantoni did most of the work – the editor suddenly went on the radio and announced that Thribb was dead. Bill Tidy was disappointed when Ingrams killed off 'The Cloggies'. 'Ingrams started "The Cloggies" and Ingrams finished them,' he said. The explanation was that Ingrams had decided that they were getting boring and asked for some new characters. Tidy, who was not bored with them, had gone so far as to introduce a new Cloggie with a beard. But after a while, the bearded Cloggie just disappeared. All the other Cloggies eventually disappeared as well. Michael Heath, who spends more time in the *Eye* office than any other cartoonist, still cannot count on much room for manoeuvre. Following the appearance of a drawing for the 'Great Bores' series, which was set in a sauna bath and considered by the editor to be improper, there was an interruption in the series.

However, both Fantoni and Paul Foot say that Ingrams is notable among editors in taking trouble with cartoonists. 'He

A drawing for the 'Great Bores' series which mysteriously appeared despite an editorial ban, causing a temporary froideur *between editor and cartoonist.*

is the only editor I know who really cares about drawings,' says Fantoni. 'He does not need an art director. The prominence he gives to artists is unusual.'

Foot remembers the hours Ingrams spent with David Austin and John Kent in order to work out some idea which would be suitable for *Private Eye*. He also thinks he is unusual for recognising the possibilities of unexpected contributors like Germaine Greer. Foot says,

I think he is a brilliant editor, although I can't bear his prejudices, which get worse as he gets older. In fact his pig-headedness is a tremendous advantage to him. He is immune to criticism and antagonistic to it. He hates office democracy. That is a strong position. He has a very sharp critical judgement of other people's work. The whole thing depends so much on him that it is inconceivable to imagine it operating without him.

Private Eye is a weathervane of middle-class opinion. As far as I am concerned this is a criticism. But I like its independence. The paper is still admirable. It never could have been left wing. But again and again it comes out on top, because he will publish things that other people won't. But if you're going to be a powerful satirical magazine your targets must be different from the rest of the media. You should attack the strong, not the weak. And under Booker's influence there is a tendency just to add a satirical gloss to *The Daily Telegraph*. For instance, I don't believe that *Private Eye* would attack Winston Churchill now as they did in 1962. Booker has gone through a 180° turn since then.

Recently the paper has become parochial. When someone turns up with a good foreign story it will go in, but it is so piecemeal. He doesn't have any good back-up people in the office who can follow up stories. He needs a few radical people who he can trust and who will answer him back. Richard's answer is in the sales figures of course. He just says 'Balls to you all'.

He's amazingly thick-skinned. He can ride out all sorts of public and private crises. Most of us are plagued by doubt in our judgements. But Richard, never. That is his strength and his weakness.

Auberon Waugh originally suggested that this book should include a chapter of psychological analysis on Ingrams. When asked what he would contribute to it, he thought for a bit, then said: 'I think he romanticises the working classes. He thinks back to his days in the Royal Army Educational Corps, and sees them as rows of earnest faces trying to spell "cat".'

Two qualities which are worth emphasising are Ingrams's humour, which always disarms criticism, and his likeableness. Candida Lycett-Green says, 'I am always having to defend him to those of my friends who don't know him. It's difficult to explain how wonderful he is, but he exudes goodness and a faint holiness.'

Holiness or not, he has a captivating charm, since the severest critics among his old friends will always respond to his re-proffered friendship after a bitter disagreement. His greatest quality as an editor is his judgement. This is something that has grown with the job. Again and again when the paper has been faced with the most appalling legal threats, Ingrams has charted the course ahead, taking advice if it suited him but analysing the risks largely by himself and usually very accurately. He also stands solidly behind his contributors.

His most baffling weakness is his reluctance to give credit to the work of others. No one can take from him the fact that he is the single most important figure in the creation of *Private Eye*, a paper which reflects his strengths and weaknesses in every issue. But he is not the only person who created it. He has been assisted in particular by Booker, Fantoni, Wells, Cook, Heath, Foot and Waugh. And he sometimes seems oddly reluctant to acknowledge that.

During the Goldsmith case he seemed to seek an unnecessary degree of isolation, becoming more and more difficult to talk to as the pressure increased. This not only proved irritating for others involved in *Private Eye*'s interests, but must have hampered everyone's efforts to some extent. John Wells says, 'the fact that he does not drink means that he never confides or confesses. That makes a real gap between him and others.'

He keeps a life-size cut out of Sir James in his office even today, six years on. When strangers first catch sight of it, behind the door, they invariably jump.

The last few years are too fresh in the memory to be seen as part of a pattern. To some extent the paper still seems to be living in the shadow of the excitement of the Goldsmith case. Its investigative side has declined and there have been more personal attacks on relatively trivial figures. The editor has ploughed an increasingly lonely furrow, but sales have reached the insane figure of 191,000.

Paul Foot's brief return in 1978, from Issue 438, was followed by a predictable improvement in the standard of *Private Eye*'s investigations. He had been with *Socialist Worker* since leaving in 1972. When the Thorpe story started to develop there was 'a slight reluctance' to pursue it at *Socialist Worker* 'because the Norman Scott aspect was considered to be anti-gay. *Socialist Worker*,' says Foot, 'was not in the foreground of exposing Thorpe because it was reluctant to be associated with anything that might look like gay bashing.'* However this was not the reason why Foot wrote the story for *Private Eye*. The source of most of the information wanted it in the *Eye*, he was not in the least interested in anything appearing in *Socialist Worker*. The story was of particular interest to Foot, who described it as a new departure, 'the introduction of allegations of criminal violence into British politics'.

Foot now considers that it was a mistake for him to go back. He found on his return that the political mood on the paper had changed and was against him. 'I didn't resent that. But I was never given the freedom to shape my own pages again, so it wasn't a very successful year. I just drifted back

---

* This placed *Socialist Worker* in exactly the same position as the national press, and made it just as useless to its readers.

Colonel Mad and Lester Piggott.

really and Ingrams always believes that everyone always goes back to *Private Eye*. After a year, in 1979, I was approached by Mike Molloy to do a column on the *Daily Mirror* and I had no hesitation in leaving again.'

Another column which ended during this period was *Private Eye*'s only attempt at racing coverage – 'Colonel Mad' written by Jeffrey Bernard. Like 'In the City', much of this had been incomprehensible to outsiders, but it caused the paper to be bought and widely read in racing circles. In October 1978 Bernard had written to point out that 'Grovel' had repeated one of his stories in the very next issue and to complain bitterly about the slovenly sub-editing of his column. 'If there are three things I despise,' he wrote, 'they are drunkenness, slipshod reporting and lazy sub-editing.' His last column appeared in December 1980 after a three-year run, and a brief stay in the Radcliffe Infirmary, Oxford. He had been suffering from alcoholism and diabetes and the hospital placed him on a strict diet. He was discharged by the matron after being caught *in flagrante delicto* with a strawberry jam sandwich. In 1981, talking to *Ritz* magazine, Bernard was asked about the ending of the 'Colonel Mad' column and said: 'I feel very sour about that now. I don't think they appreciated what Colonel Mad did for them in the racing world. . . . The worst thing about people who work for *Private Eye* is that they lack a sense of humour.'

The 'Grovel' column was the most frequent ground for complaint by those who considered that the *Eye* was going downmarket. In the view of Booker the seventies had seen a steady coarsening in the editorial standards. 'There was the arrival of the hacks [Dempster and McKay] and more stories about the media. There was also a growing streak of cruelty in the gossip, which can be traced through the development of "Grovel".' And it was mainly of 'Grovel' that Peter Cook was thinking when he said, 'Nobody could argue for the whole of *Private Eye*. I don't think even Ingrams could justify it all.' Paul Foot also objected to the pointless vindictiveness of some of the gossip and was strongly opposed to a story about Erin Pizzey which described the founder of the movement for 'battered wives' hostels' as 'a vast pudding' and a 'Lard Mountain'. This story stated that Mrs Pizzey was separated from her own husband and had just given him a severe financial mauling.

At one point Ingrams decided that his Dobermanns were getting rather out of hand and managed to set them all at each other's throats by persuading them to start writing stories about each other in their own newspapers. This scrap involved Dempster (*Daily Mail*), McKay (*Daily Mirror*), Carla Dobson (*Daily Mail*) and Olga Maitland (*Sunday Express*) and culminated in a stately letter from the latter. In his defence 'Grovel' could claim an historic scoop. In 1978 he reported a love affair between the Prince of Wales and his eventual bride's older sister.

It would not be right to suggest that the *Eye*'s new standards were set entirely by 'Grovel'. There was throughout this period the growing use of 'The Curse of Gnome', which began to resemble a scar tissue left over from the Goldsmith case. In March 1979, the newly recruited staff of *Now!* magazine were placed under the curse, including Patrick Hutber. Eight issues later the first death was reported among them, although this report later turned out to be a case of over-eagerness on the part of the Dobermanns. Then Patrick Hutber did die and Waugh crowed about the accident he had had while he was still dangerously ill. *Now!*'s editor, Antony Shrimsley, reponded to this by describing Waugh's article as a 'piece of undiluted evil', a 'wicked piece' in which he

set out calculatedly and deliberately to cause deep distress to Patrick Hutber's family.... He is publicly expressing the hope or purported conviction that others who work for this organisation will also face death or injury.... My charge against Mr Waugh and Mr Ingrams is that they are ... not muckrakers but muckmakers. The lies, half truths and sheer inventions of *Private Eye* are now so all-pervading that it is impossible for any non-informed reader to disentangle whatever fact may be buried beneath them. It serves no more to inform or expose than hard pornography. Mr Ingrams is not just some puritanical eccentric who plays the church organ for relaxation. He is an evil-doer. Instead of paying him to write in respected journals such as the *Sunday Telegraph* or the *Spectator* editors should shun his company.

Let me therefore sum up. I have said of Mr Auberon Waugh and Mr Richard Ingrams that they are wicked men. That they are liars motivated by malice who do not deserve either to be employed as journalists or to share the company of decent people. If they do not like what I have said they can always seek a remedy in the courts. My defence will be a plea of justification.

The sequel to this piece was rather different to the one it proposed. Editors did not shun either Waugh or Ingrams, on the contrary. It was Mr Shrimsley's brother, Bernard, rather than Waugh or Ingrams, who had recourse to the courts, in an action against Waugh which was later settled on payment of small damages. And on the point of lying, *Private Eye* conducted a lengthy investigation which suggested that *Now!* magazine's sales figures were erroneously high. However, as a passionate expression of outraged grief, the Antony Shrimsley piece remained unchallenged. Auberon Waugh has since said that hating people like him can help a widow through her bereavement.

There was further mention of 'The Curse' in the case of Ken Tynan, whose death, after a long illness, was reported by 'Grovel' in August 1980. He had issued a libel writ against *Private Eye* seven years before. Bernard Levin commented in *The Times*: 'The *marchands d'ordure* naturally sank to the occasion. ... *Private Eye* also stayed firmly in character; its contribution consisted of an anecdote, invented for the occasion, about masturbation.' Certainly there is something primitive about the apparatus of 'The Curse', as though the editor, by passing evil on, were avoiding it himself.

With the departure of Foot in 1979, new standards also seem to have been set for the *Eye*'s reporting. Ingrams has said that checking many stories is a waste of time, since they are simply denied and that is the end of the matter. Instead, he relies on 'the ring of truth', does the story have it or not when rapped lightly and placed next to his ear. There are a number of disadvantages to this method. For instance, in Issue 444 a story in 'Grovel' implied that Lord Kagan was a sinister and powerful figure who could arrange to tap people's phones for reasons of private sexual enjoyment. This must have had 'the ring of truth'. In the following issue a story that Kagan was merely an incompetent buffoon had the same quality. In Issue 447 something must have gone wrong with the editor's ear because several stories which had rung true were almost immediately found to be otherwise. Conor Cruise O'Brien was *not* to be sacked by *The Observer* 'in the very near future' ('Colour Section' lead). And Henry Keswick did *not* hold 'a showdown meeting' with the staff of the *Spectator* ('Grovel'). In Issue 453 it was stated by 'Grovel' that Tina Brown was *not* to become editor of *The Tatler*. The *Eye* also announced that *The Sunday Times* had discovered that their passionately Arabist correspondent David Holden, who had been murdered by persons unknown in Cairo, was an Israeli agent. This was corrected in the following issue. Anyone can get stories wrong (even I may once have erred). But it was an odd thing to suppose that the last of the above examples ever carried 'the ring of truth'.

In 1979 *Private Eye* also started to carry savage attacks on nonentities or relatively obscure figures on moral grounds, where the element of public interest was rather less obvious than it had been in the case of Poulson or Goldsmith. A campaign was started to expose homosexual clergymen in a column called 'Church Times, by The Devil'. This reached a shambolic climax in 1980 with a story about Canon Burgess, formerly the domestic bursar at University College, Oxford – the editor's old college. No fewer than ten people who wrote to *Private Eye* had letters or telegrams published in the following issue defending Burgess from the charges against him, and there were two more in the issue after that. One, from Desmond Shawe-Taylor, described the *Eye* story as 'insane libels'. In March an unusually thorough apology appeared in the paper. It read as follows:

> In our issue of 18 February 1980 we published a scurrilous and, indeed, vicious, piece about Rev. Canon David Burgess. We thought our information to be reliable. It turns out to have been totally false.
>
> The trouble is that our readers are apt to think that there is no smoke without fire'. If that is the rule this is the total exception to it. Publication of this piece was a disastrous mistake.

PRIVATE EYE

No. 236
Friday
1 Jan.'71

2/-

The article was so offensive to David Burgess's honour and integrity that an apology might seem futile. However, we give it in the fullest measure and sincerely hope that the inevitable damage to his reputation will be minimised by this apology and retraction. We have, of course, paid David Burgess substantial damages.

This was scarcely the spirit of 'Footnotes' or 'In the City'. In particular it is hard to see how a story to the discredit of a man who is previously completely unknown can or cannot have 'the ring of truth'. The fact seems to have been that the story was supplied by an unreliable informant who got it all wrong. Considerable efforts were made to check its validity *after* it was published, but none of them proved of any help.

In contrast to the almost somnambulistic way in which 'The Curse of Gnome' and 'Church Times by The Devil' made their appearance, there were some more impressive investigations. This was particularly obvious in the different treatments given to the Thorpe story and to the aftermath of the Goldsmith case. In Issue 460 the *Eye*, having wrongly identified an unfortunate man thought to have signed on for Goldsmith at *Now!*, corrected itself in these worlds. 'It seems that there were two hacks in Fleet Street called Paul Pickering and the one who fell to his death (last issue) was not the one joining Sir Jams. Still, this is no reason for the surviving Pickering to be too cocky. He would be well advised to step very carefully in the months to come ...' It was hard to believe that this paragraph could appear in the same paper as the absorbing back-page inquiry into the finances of the Liberal Party.

During all this time the Thorpe camp was engaged in an energetic cover-up, and there is little doubt that it would have succeeded had it not been for the *Eye*'s consistently accurate leaks. After one of the most damaging installments – 'The Ditto Man' in August 1978 – Thorpe even tried to get an inquiry launched. His objection was not that the *Eye*'s story had been wrong, but that it had been right. This, he claimed, was further cause for outrage and public concern. Even Thorpe's acquittal, reported in July 1979, seemed something of a triumph for the *Eye*. There was further detailed reporting, of the trial and the backstage deals between prosecution and defence which had preceded the 'not guilty' verdict, and *Private Eye* was about the only paper in a position to print the comments of Auberon Waugh: 'It was the Press which collected the evidence against him, the Press which forced the DPP to prosecute, and the Press which

Up to a point, Lord Gnome 1977–1981

Opposite: *The Thorpe affair was not the first glimpse* Eye *readers had enjoyed of Norman Scott. When Mr Scott became notorious it was discovered that the naked bottom in the background of this 1971 cover had been supplied by the celebrated male model and dog lover.* Private Eye *thereby secured another exclusive; a picture of Mr Scott's bottom.*

SIEGE MAN SAYS "I WILL NEVER QUIT"

by Our Crime Reporter
ADOLF HITMAN

Thousands of hacks today surrounded the National Liberal Club, where the so-called "former Liberal Leader", Mr Jeremy Thorpe, 47, has barricaded himself in for the past two years in a desperate attempt to "clear his name".

For weeks now, hordes of 'male models', lorry drivers, former Liberal treasurers and other underworld characters have been pleading with Thorpe to "give himself up".

Machete Man

But the beleaguered Liberal refuses to budge. Today, looking unshaven and ashen-faced, he appeared briefly on the window-ledge to shout abuse at the hordes of 'investigative journalists' who have been pursuing him for many months in the hope of establishing a connection between Mr Thorpe, Mr Andrew Newton, the late Sir Eric Miller, the late Sir Harold Wilson, Mr Sam Silkin and Lady Forkbender.

ruined the Crown case by waving money at the witnesses.'

Commenting on the decline in the investigative side of *Private Eye*, Michael Gillard says that 'you only need five good stories a year, and then keep them running.' This may be true on a 'mothball' basis but it would hardly be enough to establish a reputation in the first place. During this period at least two other *Eye* stories 'came true'. Detective Chief-Superintendent John Groves, one of Eric Miller's friends, was convicted of corruption, and Desmond Wilcox was exposed as a plagiarist in 1975. Wilcox resigned from the BBC in 1980 after the Corporation had paid out £60,000 in costs and damages for breach of copyright. He then had the impudence to sue *Private Eye* and *win*. The judge found that the plagiarism was 'guileless', and that the BBC were to blame.

The readers again made an essential contribution. They were not all satisfied by the new preoccupations of the magazine. 'Hawkeye' J. B. Easson wrote to point out that *Private Eye* had plagiarised itself by printing in January 1978 a 'Letter from Moscow' which 'bore a remarkable resemblance' to a Letter from Moscow that was printed in June 1977. One word had been altered. Mr Easson's letter was not universally welcomed in the office since the person responsible for this cock-up (myself) had until then been the only one to have noticed it. Christopher Meakin wrote a savagely critical letter in December 1977.

> Sir,
> You might feel that was some pretty smart reporting . . . to deride Wrigley's . . . for launching a chewing gum containing a new sugar substitute . . . which is now under suspicion for causing cancer. . . . Each time another sugar substitute is seen off a glow of quiet triumph and relief radiates from the American sugar industry lobby. . . . If you want to read who are the true villains of the piece I can thoroughly recommend a well-researched and totally un-challenged article in a one-time investigative magazine called *Private Eye* [on the cyclamate ban] . . .

The headline on this letter which referred back to one of Foot's classic efforts was 'Quite Right'.

Another letter was headed 'A Father Writes':

> Sir,
>
> Subject: Grovel's recent article

If a girl resists one's advances, it is reassuring if somewhat puerile, to persuade oneself that 'she has just come back from a trip to the Isle of Lesbos', rather than face the psychologically unacceptable possibility that she might simply find one repulsive. However, only one who is so devoid of any normally recognised human qualities that his fragile ego rests exclusively on his ability to seduce young girls would find it psychologically necessary to put this reassuring thought to paper and publish it in a popular magazine.

May I suggest that your correspondent grows up, learns manners, develops some human qualities and keeps a long way away from me in the future.

Yours faithfully,

Edward Goldsmith
Bodmin.

Not every reader was so unsatisfied. One anonymous correspondent wrote in October 1978:

Sir,
I am not a 'writing to newspapers' person, but I would like you to know that since my mother has been reading the *Eye* her health has improved dramatically.

For two years she had been dogged with an appalling depressive illness. Naturally an illness like this means that everybody suffers, and my father's health was beginning to decline. They are both in their late sixties.

My mother, one day, happened to glance through a couple of old *Eyes* which I had left on my last visit and, according to Dad, she was laughing hysterically for hours.

This was in March of this year, and she eagerly awaits every issue. She is more talkative and happy, and more like the person she used to be, and there have been no recurring signs of the illness so far. Her favourites are 'Grovel', 'Colour Section', 'Neasden FC' and anything about 'Brenda and Keith'. She also misses 'Dave Spart'.

Other genuine, though unprinted, testimonials were received from the widows of Donald Piers and Sam Costa, both thanking E. J. Thribb for his 'Farewell' to their respective husbands. Mrs Sam Costa said that she intended to have hers framed.

For one reader the break with the Left had become terminal by Issue 517. 'The *Eye* has no more sympathy for those who

Poetry Corner

In Memoriam
SAM COSTA

So. Farewell
Then Sam
Costa

Moustachioed Radio
Personality and
Former
Danceband Vocalist.

Keith's Mum
Remembers you
Well.

"Good morning
Sir! Was there
Something?"

That was
Your catchphrase
She says.

Was there
Something?

Yes.
But she
Has forgotten
What it was.

E.J. Thribb (17)

The Private Eye Story

Zionist Racialism

would strive to improve the lot of the working people than most other journals of the capitalist press. . . . Your magazine is written by ex-public schoolboys who seek not to change society but to make a fat living gossiping about the clowns who occupy positions of wealth and influence,' wrote David Williams, a prospective Labour candidate for Colne Valley.*

The *Eye*'s readership also maintained its merited reputation for erudition. So in January 1978, Oliver Watson, writing from an address in Gwynedd, announced that while looking for underpants in Marks and Spencer he had recognised one of their designs as a phrase in Arabic. It meant 'There is no God except . . .' an unintentional abbreviation of the phrase 'There is no God but God', which was the first half of the Muslim profession of Faith. It was written in 'an archaic and decorative kufic script. Square kufic of this type,' continued Mr Watson, 'is generally found during the Mongol Period (13th to 14th centuries AD) and later, in Persia.' This letter led to the Islamic Council requesting Marks and Spencer to withdraw the design since it might injure the feelings of Muslims.

And in 1977 a learned historical controversy broke out in the 'Letters' column as to whether or not the late Queen Mary was a hazard to the antique trade by reason of her demands for free gifts. According to Sidney Sabin of the Sabin Galleries this story had been thoroughly investigated by the British Antique Dealers Assocation and found to be mythical. However Roger Thompson, writing as a wartime evacuee to a great house in the shires, remembered that the myth was powerful enough during the war for an early warning system to be devised if Queen Mary was in the neighbourhood, so that all valuables might be hidden before she dropped in. And Alan Ware recalled that his grandfather, a royal farm manager, once entertained her and, while she was out of the room, one of her attendants had suggested that he might like to give Queen Mary a particular Queen Anne chair in recognition of the honour of her visit. Mr Ware's grandfather declined this suggestion.

Another correspondent was less fortunate. In 1977 Martin Amis invited Ingrams to contribute to the *New Statesman*.

* Very true, but not even Auberon Waugh was quite the right-wing stereotype this suggested, as witness his discovery that Prince Andrew, 'although a healthy enough boy in other ways, has never actually learnt to speak. When he opens his mouth, a noise emerges which has been compared to the honking of angry geese or the trumpeting of elephants on the rampage, according to the time of day.'

He offered £40 for 1000 words. His letter was published with the headline 'On the Cheap'. On a previous occasion Andrew Knight, the newly appointed editor of the *Economist*, wrote what was clearly intended to be a confidential (if slightly over-excited) invitation to Ingrams, whom he knew, suggesting that it would be to Ingrams's benefit if they met. Ingrams also published this letter; the headline was 'Good-looking'.

André Deutsch, not only a reader but a fellow publisher of Pressdram, starred in an item in 'World of Books'.

> We knew that times were hard at André Deutsch, but I am distressed by a memo which André has sent to all his staff and which has belatedly reached me.
>
> 'When you use whisky, gin, soda water, ginger, bitter lemon, etc., please screw the tops back properly so that oxygen does not get in it and it remains good for the next time. The two worst culprits are Piers [Burnett] and Bill [McCreadie]. . . . we also consume wine and I frequently notice that at the end of lunch half-used bottles are not recorked. . . . it might interest you to know that earlier this week I had lunch with the Chairman of W.H. Smith . . . it was a very posh affair with other guests. At the end of lunch, Peter Bennett, Simon Hornby and two other Smith's colleagues were all screwing and replacing corks.'

As time passed *Private Eye* was left more and more of the field in the aftermath of the Goldsmith case. In February 1980 it discovered that there was something very fishy about *Now*'s sales figures. Advertising was sold on the basis of a forecast of 250,000 copies, but actual sales fell far short of that figure. Goldsmith issued a libel writ at once, but as the weeks passed it became increasingly apparent that the *Eye* had got it right. *Now!* magazine was closed in May 1981, presenting the *Eye* with a cover and a 'Business News' lead. The reaction in the national press was unusual. Many papers made the closure front-page news, a reaction hardly justified by their previous interest in the paper, but quite revealing about the extent to which the *Eye v. Now!* battle had gripped the world of Fleet Street. An offer Goldsmith made to pay *Private Eye* £15,000 was tested and found wanting. He had told *The Guardian* that *Private Eye*'s legal costs against him were more than £100,000 and that if they were audited and found to be below that sum, he would pay *Private Eye* the balance. The final figure invoiced by the *Eye*'s solicitors was £85,000. But Goldsmith continues to dispute his liability to pay the

£15,000 balance. Towards the end of 1981 he was reported to have left the country and bought a ranch in Paraguay.

But his ghost has haunted the pages of *Private Eye* ever since the case. Only two issues after the grand settlement, 'Business News' carried a story attacking both Goldsmith and Tiny Rowland (who had donated £5000 to the 'Goldenballs' appeal). This was reassuring, and showed that it was business news as usual, but subsequently a long, drawn-out score-settling process got underway. There were attacks on Simon Jenkins, who had played a difficult role in the settlement negotiations, and on Mr Justice Wien who had started it all. The attack on Jenkins continued into 1978, and then Anthony Blond, a director of Pressdram who had also attempted to intervene in the argument, got his. Charles Benson, who would have been a vital witness for the defence if the case had come to trial, and who was almost the only member of the Lucan circle prepared to stand up against Goldsmith, was described as 'the porcine hack' by 'Grovel' in the same issue.

On a more defensible level, close attention was paid to John Addey who had, incredibly, managed to get himself appointed as a magistrate in East London. This appointment was to last little more than a year. His resignation was announced in December 1978. Eric Levine's various troubles with several investigatory bodies were also probed. This eventually had some success. Although Mr Levine was never disciplined by the Law Society, he was reported in 1982 to have moved his interests to the New York property world.

Light relief was provided by the transcript of a telephone conversation between Peter Bessell and David Holmes, which subsequently formed part of the evidence in the prosecution of Jeremy Thorpe.

> Holmes: There is one marvellous piece of news . . . Jimmy Goldsmith has actually got criminal libel proceedings against *Private Eye*. . . . Already cut its circulation by 70%.
>
> Bessell: Good God. . . . Oh that will be nice. . . . Oh my God, that would finish them, which would cause me no grief.
>
> Holmes: That has cheered me immensely. . . . Goldsmith, mercifully, is a multi-millionaire.
>
> Bessell: That's splendid. More power to his elbow.
>
> Holmes: I know. That cheered me up no end.
>
> Bessell: Yes. I should think so.

By coincidence two barristers who had proved good friends to *Private Eye*, James Comyn, QC, and Ronald Waterhouse, QC, were made High Court judges on the same day in 1978. In the same year Goldsmith's counsel Lewis Hawser, QC, also became a judge, though of a slightly lower degree. *Private Eye*, curious as to why this distinction was made, dug up an interesting story about Mr Hawser's conduct as a criminal defence lawyer, which was advanced as an explanation.

Finally, in April 1979, an obituary for Leslie Paisner was printed. He was in a sense the chief victim of the battle between Goldsmith and *Private Eye*.

Early in mid 1977, at the end of the Goldsmith case, the sales of *Private Eye* had sunk to eighty-nine thousand, equal to their lowest point since 1971, and well below the previous (1974) peak of 117,000. They continued to sink until the end of 1977. It was not to be until 1979 that a recovery was truly under way, with a final figure of 116,000. Then a sales boom started in earnest. The figures rose until, by the end of 1980, they had reached 144,000. By the end of 1981 the sales were 190,076. The cash registers rang out merrily and there were £££££ signs in every eye.*

There were some notable jokes. 'Dear Bill' written by Ingrams and Wells became one of the most popular features the *Eye* had ever run. It had started within a month of Mrs Thatcher's election victory. In the 'Colour Section', 'Colonel Mad' revealed the existence of an astonishing phenomenon, 'the Rigid Man of Cheltenham Racecourse', alias Geoffrey Wheatcroft, who could pass out balanced only on a crate of tonic water bottles, and still remain entirely rigid.

The IRA received unsympathetic treatment. In April 1971 there was a spoof extract from the *Observer Magazine* series 'A Room of My Own', with Bobbie Sands, the hunger striker on the blanket protest in the Maze Prison, preferring a 'simple pastel brown wall decoration that had cost him next to nothing'. This was written by Ian Hislop, a recent graduate of Oxford. He now contributes regularly, possibly the first of a new generation of satirists to join the original collaborators.

* A significant number of new readers appear to be sixteen- and seventeen-year-olds. Michael Heath was told about three schoolboys on a train. One was reading *Private Eye* and the other two snatched it away. ''Ere', said the first schoolboy. 'Give me back me comic.'

The Book of Begin

Chapter One

1 Here beginneth the Book of Begin.

2 And Goldamiah begat Rabin.

3 And Rabin begat Begin.

4 Now the Israelites had lost their way in the wilderness, and they were sorely vexed. And the inflation rate was nigh unto four-score-and-three percent.

5 And the Israelites chose Begin to rule over them. For they said among themselves, now it is time that we should choose a man who is without fear and who will go out and smite the Syrians and the Egyptians and the Trans-Jordanians and the dwellers in Lebanon like they have never been smitten before.

6 For did God not say unto Moses that the people of Israel have a perfect right to smite anyone they like in order to ensure that they should be able to sojourn in safety in the Promised Land, they and their children and their children's children and their children's children's children. *(Get on with it – God.)*

7 And lo, Begin ruled over the Israelites for many years, and did a bit of smiting from time to time, and the children of Israel were pleased with Begin.

8 But there came a time when the children of Israel took counsel among themselves and began to say, Begin is full of years and passing sick. And the inflation rate was now nigh unto five-score.

9 And some muttered and said let us choose Shimon-Peres to rule over us. For he is a man full of the milk of loving kindness and will not smite the Arabians.

10 For we are weary with this constant smiting and wish only to live in peace with the tribes of the Arabians.

11 But Begin saw what was afoot and determined in his heart that he would show the children of Israel that he was one whose days were not yet numbered.

12 And privily in the night Begin girded up his loins and smote the Children of Lebanon, and there was much weeping and gnashing of teeth.

13 But Begin was not yet wearied with his smiting. And again he girded up his loins and smote the Iraqis, even unto their nuclear reactor.

14 For he said if we do not smite them, they will smite us.

15 And this was talk that the children of Israel understood.

16 And they took counsel among themselves and said: This man Shimon-Peres is an weed.

17 Let us therefore choose the mighty Begin to rule over us, and our children, and our children's children etc.

18 For he will continue smiting all the days of his life, even until all the nations of the world have been smitten to ensure that the children of Israel may lead a quiet life.

19 And they chose Begin and he was, verily, over the moon.

20 But Shimon-Peres was cast into outer darkness. And he was sick, even as an parrot.

Here endeth the First Lesson

There was also a new series by Michael Heath, 'The Gays', about the home life of a male homosexual couple. And there was 'The Book of Begin': 'For he will continue smiting all the days of his life, even until all the nations of the world have been smitten, to ensure that the children of Israel may lead a quiet life.' One man who untypically lost his sense of humour was the cartoonist Mark Boxer. Stung by 'Grovel's' account of his impending divorce and his affair with Anna Ford in Issue 501, Boxer told Smirnoff Vodka to withhold the ad which he regularly drew for the *Eye*'s page 2. No cartoon appeared in Issue 502. But then, under the calming influence of his fiancée, he began to see things straighter and the series re-started in the next issue.

Issue 465 showed to what extent *Private Eye* still provided a completely different view of the world. So Claud Cockburn,* not a big Pope man, pointed out the way in which the

---

* Claud Cockburn died in December 1981. The *Eye*'s obituary, signed by Richard Ingrams, said: 'He was an inspired journalist ... [who] more than anyone else was responsible for turning the *Eye* towards factual as opposed to satirical journalism.'

British government and press had enthusiastically praised the Pope's strictures on the IRA while turning a deaf ear to his remarks about the moral responsibility of the government. 'Grovel', not a big IRA man, corrected the hagiolatry of the late Earl Mountbatten by revealing that he had been a raging queen, and also revealed that the cuddly new Archbishop of Canterbury had been nicknamed 'Killer' because of the number of Germans he had despatched while he was a Scots Guards officer.

An opportunity for a memorable cover was missed in the 1980 Christmas issue. The printed cover showed Lord Kagan threatening to go on hunger strike, but after Christmas. The first idea had been to show a picture of the current IRA hunger striker saying, 'Oi tink oi moit fancy a bit o'd Christmas pudden.' This cover was not used lest it draw unwelcome attention from the IRA. But by the time that issue was on sale the hunger strike had been broken.

The libel front was fortunately unable to match the excitements of Goldsmith. The most notable legal development of 1978 was a considerable victory over Sir Richard Marsh, masterminded by Foot. Getting wind of a damaging article about a medical company, which was backed by the National Enterprise Board and of which he was a director, Marsh won an *ex parte* injunction against its being printed. This was achieved entirely on the strength of the fact that Marsh had been questioned on the telephone by Paul Foot. It happened at 2.30 pm on press day with a 7.00 pm deadline. The *Eye*'s barrister Desmond Browne immediately went to the same judge and argued against Anthony Hoolahan, QC, over each of the various allegations in the article, every one of which would be justified said Mr Browne. Mr Hoolahan claimed that the article was 'gravely defamatory and a gross abuse of the freedom of the press'. The judge rescinded the injunction. The article went to press that night, and not a squeak more about libel was heard from Sir Richard Marsh or Mr Hoolahan. The whole incident illustrated the frightful danger of 'checking' facts.

The most unexpected turn of legal events occurred in 1978 when a BBC radio contributor, Wilfred De'Ath, came to the office with a sorry tale of how he was being sued for a piece he had written for the *Hampstead and Highgate Express.* The paper was not defending him from the action adequately; instead its lawyers, the notorious firm of libel suers Oswald Hickson, had advised De'Ath not to accept service of the writ. The plaintiffs who he was alleged to have libelled, a gang of BBC radio persons, were being advised by the *Eye*'s lawyers, Bindman & Partners. The *Eye* thereupon offered to defend Mr De'Ath against the attentions of Bindman's. The outcome was that the radio gang were paid damages by the *Ham and High*, and further abused in the *Eye* for getting them, while the action against Mr De'Ath was dropped.

Despite *Private Eye*'s commercial position it is not a big machine whose future is endlessly assured. It remains the product of a handful of individuals. If they lose interest in it the paper will close. As the unaccustomed perils of success loom larger there is a growing temptation to risk everything on a gloriously protracted libel battle and go down with guns blazing – after all.

Its twentieth year, 1981, ended with the first-ever glossy cover and the news that after years of boardroom butchery Jocelyn 'Piranha Teeth' Stevens had at last been fired by *Express Newspapers*. It had taken 522 issues, two thousand libel writs and millions of pounds, but if 'Piranha Teeth' had finally learnt that firing Candida Betjeman from *Queen* magazine was just not on, it had been worth every moment.

Specially drawn by Nicholas Garland.

A NOTE ON THE ENDPAPERS

From the start *Private Eye* has relied heavily on the contributions of cartoonists and illustrators. The earliest issues were monopolised by William Rushton. He was joined in Issue 11 by Ralph Steadman, and then by Michael Heath, Wally Fawkes (Trog), the late Timothy Birdsall, and Gerald Scarfe. The endpapers carry a selection of drawings by many of those who have been regular contributors and who are not represented elsewhere in the book.

In the early days it soon became known in the small world of cartoonists that this new magazine would print anything considered too indecorous for *Punch*, where propriety and sanity reigned. Since cartoonists were paid remarkably little for their work *Private Eye* was also able to match the top Fleet Street rates for cartoons long before it could pay other contributors properly.

Some such as Steadman ('I'll sue the bastards' – *back middle*), Barry Fantoni ('Shakespeare' – *back left*) and David Austin ('Press' – *front middle*) first established themselves in *Private Eye*. But the magazine was not only a vehicle for new talent. Veterans like Osbert Lancaster ('Connie Lingus' – *back middle*) also submitted jokes which had little chance of appearing elsewhere. Sir Osbert was a subscriber from the early days. He once said appreciatively that his copy wafted through the letterbox every fortnight, 'like a breath of foul air'. Mark Boxer, or Marc ('Maudling' – *front middle*, and 'Longford' – *back middle*) also offered drawings which had been rejected as too strong by *The Times* or other papers. The *New Statesman* commissioned Marc's portrait of Lord Longford at the time of his report into pornography; without *Private Eye* it would have ended up on the spike.

There was at least one other category of joke which the magazine made its own. The work of a group of cartoonists – which included Bill Tidy, Larry, Hector Breeze, Maclachlan and Maddocks – appeared all over the country in the national and local press. They were very prolific and their jokes for that market were, as one might expect, conventionally funny. Encouraged by Richard Ingrams they developed a surrealist line of humour which was the more effective for being harnessed to their usual pictorial style. The best representative of this on the end-papers is Maclachlan's famous Hedgehog joke (*front right*).

Of the topical jokes Lady Antonia Fraser imitating Christ (*front right*) was drawn by Bert Kitchen after she had read from *The Imitation of Christ* in Westminster Cathedral; Lord Goodman as a press baron by Scarfe (*back left*) illustrated his joint role as chairman of *The Observer* and leading libel lawyer; and the nude Macmillan was drawn by Scarfe (*front right*) at the time of the Profumo affair.

Index

DO YOU HAVE A COPY OF SHAKESPEARE? Zgikspon?

FOYLES

THE PRESS GOD BLESS IT

"I'll just have one more try before I make my vow of poverty"